I applaud and respect your honesty – it must have been extraordinarily challenging to relive the experience, and I salute you for it. It's a high emotional impact book.

Celia Taylor
❖❖❖

I began reading *Romance Scam Survivor: the whole sordid story* and have been compelled to continue.
My heart is breaking for you as I am amazed by your strength.
This is more than a memoir. It has great honesty and openness and contains much useful research and advice.

A friend and editor
❖❖❖

Romance Scam Survivor
the whole sordid story

by **Jan Marshall**

Romance Scam Survivor: the whole sordid story
First Published 2018
By Sangam Enterprises Pty Ltd
ABN: 97 058 176 453
For Jan Marshall
Bundoora, VIC 3803 Australia

Copyright © 2018 Jan Marshall
The right of Jan Marshall to be identified as the author of this work has been asserted by her under the Copyright, Designs and Patents Act 1988.

All rights reserved. No part of this book may be reprinted or reproduced or utilised in any form or by an electronic, mechanical, or other means, now known or hereafter invented, including photocopying and recording, or in any information storage or retrieval system, without permission in writing from the publishers.

ISBN: 978-0-6482336-0-2 (pbk)
ISBN: 978-0-6482336-1-9 (ebk)

Printed and bound by Ingram Spark.

To Amitabha

For your understanding and love

You are in my heart

Preface

"How could you give money to someone you have never met?"

Many people, when I first told them of the scam, asked that.

It's a fair question, and hard to explain. I did not fully understand it myself at first. It is nonsense to send money to someone you do not know. But others do not understand what goes on in an online romance scam. They think you must just be stupid, then push it away as something they would never do.
After I realised I had been scammed, in sequence, I compiled the records I had of all of my interactions with my scammer. It took several months to put Part 1 together, as I worked mostly on weekends and holidays, from late 2012 through to early 2013.
My purpose in writing at that time was to develop some understanding, of and for myself, of the sequence of what had happened. It was an attempt to answer the burning question - how could I give money to someone I had never even met?
Once I had written this I could not look at it again until years later, after more healing had occurred.
This book comes in multiple parts. The first is the detailed records I have of the scam, the emails, messages and SMSs that I compiled in that early writing during 2012-2013. I provide it, often with some limited commentary, trusting that it tells the essential story.
Rather than try to distinguish between the types of interactions, I have distinguished his, my and other interactions so that the nature of these exchanges is clear. Any names have been changed to protect privacy.
Where there are no records, for example, phone conversations, where I could not remember the dialogue, instead, I have written a general piece about the content. I regret that these pieces lack the detail. Luckily, the written records carry the story sufficiently, without my having to explain every nuance of how I was feeling at the time.
Throughout this book I maintain the purpose of understanding both what happened and how I could give so much

money away. I hope you may also gain some understanding.

It is important that you know I entered the relationship with the scammer, the person I knew as Eamon Donegal Dubhlainn, sincerely, openly and unquestioningly. I desired love and partnership, and I include the words we exchanged here in the same vein.

As I bared my soul to him, so I also do to you. I ask you not to judge me harshly for the errors in judgement and missed discernment through this time, but instead to see my behaviours in the context of the scam.

The second part details my reaction to the scam, and the process of realising the true nature of a scam. During this time, I did a lot of research and I have listed much of this for your reference if you want to explore further. This will also help you understand my process as I uncovered the truth. Some of this research, as well as more general reference material, can be found in the Appendix. This information is useful if you want to review what scammers generally do, if you are contemplating online dating, or if you have yourself been subject to a scam, of whatever sort.

It is not my purpose to write this as a 'how to avoid the pitfalls' manual. There are many such materials out there on the web, of much better credibility. Check out some of the websites listed. If you are on a dating site yourself, I suggest you look out for information provided on scamming and how to avoid it, or go to your national government site on scams.

You may also have questions about why I didn't do something you might have done? Some of the research may provide answers. Emotions also played a big part. I was very resigned and affected during the period after realising I was scammed, as I quickly realised there was little I could do.

Part three deals with the financial consequences of my actions in accessing funds to which I was not legally entitled. I had to deal with these consequences through 2013 and 2014. This section describes the legal transactions with the Australian Tax Office, either by me or on my behalf. This content is often legal and dry in nature, and I have tried to provide just the salient sections to mitigate this.

Full documents are provided at the end of the book for those who would like to see the detail.

It was not until I took on the task of developing my own formal objection to the private ruling from the ATO that I came to understand what 'scam' meant, and how it was perpetrated. I trust again that you will appreciate my intention for inclusion of this material, to show how I came to better understand what had happened to me. It was not until this point that I was able to appreciate that I was a survivor of a professional fraud.

Lastly, you will see my section on who is culpable and what needs to change, headed Analysis. This section is included because, as I proceeded through writing Parts 2 and 3, I realised there was much that needed changing in the realm of online dating and scamming. It is my intent to go on from here, on this personal journey, to focus more on what it takes generally to recover from scams and, more generally, how the stages map out in this process of being scammed.

There is enough information out there on the nature of scams, how to identify and prevent them. There is, however, precious little on the recovery process. Yet there are thousands of people impacted and millions of dollars lost to scammers.

It is my intent to shine more light on the recovery process with a subsequent book. As has been the case in changing societal attitudes to rape, and the move away from blaming the woman for wearing clothing which is too alluring, or for drinking too much, the shame needs to be taken away from those who have become ensnared in a scam. Responsibility and culpability must be directed squarely at the perpetrators, the fraudsters.

Contents

Preface i
Contents iv
Prologue 1
Part 1: The Scam Diary 6
   My Whole Sordid Story 7
   The Start 7
   The Love Bomb 16
   A Marriage Dream 63
   The First Request for Money 76
   Are You Real? 88
   Hot Sex 96
   The Cheque 102
   More Taxes 110
   Robbed 115
   Paying out the Employer 127
   Tickets 134
   Car Accident 138
   The Realisation 144
Part 2: Aftermath 148
Reactions - Mine and Others 149
   Immediate Aftermath 149
   In my Journal 151
   Reactions of Family and Friends 155
   Dating Continues 157
   It Wasn't Personal 170
      Typical Characteristics of Scammers 176
   Trying to Find the Trail 180
   Surviving 184
   Financial Management 187
Part 3: Survivor 192
Dealing with the Consequences, and Recovery 193
   Step 1 – Making an Undertaking 193
   Step 2 – Closing the Fund 204
   Step 3 - Asking for Discretion From the ATO 213
   Writing my Objection, Becoming a Survivor 217
   Recovery Begins 234
   My Survivor Year 241

Part 4: Analysis 251
   Who is Culpable?.. 252
      The Victim... 252
   What/Who Are Those Other Parties? 254
      The Scammer 254
      The Websites... 255
      The Local Police (State-based in Australia)............ 257
      The Banks.. 258
      Money Transfer Agencies/Agency Operators......... 259
      Regulation Agencies Who Oversee the
      Banks and Money Transfer Agencies...................... 260
      Governments 261
      Society at Large... 264
   What Needs to Change? 266
Appendix 271
   Additional documentation:... 272
      Item 1..
   272
      Item 2 275
      Item 3: ATO/SMSF Documentation 277
      1. Wording from ATO's first response
          to my self reporting. 277
      2. ATO Request for fund review
          documentation... 279
      3. My 'Statement in Writing' in response
          to the ATO... 282
      4. Scammer bank statements (x 2)....................... 286
      5. ATO Notification of Escalation to Audit 288
      6. Lawyer's letter asking for discretion. 290
      7. My letter to ATO 295
Useful Information 301
      Websites... 301
      Books 303
Acknowledgements 305
Author Information 307

v

What follows is my story, as I experienced it.

You will likely notice poor grammar and typographical errors and ask, why didn't she correct them?

Because this is my story, and I want to tell it as it was for me.

So the emails, messages and correspondence between me, the scammer, the authorities and those I went to for help have not been edited. They are present without having been cleaned up or sanitised, just as life is, unedited.

I was scammed.

And this is my story.

Jan Marshall
http://romancescamsurvivor.org

Prologue

Wednesday, 24th October 2012:

> Boarding the plane my love.... I love you sooo much and thanks for everything.

That's a bit dismissive, I had thought. But I persuaded myself that he must have meant for the help I had given in Dubai, and that I would soon hear from him in England, as he had promised.

Now, four days later, I had finally and quietly to myself, realised.

I had been scammed.

That was the end, and I had been completely, totally and resoundingly SCAMMED. I was never going to get my $250,000 plus back!
I had felt good that day. It was warmer, so I had worn my bright fuchsia jacket. I looked and felt good, and thought I was doing well at work. But underneath I was going into shock.

Stop feeling.

Don't feel anything. Detach from all that.

Keep the front up and get through the day.

I called Mum. She was disbelieving and, unsurprisingly, shocked. There was no way she could understand. It was not understandable.
"How could I have given away all my money to someone I had never even met?" ALL my money! And more. I wouldn't even tell her how much.
My first response was to email to him. I'd been writing many times a day so that was normal. Was he reading them now? I

Romance Scam Survivor

didn't know. Perhaps he would want to know what reactions I was having, to see if he needed to protect himself in some way? Anyway, I needed to write.

Before I sent it, I wrote the subject as "Back to you..."

> I have realised today that you are not going to return my money are you. That "thank you for everything" was a last dismissive good bye.
>
> You would leave the woman you love with not enough money to buy food. That's how short of funds I am right now and you knew it would come to this.
>
> I wouldn't let you go without but you would let me. I guess that's my fault though, for choosing love over money.
>
> I'm in shock of course, haven't yet allowed myself to feel. The loss of your love will be the most painful, because I know, even if you scammed and manipulated me, that you loved me too. I know that, because I felt your heart with mine. And you confirmed it in your last message.
>
> Part of me hopes you will just turn up on my doorstep, surprise me, make it all alright, and we can be together the way we'd promised each other, forever. Deluding myself again...
> Was any of what happened true, or was it all a manipulation? I certainly believed it, you made it so believable. I guess I will never know.
>
> Who are you, are you real? I still believe you are. More fool me.
>
> If I have it wrong, please get in touch. If I have it right, please get in touch.
>
> Otherwise I guess I draw my own conclusions, broken heart and all.
>
> I am your woman, always, all ways. Now we have to wait another lifetime to complete this bonding, promised to each other for lifetimes past.
> I know in your eyes all of this must sound pitiful, you are

The Whole Sordid Story

probably laughing at me, at how easy I was to manipulate, but I know my love was honest and true, full and generous, and sexy, and I stand strong with that.

With an open invitation – turn up on my doorstep some time...
Back to you... I love you sooo much. Thank you for everything.

Then I went to check my finances. They were appalling. Already two of my accounts were overdrawn, and I only had $200 cash to draw on.
I had $2700 in bills due before my next pay of $3500 came in, and another $3200 due in the week after that, including my rent and mortgage payment. I had no idea how I would afford food during that time. I calculated I might be able to pay some bills on Amex, but that might come back with a sting with the next statement if I was unable to pay it all then. I could delay one or two, and maybe pay later.

I emailed him again, desperately calling this one "Bills."

> Just in panic reviewing my bills due over the next few days - $3500 worth that I cannot pay because you have my money. That I believed honestly you would be paying me back by now.
>
> Is there any way you could send some to me – cash in a card if you don't want me to know where it has come from.
>
> Eamon please.
>
> That's after I have spent my next pay cheque on rent for my place here, and does not include food and living expenses. My accounts are already $200 overdrawn, so perhaps $4000.
>
> It's not much to ask after all the money you have from me...

Did I expect him to do this? Part of me wanted there to be some caring for me from him. I've not emailed him again.

Romance Scam Survivor

How did I get myself here? I was warned. Strongly warned about these exact types of scams by several good girlfriends and numerous family. So, I had no excuse.

How could I have given away all of my money, including all of my superannuation, to him?

How could I have taken an additional $25,000 credit card debt, to give the money to him?

It's hard to explain how. It needs the full story to make sense.

The Whole Sordid Story

Part 1: The Scam Diary

My Whole Sordid Story

The Start

I was ready. After twenty years of being an independent and lone woman, I was ready. I'd seen it was possible. My landlady in Brisbane had done it, found a nice man, gone travelling to Europe for three months, then settled down to reshape the garden in his new home on the Gold Coast together. And then retired at sixty-five. Age was no barrier.
I'd tried one of those "attract your soul mate" eBook courses last year, but wasn't ready then. I only reached day sixteen of thirty.
There had been a big change and I was ready. I had left Brisbane and moved to Melbourne. I found a good job, a nice house, and it had all gone very smoothly, not one problem. I had returned to my teenage stomping ground. Family was nearby, and pleased to have me back.
Couldn't I also have someone to share my life with? Of course, I could. I deserved it. At age fifty-nine it still wasn't too late. All other areas of my life had been going so well, this would go well, I told myself.
Last year I had gotten a cat, a lovely ragdoll kitten I called Cookie. Having Cookie to look after every day opened up my loving nature, my heart. I loved Cookie and knew I could love someone, given the chance. I was ready for love.
I'd looked at 'Plenty of Fish' (PoF) once before, years ago, so went back there. No money to exchange. I had one good photo to use, the same one I have on Facebook and LinkedIn. A nice laughing face, with pearls.
The first decision, a pseudonym. I was new to this big city, I would use that. Jannew2melb. Yes, that was me.
I was a fifty-nine-year-old Leo, non-smoker, with 'A Few Extra Pounds' body type, looking for a long-term relationship.
Before I had even completed my profile, there were people wanting to chat to me. I ignored them. I wasn't ready. Chatting was a bit too immediate.
I got some help from a friend. "Tell them what you admire in a man," she said, "they like that."

Romance Scam Survivor

I finally settled on:

> I left Melbourne many years ago, and now I'm back, and want to explore and experience all that's wonderful about Victoria. It feels like a new phase in my life.
> I like social cycling, and a weekend away, walking, cycling, enjoying good food. I'm looking for good company to do this with and a partner to share my life with. I'm keen to be fit and healthy, and get into a good routine to support this.
> I'm interested in property investment, to build my retirement income, and would love to build or renovate a home here.
> I'd also like to get back into some creative activity, painting or drawing. I also enjoy wandering around a good art exhibition.
> I admire a man who has a good intellect, clear ideas, and can carry a good discussion about what's important in life. I think a friendship grows from shared values - mine are left of centre. I'm also content with silence, when that's appropriate.
> I'm attracted to someone who has a strong sense of who they are, have a positive attitude to life and the challenges it brings. Someone who wants an equal partner in life, and can allow me to be myself. As well as being interested in the financial markets, they would be well read, socially and spiritually aware, and may belong to some group with a cause or topic that they are passionate about.
> I'm not a social butterfly, more a home body, but love to be tempted to go out for movies, theatre, or a good restaurant. When home I'm a TV watcher, mostly ABC or SBS, and I love Radio National in the morning and afternoon. I'm not much for watching sports, except for Tour de France and the Olympics. I have a cat, a ragdoll, on whom I lavish my love and affection, and I am happy with who I am and where I am in life.
> I know there could be more. I'd love a partner, companion, lover to share my life with, perhaps find a project to work on together. Will that be you...?

Within a day there was a contact from a good-looking man, from Burlington, Canada. I was surprised to be contacted from someone so far away. I wrote back, asking did he know I was over here in Australia? He replied that it was no problem, he would be willing to relocate for the right woman.

He had four nice photos on his profile, one in a suit, looking respectably grey, one at the wheel of a yacht, and two casual photos. He had a dimple in his chin, a bit like the one Cadel Evans the cyclist has.

What was striking about his profile was that it was prolific. He had written a lot, which most men do not do, but of course women like, and I certainly did. A couple of things I remember were that he liked to eat ice cream, and he liked sunsets. He was about ten years younger than me. There was something inconsistent about the age on his profile too.

Within a short time he was suggesting we continue connecting via email, as it was cumbersome to write on PoF. I agreed, not knowing that this was a usual scammer's ploy. Luckily it now means I have a good record of what happened.

I emailed him, Sunday, 12th August:

> Hi Aemon, (name spelled incorrectly at this stage)
> I am ok to keep emailing back and forth, I certainly think writing is a good way to start getting to know each other.
> I certainly admire your persistence in writing back to me.
> This is new to me and I am a little wary of your motives and the logistics could be an issue. It's a bit more of a trust issue, in my mind, than if you were local (why this is so is perhaps something I should question).
> Let's see how it pans out.....
> A couple of things... You have on your profile that you are interested in 'dating', but you are saying to me that you are looking for the longer term.?
> Also, POF would be saying you are 60 if it is reading your birthdate as 1952... Which by the way is closer to my birth year, 1953.... Meaning I am a little older than you. It's not an issue for me if it's not for you?
> I have just moved from Brisbane to Melbourne, so I know what it's like to move a bit, though it's not the same as country to country. It took me 4 days to drive down, staying with various friends and family along the way, and to give my cat Cookie a rest from the car. Settling nicely into Melbourne now though, and I'm 3 weeks into a new job.
> I also was in the US and Canada earlier in the year. I went to attend a work conference in Las Vegas, took some extra time with a US based cousin touring the grand canyon, then was up in Vancouver Island visiting relatives I had not met before. They are also originally English, as are my parents, though only my mother is now alive. I was actually

conceived in England, and my parents then immigrated to Australia, and I was born here.
What sort of project are you on in Canada?
Tell me more about yourself...
Jan

He replied, Tuesday, 14th August:

Greetings to you I truly appreciate you taking your time to write back to me and letting me have your personal email address, it felt good to read your response.
Here's a little more about me.
I am a civil Engineer, I am into building and constructions, I handle my job in contracts because I am self employed. I'm renovating and building new offices for a company here
My daughter is 15 years, she lives with me in my base, Manchester England. She isn't with me now, she's home.
I got married 16 years ago and it lasted for just 10 years. My divorce was quite difficult because I loved her so much and never saw it coming, it cost me alot, my concentration and so on.
I have not felt the love of woman for long now, and I really miss it, to be sincere, I'm quite scared, but just want to be bold. As the saying goes, no risk, no reward. Age is not an issue for me because you aren't much older than me, I am 50 years old.
Does it bother you?
I am a man who believe so much in love and fun. I am a one man to one woman relationship type, and when I love, I love real hard, I listen to my partner , respect her points of views and understand a lot.
I'd like us to have a good communication based on honesty and see where it leads,
I'm sure it will get somewhere good.
Keep well
Eamon....

So far so good. He sounds interesting, open, willing to communicate honestly and shares about himself in a very engaging way. Even his name is exotic, Eamon Dubhlainn. Emails went back and forward.

I replied, Tuesday, 14th August:

The Whole Sordid Story

Hi Eamon,
thanks for sharing with me about yourself. I was touched. A little about me in return.
I don't have any children and I have never been married. In fact I have been without a partner for many years. When I was younger this was distressing, but for a good few years now I have been comfortable with being on my own.
I am an Organisational Change Manager, working on large IT implementation projects. I worked in Queensland in govt departments for 6 years, until the state government changed in March and the policies of employing contractors changed. I took this as a hint it was time to move back to Melbourne - more work down here.
Most of my family is here, except for my Mother, who is in an aged care facility in northern NSW. I am in the process of moving her down too, to a facility nearby. She has a degenerative motor neurone disease, and her health is declining. Another reason to be closer to family. I have been her primary support.
The move has gone really well. I found a lovely house, not far from my brother, and I had a job organized down here before I left Brisbane, and had several weeks to unpack and settle in before I started work.
Coming down to Melbourne feels like coming home somehow. I haven't lived here since I was 17 yo. It also feels like its time to find a special someone who can complete me, who I can share my life with, and that this will happen now. I have a lot of love to give, but I am also scared. I know I don't have a lot of baggage in other areas of my life, but I don't know what might come up in a relationship. I just have to trust that life experience will be enough.... I want a partner in the true sense of the word - someone to do things together with, to share projects, plans goals with.
I'm a sensual person, and I want to be able to touch and feel.... And be close.
I'm saying things i haven't said before, perhaps not even admitted to myself....
Enough for now, it's getting late.
Looking forward to hearing more from you,
Stay safe
Jan

Romance Scam Survivor

And he replied, Thursday, 16th August:

> Hi,
> It was really nice receiving your email, I hope you slept well and had sweet dreams. thanks for sharing with me so much about you, was really really nice to receive your email. I'm happy to know that you are ready to share your life with someone, that means you are ready.
> I've never done this before and I'm thinking of what to share, for you to get to know more about me, so I thought I'd write out some of my likes and dislikes, not implying that you have to be this way but it will give you an idea about the man you are communicating with.
> Interests: I tend to have a variety of interests, such as the following: I enjoy the outdoors. I love spending time by the water (lakes and oceans) as the water grounds me and provides me with inner peace. I too enjoy a nice sunset especially by the water (romantic). I enjoy cooking, walking, swimming, anything with outdoors involvement and playing like a kid when am with my partner. A swing is always lots of fun especially if someone is pushing you. I have a playful spirit. I enjoy quality time spent with my daughter. I enjoy a good movie, all types of music, reading, some sports, different types of foods. I am open to trying new things. The bottom line is I am active and have a tremendous amount of energy to expend.
> Passions: I have a few passions in my life and I would have to say that I am passionate about being a good father, about my career, about developing relationships (in general), and I really look forward to being passionate and having a passionate intimate relationship someday. I tend to be passionate about all things that are attached to the heart, my heart. Generally, this is my love and passion for humanity and for those that will come into my love life.
> Likes: I like many things as I am open minded and flexible person. Generally, I like everything providing that there is no dislikes of mine infringing on the likes. Some of my favorite food (restaurants) consist of Chinese, Mexican, Italian with Jamaican sauce and rice being my favorite. I love red licorice and my favorite flowers are carnations. I do enjoy traveling and thanks to my job. I would like to see castles close up some day and stay in a beautiful hotel close to the sea. I am thinking about a holiday over at the Caribbean. Not sure where I would like to go for now...

The Whole Sordid Story

Dislikes: There is not a whole lot that I dislike, however; the things that I do dislike seem to be based on values and character, allow me to explain. There are certain things that I have no interest in, however; these are the things that I clearly dislike or choose not to tolerate are: disrespect, unfaithfulness, dishonesty, lying, cheating, mean spitefulness, being judgmental, callousness, harsh words, hurtful acts, untrustworthy people, displaced anger, unfairness, injustice, selfishness, being inconsiderate, blaming, not taking responsibility, self-centeredness, rigidity and anything else that can cause damage or be damaging to another human being.

Relationships: Give 100%, if this can not be given, then you are not that true friend, lover or husband/wife. Be true to yourself, and your love ones. Honesty, communication, and understanding along with patience will make the difference. This is just my opinion mind you. Sharing, is more than finance, material assets, more importantly, it is the sharing of yourself, time, and love. Giving always more to the other, and they will give back. It is a forever revolving door of giving...

Let me see, what else can I share about me? I have a strong work ethic and I never give anything less than my absolute best. Oh, one more thing . . . in case you hadn't figured it out already, I am a hopeless romantic. I love the little things about a relationship -- holding hands and doing nothing, picking flowers in a field for the table for dinner, watching a butterfly go by as you're walking! I know, it probably sounds silly but it's me.

I trust that you are having a good week. I would love to hear from you and if there is anything else you would love to know or share about likes, dislikes, passions, and interests, do not hold back, am glad we are having this conversation, it will help in bring us closer.

Your in my thoughts,
Eamon

Are these things any woman would respond to? I certainly did!

- He's passionate – yes!
- He's a romantic – yes!
- He's articulate about what he wants – yes!

And he says he has not done it before, so it seems real. He emphasises openness and honesty. That's what I want too. I was already getting hooked.

Romance Scam Survivor

My reply, Thursday, 16th August:

> Hi Eamon,
> what a lot of information you have provided. So wonderful to read it all. I am so honored by the time and effort you have put into all this. And that you have been able to be so clear about things.
> I'm not going to manage to provide as much about me back in one go, as it's a bit late. There's a weekend coming up, so I will be able to have a good go then and take the time to respond as I would like. I have a friend from Brisbane staying tomorrow (Friday) night, but she is going back early on Saturday so I should have plenty of time then.
> Suffice to say that there is nothing in what you have written that jars with me. Quite to the contrary, I am thrilled by it all. It's not all the same as for me of course, that would be boring anyway, but there is enough in what you have said that has a form of echo with me, that I will respond to when I have some more time to find the right words. I wish to honor you in the same way that you have honored me (sorry the spell checker keeps americanizing....)
> Time for bed now, and I will dream of butterflies, water, sunsets, swings, and holding hands...
> Jan

And then the final tug on the hook, 18th August:

> Hi there, thanks for your very informative email. [I didn't give much information so this comment seems a little strange, but I let it go...]
> I have enjoyed my time responding to your life with mine, your thoughts, wants, needs, dreams and more. I don't know you other than a small amount of correspondence. I will say my heart tells me you are one very special woman. Whatever will be between you and I, please know you have a friend for life regardless of the miles between us. I feel very blessed that you responded to my email, that I will cherish forever. In our walks of life, it is not often you come across another who still has morals, family values, respect and continues to follow their dreams.
> I want you to know that I will not be communicating with any other woman on the dating site for now, because I want to concentrate on getting to know you, I cannot communicate with more than one woman at the same time, please don't

get me wrong, I am not trying to impose it on you that we must have something, I just want to have my attention on you and see where it leads us...
I want us to continue this communication, because there is much to know about each other, though we are far apart, but if we keep communicating good, we will be close to each other in our hearts...
I am offering you the flower of my heart as a friend. It's always growing and searching for perfection, always reaching for the sparkling rays of the sun but only if you can give it the care and nourishment it needs to thrive, give it your light and I pray it blooms forever.
I will be leaving for England 10pm today, I have been here for 7 weeks now, I rounded up my job here in the morning, please don't let that scare you ok
I don't know if you have a yahoo account, so that we can chat through the im, it is a fast means of communication, we can instant message ourselves ,ask questions about each other and get instant answers, if you don't have one ,I will appreciate if you will be able to sign up for one, it is free and easy...
I wish you a wonderfully blessed day ahead...
Warm thoughts Eamon

I had checked out other profiles on PoF, and expressed some interest in meeting at least two local men. Both declined, one saying he was too busy, the other was already in a relationship. I was surprised that Eamon was saying his attention was now exclusively on me, as we didn't know each other well yet, but it was flattering to be thought a person of interest. When a man says he can only focus on one woman, any woman would like that. It's a bit contrary to the 'men cannot commit' myth and that they want to always play the field.

I didn't feel ready to take my PoF profile down though. Looking back, I see that I had focused on, '*I just want to have my attention on you and see where it leads us...*' rather than any of the inconsistencies in this email.

I had looked for him on the internet, and found nothing. This was a surprise. Self-employed people would normally promote their skills and capability online.

All I found were references to the Irish/Gaelic translation.

The Love Bomb

By this time, I had been exchanging emails with Eamon for just seven days. I was certainly intrigued and interested.
I continue to engage with him, exploring the dream of love that was developing, and opening up myself.

19th August:

> Hi Eamon,
> I just found this in my junk email box, so sorry I have not responded to this in the email I have just sent.
> I will think about the yahoo IM, not there quite yet....
> Happy travelling.
> Jan

And even to use this as a chance to uncover for myself what I am interested in, though this crosses the last email.

> Hi Eamon,
> finally I have some time to sit down and write to you. I had an unexpected invitation to go to my aunt and uncle's for lunch today, as my niece was calling in. I have just got back from there, having spent a nice afternoon chatting and catching up. My niece is a beautiful 25year old, and having spent several years travelling and working around the snow fields, she is now looking at going back to Uni, and is looking at Civil Engineering as a study area... so I'm getting to this much later than I thought.
> In order to write, I have had to do some soul searching myself, peeling back the onion on areas that I haven't thought about directly. As I have been alone for a long while, I have been/am very independent, and so have not been so clear about myself in relation to close others, as you with your daughter and wife have been. I did encounter some 'he won't be interested" gremlins along the way too, that I had to fight my way past.   It's a process of opening up myself, and my heart. So here goes...
> Interests: cycling: I am a social cyclist, and bought a new bike in January planning to get fit to do a 9 day tour run by Bicycle Queensland in September with my cycling mate Lynette and 1500 others.   I did a similar one in Victoria several years ago, from Portland to Geelong along the great

The Whole Sordid Story

ocean road. So I've been getting fit and loving to ride my bike – but all this interrupted by the move to Melbourne, starting a new job etc. I've been out once since I got down here, but want to do a lot more....

Property Investment: I am interested in this a form of building wealth, have one house currently rented out and want to get more as part of my superannuation. I also am very interested in house building and renovation – any related programs on TV I love, especially Grand Designs. I have built one house (with a builder, not with my own hands), and would love to do this again.

I like to go to the theatre, go out to art galleries, but need to find some new friends to do this with here, hence PoF...

I like to cook, when I have people to cook for, and play word games like scrabble, crosswords, codewords etc. On the weekend I like to relax having a good read of the newspaper or a magazine, as well as get out and do something active, cycling or walking, anything outdoors. I enjoy time with family, as this afternoon, and love a good picnic or BBQ.

I enjoy gardening too, when I have one to work in – a the markets today I bought some parsley and mint to pot up and get going, and I will get some flowers too to grow in pots.

Passions: That's Interesting...   Certainly my work as an organisational change manager. I have been part of the professional practice group Change Management Institute here, including running professional development events, and being the chapter lead in Queensland, promoting change management as a profession. I have also gone to a number of conferences.

Then there's my cat, a ragdoll breed, called Cookie. He is just 2 years old and I have had him since a kitten. I credit him with opening up my heart, giving me something to lavish my love on, unconditionally, with unconditional love coming back.

I think, once I am in a relationship, I have a lot of love to give, passions to share, but part of me wonders if this will ever happen for me.... But hidden deep is quite a fire burning, just needing some oxygen...

I have a very close relationship with my mother. She is 83 next week, and suffering from a form of Motor Neurone disease, and is progressively losing her capacity to use her hands and feet. She is in an aged care facility, and I hope

to be moving her down to Melbourne in the next month or so. Being closer to family will make a huge difference for her I think, and me as I have been her primary supporter.
I am generally a very adaptable and accepting person, I do not react to people or things very much. People would describe me as very grounded and a calm person.
I'm left of centre politically though, and disliking of right and extreme right views. Here I am a Labour voter, and would be similarly in England, as my folks come from good east end of London working stock. I would react against forms of institutionalised persecution, especially religious forms of this. (see that some of these comments contradict my comment above... I guess we are sometimes full of contradictions)
I like many food types, would love to travel down the rivers in Europe on a boat, or cycle along the boat paths.... I'd like to explore Canada more, maybe by rail....
I've done quite a lot of personal growth and spiritual development activities in my life, including spending some time with Rajneesh/Osho/The Orange People during the 80s and 90s. Though not currently doing any form of meditation practice myself, I have been close to some of the current day spiritual teachers and enlightened ones over the years, and value an interest in spiritual awareness and practice, and the self-awareness and responsibility this brings.
I admire your willingness to be a proclaimed romantic. Its refreshing. I'm sure I would respond to it, and want to, but I know I am still a little wary about opening up my heart too quickly – I know I could easily 'fall in love' and loose myself, based on an idea of something that may not be reciprocated. I tend to trust too early.... And have little experience to help me to validate what's real or not. So I may seem a little reserved....
Eamon, on the one hand I am enjoying this discovery and getting to know you activity, and writing is a great and safe way to do this. I like what you are communicating, and think that it would be lovely to meet you to see if this could become an abiding friendship, and then more. One of my motivations for joining up with Plenty of Fish was to find a companion to do things with here in Melbourne. This goal is being mightily thwarted with you in Canada. How, if you have any idea, do you think this might unfold?
Hoping you are having a good weekend, out somewhere in

The Whole Sordid Story

the outdoors, with nature,
Intrigued and wondering where all this will go...
Jan

To my friend who helped me with my PoF profile I write:

Hi Rosie,
I thought I would give you a quick update on my progress with PoF.
I have continued to communicate with
Thosesummertimes7 – Eamon Dubhlainn. Though at the time he was in Canada, he has now returned to
England. He seems very keen on me – saying he will no longer look for contacts on PoF as he is only wants to focus on one woman..... I'm trying to go slow with it, but I must admit he is tugging at my heartstrings.... I find I am not looking at contacts on PoF either....
The only other fellow I was interested in on there has not responded.
He has been forthcoming about himself, his likes and dislikes etc, and is a self proclaimed romantic.... I have been up front about being a little wary and reserved, but underneath that, I have been touched by what he has been writing. I did put out in my last email that I was looking for someone in Melbourne... asking what he thought could be done about this....
He's keen now to get onto instant messaging on Yahoo so we can chat. Part of me in reluctant, but I think that's the part that doesn't want to change, to open, to keep hiding away. So far I cannot find any good reason not to continue to explore.... And it has been an exploration of uncovering parts of myself.... Which is good.
I feel a bit like I am jumping in the deep end..... or off the abyss...
Wish me luck
xxxxx
Jan

There is a very quick and strong response:

Hi Jan,
Have been wondering how you are getting on.
Darling I'm sorry to say this, but there are red flags here for me. What's he up to? Has he mentioned coming to

> Australia?
> If he hasn't, I would ask him straight out why he is romancing you. Hard for me to get a sense of him as I can't get his profile; if you send me your login I will have a look. Jan he doesn't know you, the fact that he is so keen on you before even speaking that he is saying he isn't looking anywhere else, at anyone he could meet as a real person, actually isn't good. He is living in a fantasy, he cannot know you well enough yet to genuinely be in that place. So you have to wonder what he's about.
> Already you are feeling something, he's "tugging at your heartstrings, I find I am not looking at contacts on PoF either" ....this worries me!
> Darling you are very vulnerable, there are predators out there. I' m reluctant to say more as I know how long it's been since you explored this side of yourself but it's very unwise to focus on one person so early.
> PoF isn't a high quality site. You could continue to explore with him, and also put up an RSVP profile, I think the quality can be better there; although they all have men looking for casual sex, I think they all have women looking for that too. ....but the quality men I have met were all from RSVP or Oasis. Even Oasis......not sure. The thing with RSVP is that they need to pay to contact you beyond the hello kiss, so it weeds out some people. PoF and Oasis are both free.
> I really don't want to rain on your parade Jan so won't say any more; but would you allow me to use your login so I can check him out? I just have alarm bells going on this one.
> That reluctance you have to go on Yahoo with him may be your own alarm bells. Don't let him push you until you feel it's the right time for you.
> Keep in touch, I feel protective! I remember Susie feeling protective of me when I first met Andrew. Same thing really, I liked him so much right from the start, and although I grew a lot in that relationship, it was very painful too
> Any way let me know what you feel about your login,
> Rosie xx

Her warnings were not enough to put me off, he did not feel like a predator to me. Within a few days I am writing.

> Hi Eamon,
> missing our email exchange this week. I had set up yahoo messenger earlier, but not seen any time when you've been available. Friday am here, I am on the train to work.

The Whole Sordid Story

Weekend now coming up so I was wondering if there is a good time for us to connect?
Thinking of you

And our first (Yahoo Internet Messenger) IM chat as a result.

21st August, 8:32:34 pm:

    E: Hi are you there ?
        J: Yes I'm here
    E: Wow Wow
    E: So nice to meet you onine
    E: online
    E: You having a good day ?
        J: I've missed our 'conversations ' this week
        J: End of the work week for me. I'm relaxing with a glass of wine. What have you been up to ?
    E: I missed it too , what were you doing before my IM message came in
        J: Just watching some TV. Friday nights is just a relaxing night.
    E: How was work today ?
    E: Good Good Good
    E: Glad you are relaxing
    E: So tell me, what's been your online dating experience
    E: ?
        J: Work was ok. Met with my boss yesterday and got the ok to move forward with some ideas, so able to flesh them out a bit today.
    E: That's awsome !
        J: I was a bit overwhelmed by the 'chat' contacts first up. I did not respond to them. You are the only one I have any meaningful contact with. A couple that I thought interesting and put out requests to meet each came back with nos.
        J: And you? What have you been up to since back home?
    E: I can say that you are my first experience because, I signed up for the dating site, 2 weeks before I met you, but didn't have the time to use the site because I was busy with work until 2 days before I wrote you, I first wrote a lady who had a problem with the distance, then I wrote you
    E: and here we are chatting
        J: I has joined just before we connected too. I haven't done much of it. And actually haven't been our with anyone.
    E: Tell me about your work
        J: I work as an Organisational change manager, helping

prepare people for major change, often due to new IT SYSTEMS.

J: I have been in my job for about 4 weeks so still finding my way in a new Organisation

E: Oh ok.... So what were you doing before you started this job

E: ?

J: I work in the superannuation industry , and there is new laws coming in next July that people have to update their systems for.

E: Have you been enjoying the 4 weeks so far ?

J: Before this I worked I queens

J: Queensland that is

J: For a government department, again doing OCM for IT systems. I was on the same project for 6 years, and will go up for a celebration on 7 sept.

J: Just this week getting a feeling that I can do this job, getting an understanding of what needs to happen and who to connect with

J: And you?

E: I'm basically into constructions, the reason why I travel for work is because I am self employed, so I go work wherever I get a contract and I can base anywhere because I can work from anywhere

J: What sort of construction do you do?

E: I love being creative and my job gives me that opportunity, so yes I enjoy it soo much... Especially the part of being my own boss

E: Any type of building construction

E: Houses, roads etc

J: Yes nice to get the opportunity to travel too

E: Very correct

E: How will you describe your ideal partner ?

J: That's a big question...

E: ☺

J: I want someone who i can't have a good conversation with, and we are already doing this

J: I want someone to share the everyday things with, cooking, being friends going out and exploring restaurants, the country side. I want to make a life with someone and share projects - I would especially like to share a house construction project

J: I want to be physically close, cuddle and make love

J: I want to go cycling together exploring bike paths....

E: I want someone honest, caring , loving , down to earth and

The Whole Sordid Story

has a good sense of humor , a woman who will respect my point of views and I will reciprocate that, she will love my daughter as her own and I will love her kids, if she has, as mine. She'll be open minded enough to always tell me what I need to hear and not only what I want to hear. She would be to be not only a lover but also a best friend
E: for your ideal partner, that will be me
    J: Will your daughter allow another woman into her life?
E: Of course she will allow it...
    J: I have a lot of love go give, and I am very practical and down to earth. I've had to be as I've looked after myself mostly. Now I'm wanting to share more.
    J: I have no experience with kids, but I can certainly connect to a young woman, woman to woman.
    J: I will certainly tell you the truth, even if so
    J: Si
    J: Sorry
E: Of course you will connect to her
E: she is a very cool kid
E: you will love her, trust me
    J: Even If sometimes it may not be comfortable. I'm not going to play rescue games, and would expect you to be straight with me to, we must both be responsible for ourselves and our own feelings
    J: I'm sure I would love your daughter
E: That's very correct
    J: Who looks after her when you are away
E: I employed a nanny who looks after her while I am gone for wor
E: work
E: Do you have a large family ?
    J: I have two brothers, one older, one younger. My younger brother lives five mins away, and he has been great helping me settle in here. I'm invited for a roast on Sunday
E: Nice
E: My daughter is the only family I know
E: I guess you are wondering why
    J: My older brother lives 100 k east of Melbourne. I
    J: Yes
    J: I also have an auntie and uncle not too far away, and there are numerous cousins too.... But I have not lived near by since I was 17
E: My dad died in a car accident when I was only 3 years old, it was my mom who drove the car when the accident occurred, my dad's relatives blamed her for his death and threw her our

of his house, that is how she left with me from Ireland to England. I am Originally from Ireland but grew up in England. Until my dad died, I was the only child and mom never remarried....My mom didn't know her own relatives too because she was raised by an orphanage in Russia, my mom was Russian, my dad met her there before he married her she died 7 years ago

J: That's sad. My mom has a form of motor neurone disease and is increasingly physically disabled. My parents separated when I was about 5 . My father who I was not close to died in 1977. I'm very close to my mum

E: I'm so sorry about your mom's health

J: We are still waiting on a place in an aged care home to be able to move her down here.

J: Tell me again what happened with your daughter's mother

E: Ok

E: Uhmmmm.. Can I please tell you about that later, I forgot I have a dentist appointment.... Blessing just reminded me

E: Got to go now.... chat later ok

E: Sorry for cutting this..

J: Ok, I'll be off to bed soon.... Till tomorrow xxx

E: ok.... have sweet dreams

J: Try me when you get back to see if I am up [9:32:25 P]

But email is still our main communications. See also my responses to his email within the email below.

26th August:

> Hi Eamon,
> yes I also slept well after talking to you, it was good to connect again. Today I have been planting out some herb seedlings (2 types of parsley and Thai mint) I bought last week at a local market – just in pots as I am only renting here, but I do love to have my own things growing. When I went to get the larger pots and soil, I could not resist getting a dwarf lemon tree as well. I still have to find the right pot for it – a bigger one that it can then settle into. Today I also found a large pot in my garage that I had forgotten was there, so went to buy some tomato plants to put in it. I had to buy some basil too. Its great time to be planting things now – its spring here next week.
> So my little garden is growing – I have one sunny corner of

my outside area, and they are all gathered there.
So nice you are feeling at home there in Manchester. As I have moved back to Melbourne I have felt that I am coming back home here   I grew up here in my teenage years.   I wonder where we will end up – I like your idea of mutual visits – it will be important to see each other in our 'home' environments.
Thank you for your questions.   I have put some answers to you questions below....>>
Another way to get to know each other might be to say what we don't like, and to talk about those value areas – politics, religion, etc.
I had thought to pose some back to you but I'm jumping in the bath now before going to my brother's for a roast dinner, so have to go... ☺✍
I'll be thinking of you as I go to bed tonight.
Jan

From Eamon, and my responses to his questions:

Hello Dear,
       How are you and how is your day going ? I hope you did sleep well and wake up beautifully after our chat last night, my night was wonderful as your thought fills my heart, Blessing is so happy seeing me by her side, all we have been doing is talking and laughing, she enjoys playing the drum, she loves soccer and play in her school as well and she enjoys bowling a lot.
Went for my morning road walk this morning and was feeling strong when i got back, feeling the air of Manchester again....lol, it's really nice to be back home again, wish you where here with me right now...lol, but i know a time will come when you will come visit after i have been down there to visit you at first...
Was thinking about us all day and decided to ask some few question to put a spark to what we are building here which i already gave my answers to, please do not be offended by any of them, am so happy and in love with our communication and what we are trying to build here which is friendship.
1.   What is your idea of the perfect romantic date?   My answer   Dinner for 2 at a quite candlelit restaurant that lasts for a long time, just talking followed by a nice walk in the moonlight and at the end, since it is a romantic date, a

soft sweet kiss should end the night.

>>I certainly like the idea of a nice meal, and definitely a walk afterwards. I don't mind if it's a picnic though, and a walk in nature. The kiss sounds very nice.

2. Have you ever been on a cruise before, if so where? My answer No i have not but would love to and with somebody very important

>>No I have not been a cruise, I would like to but it would depend where. I'd love to do an Alaska cruise. I would also like to do some of the walks across England eg Yorkshire Moors, or cycle the river paths of Europe. As I'm often sitting at work, I like holidays to be a bit active and totally different.

3. What is your favorite food? My answer Sea food, then white rice with Jamaican sauce

>> I cannot say there is a definite favourite. I like all sorts of food, and we have such amazing choice here. I do like seafood – a lovely grilled fish, or prawns. I also like a good steak, and we have good Thai food here as well. A little spice but not too much. Too much chilli makes me hiccup!

4. How would you describe your personality type?? My answer Friendly, sincere, open-minded, giving, understanding, sharing etc..

>> I'm calm, grounded, practical, sometimes I can be too serious until I really relax with someone, and then I will be playful. I'm a little reserved in the beginning until I get to know someone, but over time, people really appreciate me.

5. What are your favorite physical activities? My answer I like to hike especially in the woods or walk on the beach, also dance around the house and when I get in the groove I like to workout swimming, biking and travelling

>> My favourite physical activity is cycling, though I have only been out once here in Melb. Its been a bit cool. I have set up my old step through bike as a trainer, and did some time on that this morning. In Brisbane I was working with a training, doing weights too, but I haven't got into a full routine yet. I also like to walk and if I cannot get somewhere near nature, even around the suburbs is good, just to get the body moving. Your dancing sounds like fun. In the past I have done swimming as a workout, and certainly like being in the water. Not so

The Whole Sordid Story

much heavy surf – I prefer a river or pool. I love walking on the beach too – always revitalising, even if the weather is not so good, it blows your cares away.

6. What is your idea of a ideal relationship? My answer   First and most important is being best friends with someone that you feel comfortable with and being able to talk to them about anything. Equal partner relationship where both parties respect each other and grow to love each other more each day.

>> I would say exactly the same – friendship is very important. I'd also say that its important to be open to finding/revealing the parts of oneself that are habitual or wounded, and healing these though a loving relationship. I see a relationship as a process of growth, and spiritual sharing, and its important to have each moment be new.

7. What have you learned from past relationships?   My answer   I have learned that I love completely, mind, body and soul, I don't know any other way to love..

>>I have learned that I can easily 'fall in love', that the love comes from within me, and may have nothing to do with the person outside. Its easy to be in love with the idea of being in love.... And to put the other person on a pedestal so you think its about them. Because this has been a struggle for me in the past I tend to be a little wary and reserved.... If/when I am reserved, it really means that there are feelings underneath... but I keep them to myself.

>>I do know that when I love fully and openly, it is a big love, unconditional and generous. And sensual and physical.

This are my questions and answers, i hope my answers are appealing to you, will wait for your own answers, it will bring us closer and give us the opportunity to know more about ourselves, when I give into something, i give fully, so that's me.

Work as usual but please do not work yourself to hard, i will always be here waiting for you when ever you are free to talk, am home now and less busy, no job for now and am not working on anything for now, all am doing now is putting things together in my home office and home workshop since i have been away for a while, so do call me anytime when you are online or want to talk on phone..

> My warm thoughts are for you,
> EAMON.

I finally find my friend Rosie's warning email, and respond to it:

> Hi Rosie, somehow I missed reading this earlier in the week – was checking emails on iPhone and probably disregarded PoF reference.   Thanks so much for your thoughts and concerns, and protectiveness.   He has now talked about coming, but yes, my sense is that he cannot know me yet and that he is projecting on to me the love that he wants.   He says that he is no going to contact anyone on PoF now.   His profile there was thosesummertimes7.   What more I have gleaned is
> He is a single child of Irish father and Russian mother.   Separated from father when he was three, brought up by mother, who died 7 years ago.
> He has a 15yo daughter – split from wife some years ago and was devastated. When he is away working a nanny looks after his daughter.
> Lives in Manchester, self employed - works when he gets contracts as civil engineer, construction of buildings, roads, etc (I wonder if he is just a builder but talking it up – his profile says he has high school education.   Nothing wrong with builders though)
> I certainly like what I have seen of him so far, but would want to meet him first.
> I'll look at RSVP, I think that's a good idea.   The only people on PoF I have been interested in have come back and said not interested.
> I'll keep you posted

I send through to Eamon some pictures of my house inside. He is interested to see where I live, and I am eager to share.

The Whole Sordid Story

And another chat, 27th August:

J: Hi there, sorry I got caught on the phone with an old neighbour from where I lived in QLD.
E: Oh ok
E: How was your day?
E: I'll wait by the computer for 30 mins
J: A little frustrating. There was a meeting that I wanted to have that was rescheduled to Thursday. I really want to get on and do things but need to get the ok to continue with my plans. Now I have to wait a few more days..
J: What have you been uo to?
E: Spending time with my daughter, thinking of you
J: I see from your photos that you have been sailing. Do you do that regularly?
E: Yes I do quite often
E: do you like sailing?
J: I have done some when I lived in Sydney. That's a lovely place to sail. I haven't done any recently, but I do like it when I do.
J: What were you doing with your daughter today?
E: doing nothing much today, just chilling
E: what time is it there now?
J: 9:58 pm. I go to bed soon, as I try and get up about 5:30 to exercise before going to work
E: Oh ok... Do you have a couple of mins to chat before you go to bed?
E: I wanna know good times to chat with you so I do miss you on IM all the time
J: Yes, ok foe a little now
J: I look for you on my way to work of a morning - between 7:30 -8:15
E: So tell me, when was the last time you were involved in a relationship
E: ?
J: I'm home about 6:30
J: There was one man who was interested in me about 4 years ago, but he was married and it went nowhere.
J: Prior to that nothing for many years
J: I have not 'lived' with anyone for a long long time.
E: My marriage ended 6 years ago, it ended because she was cheating and it was my daughter who caught her in the act, One day while I was gone for work, my daughter was ill in school and needed to go home, before she could call her mom to come get her from school, one of her teachers volunteered

to take her home, getting there she finds her mom having sex with a man in the living room. Her teacher saw it too
    J: Ouch! Not nice for your daughter or you.
E: Yes it was terrible for her. I thought I had the best marriage until this happened, she was a good pretender.... 30 months later I got involved in another relationship, which lasted for only 6 months, it ended because she didn't want to get married to anyone older than her with more than 5 years, I was older with 7 , silly excuse huh
    J: Yes, that's a silly reason. Especially when you cannot tell the age difference to look at people.
E: True....
E: On a lighter note, tell me about your house, car you drive etc.. Asking because I wanna have an imagination of the world around you
    J: I hold commitment as important, when you (we) commit to a relationship I think that's what you should live by. But people do change too, and you need to be honest about that....
    J: I have a small but quite spacious red brick single story house, 3 beds. I'll attach some photos. Let me try
E:: Are you there ?
E:: Did you send the email with the pictures yet ?
    J: Sending on IM but they are still transmitting on my iPhone.
E: Sending on IM?
E: I can't see anything here
E: I don't know if there's something I'm supposed to do, I actually don't know how it works
    J: Yes, probably not there yet...
    J: It still has the sending symbol on it....
    J: I've included a pic of my cat Cookie too.
E: I can't see it... How about you just email it
E: wouldn't that be better?
    J: I have a Kia Sportage car. A soft reader SUV, White.
E: I live in a 5 bedroom en suite house, in a suburb 10 miles away from the city of Manchester, I love my house because I built it, it has a half Olympic size pool, a Very big living room and a small one, I got a pool table in my living room. Just in case you don't use the word " en-suite " there, it means a room that got it's own bathroom
    J: I don't think I can stop it, and the photos are on my iPhone and it would take time to send on email as well. I'm sure they will appear.
    J: One thing I love is that my bathroom is accessed off my bedroom, as

The Whole Sordid Story

E: I drive an Audi A5 sportsback and Range rover sport Sc
E: they both 2010 model and Maroon color
    J: Not quite a ensuite, but works as one
    J: Nicevcars
    J: Keep typing v instead of space.....
E: Thanks a lot
E: It's ok
E: I probably should let you go to bed now
E: I'm happy we got to chat today
    J: Photo sending icon is still going- i sent 5 or 6 I think.
I'm sure they will appear.
    J: Did you design your house too
    J: Yes I'm also happy we got to chat.
E: Yes I did
E: I designed my house
E: I hope it comes through
E: Do have sweet dreams ok
E: I carry you in my thoughtd
E: thoughts
    J: Thanks yes, with a big sigh.... Goodnight.... Keep watching and send a message if they come through
E:
    J:

The content of the emails is now getting stronger and more direct, and now, some slightly sexual references. Enough to tug on any girl's heartstrings, or it does mine. References to the daughter though make it seem very normal and safe.

28th August:

Hi Dear,
Thanks for the beautiful pictures you sent me, Presume your day has ended and you had a good one, I woke up with thoughts of you this morning and my thoughts were of us cuddling, your head on my chest, whispering sweet words you would love to hear into your ears, simply wish i was there with you, am sorry if this seems too soon for me to say but it's just my heart pouring out what it feels.
My day has been beautiful and a little bit stressful, went for my morning road walk and when i returned i rushed down to my laptop to see if there was a mail from you, you should see me, i was such in a rush...lol, am really glad we are having this conversation.

> Right now I'm about going shopping with Blessing, she has really missed shopping with me, guess am trying to be the best dad that i can be...lol, i guess when we meet and go shopping together, it will be fun because i will be there to check you out when you go through the clothes you select...lol...
> Please dear one, no matter what you do, don't forget that there is someone out here who cares so much about you. Take good care of yourself and don't forget to always smile cause that's the best thing we can do with our lips....lol, I like this line a lot, although there is something else we can do with our lips.
> Lot's of kisses and a big hug from Papa bear to Mama bear.
> Eamon....

I must have received this early in the morning, responding on the train, on my way to work.

29th August:

> Your words make me feel so warm inside. I feel your love all this way across the other side of the world. I woke up with thoughts of you beside me in bed. It surprises me that I am responding so strongly to you.
> I know it's just yr feelings, but you don't know me very well yet. I think you are a bit on love with the idea of being in love, and worry a little that when we meet I won't live up to yr idea of me.
> Have fun shopping. Looking forward to our next chat. I'm also checking emails and IM.as soon as I wake up or get free fr work.
> Train arriving CBD got to go.
> Xxxxx
> Jan
> Sent from my iPhone

And his response, 29th August:

> Hello Dear,
> How are you and how was your night? hope it was lovely, my night is always beautiful because i always do take you with me into my dream world, was hoping there will be an email from you this morning and here there is one, receiving an email from you always do make my day, so don't stop...

The Whole Sordid Story

> Woke up this morning and was feeling so strong, have really had time to rest, just returned from my morning bicycle ride and decided to write you with so much joy before going into my home workshop, done putting my home office in place.
> Yesterday was fun for us while shopping, she has really missed shopping with me, we almost shopped everything that we came across, she is so happy that am back home in all ways.
> Can we always chat on daily basis? it will definitely make my day perfect getting to talk with you, sometimes it baffles me that I can't get you out of my thoughts in a day....hahahahaha and I want it that way, I want you always be part of my day.
> Well, will have to go into my home workshop and put somethings together, I hope you wake up sound and healthy.
> My warm thought are for you and you alone,
> EAMON

The frequency of contact increases, we are now talking two or three times a day, via email, phone and IM.

Still 29th August:

> So lovely to come out from work and find email from you on my phone. I'm on the train now and will be home in about an hour. I want to exercise, so perhaps we can chat after that, about 7:30 my time, or later if that suits you, as I'll also have to get some dinner.
> I am already looking forward to it.
> Xxxxx

And later on IM:

>   **J:** [7:52:12 PM] Are you there Eamon?
> **E:** [10:00:57 PM] Yes sweet one
> **E:** I'm here
> **E:** How are you ?
>   **J:** Just sending you some photos.....
> **E:** Yes sweetie
> **E:** I saw them and I'm loving them
> **E:** I've been thinking about you all day and missing you
> **E:** Do you think it's time we exchange numbers and start

33

    talking on the phone ?
       J: Me too. I even missed my train station, and I never do that lol
    E: You make me smile
    E: You've been a great source of joy to me lately and I appreciate you from the dept of my heart
       J: You are so.... I don't know how to even describe what you do to my heart. I do so want to love and be loved too. And I've never believed it possible for me. believed
       J: This is moving quickly and I want to go with it. The thought of talking on the phone is tantalizing, and scary as it means we are going to another level. As I open my heart more and more to you it gets scary....
    E: So do you think it's cool for us to start to get to talk on the phone ?
       J: +61 3 ▇▇▇, is home. Mobile is +61 401 ▇▇. Cool or not......
       J: Did you just call my mobile? The call dropped out......
    E: Yes I did
    E: I just tried to call
    E: I heard your pretty voice for a minute and then it got disconnected
    E: I hope you do like my accent when you hear it because I got an Irish/Russian mixed accent
       J: I'm sure I shall
       J: Try again
    E: Don't know what's wrong with my network
       J: I heard you walkin
    E: You wanna try calling me ?
       J: Up or down stairs
       J: What number?
    E: +447700028168

Our first phone call. I don't remember exactly what we talked about, but it felt good. At the time I think his accent is very northern European.

    E: 10:41:42 PM The sound of your angelic voice made my day... Thank you. Mwaaaaaah
       J: So lovely to hear your voice.
       J: Good night 😊

Very clever, got me to do the calling, I think later.

The Whole Sordid Story

More questions, and he sends me a song.

30th August:

Hello there,
　　How are you and how was your night? I hope you did sleep well? Thoughts of you has not left my mind for a minute since I spoke to you on the phone today, the sweet sound of your voice really really made my heart melt. I just got home not quite long, from running errands and decided to write you with utmost joy, I have added some questions as well, I want you to relax and take your time to answer this questions so I can get to know you more better, will send you back my answers when I receive your response, I want us to be as one, I want to look at you and see me through you and you through me, and the only way I believe this can happen is by being faithful, honesty, humbleness and answers, so sorry, hope it doesn't sound like an interview!)

Do you like to dance?　　Slow dance or fast?
Favorite type of music, groups, band?
Do you have any close friends in England?
What was the last date you went on - or last relationship you were in?
Favorite childhood memory?
What do you find most romantic?
Do you like things tidy/clean - or are you messy?　　(lol)
What's your favorite type of house?　　(new construction, old/vintage?)
Do you have a bad temper - or are u easy going - mellow, difficult, strict?
How about possessive, jealous?
Do you ever curse (say bad words)?　　(lol)
Do you like to drive fast/slow?
Favorite car?
Do you like to kiss, hold your man, hold hands, be affectionate?　　How about in public?
What is the most attractive feature on a man that you like?
Are you generous to people, helpful?
Do you think you're nurturing - do you take care of someone when they are sick, be by their side?
Do you worry about things - give an example of something that makes you worry?

Romance Scam Survivor

> How often do you work, what is a typical day for you?
> Where do you see yourself in 1 yr from now?
> and what's your middle? or let me know what your full names are Just curious...!
> Have added a song for you to listen as you answer my questions...lol,
> http://www.youtube.com/watch?v=kkWGwY5nq7A
> --
> Thank you.
> Hope to receive your answers soon...lol.
> A man who cares,
> EAMON...

The song definitely tugged at my heart strings. It reinforced the whole story, and a quick phone call whilst I'm on the train to work reinforces it even more.

> Good morning Eamon. So lovely to hear yr voice this morning. I had wanted to confirm that you were there, but didn't feel confident enough to call you yet, so it was wonderful to get a call from you.
> I'm now on the train...
> An interesting set of questions you have posed. I will ponder them through the day and reply tonight.
> I will be home later than usual, as I'm going to a Change Management Institute networking night with others of my profession.
> Have a wonderful sleep and talk again yr tomorrow
> Cxxxxxx

And another from him in the evening:

> Just a line to let you know that you are in my thoughts. I don't wanna call so I don't distract you from anything. I am so looking forward to connecting with you later...
> Kisses, lots of them
> Eamon

A quick reply that evening:

> Hi Eamon, thanks for your consideration . I'm home later than usual this evening after being at a networking event for my profession. I've had something to eat, but after a couple of wines at the event I am a bit tired, so think I will go to bed

The Whole Sordid Story

early, and cuddle up with my cat thinking of you. I will get to your questions, but not today.
I hope you had a good day, and I look forward to talking with you tomorrow, the end of another work week for me. I look forward to hearing your gravely deep exotic voice...... J
Ps, no middle name, just Jan, but more about names another time..... Xxxxxx

His reply, and another song. Just another blast to the heart and what every girl wants to hear. Especially me as I was wanting someone to explore my old stomping ground with.

Hello dearest one, I just woke up now with you on my mind I had a very very good sleep, my night is always wonderful cause I do go to bed with you in my thought.
I'm here missing you , wishing you were close to me, so I thought I'd give me own answers to the list of questions I sent you, I hope it makes you know more about me.
I've added a song for you as you go through my answers,
http://www.youtube.com/watch?v=5FnTclqb6Yc
(this now shows as Private, but was Rascal Flatts video of Bless the Broken Road. Other versions are available on You Tube)

Do you like to dance?   Slow dance or fast?
I love to dance to fast and slow music, music is fun and lovely.
Favorite type of music, groups, band?
I love all kind of music, as long it brings joy to the soul and can move to the beat, but I don't do hard rock .
Do you have any close friends in England?
Have not really had close friends since my divorce, decided to concentrate on my daughter and job, friends i had weren't true friends cause they never kept their promises.
What was the last date you went on - or last relationship you were in?
Last relationship I was in lasted for 6 months, this was three years ago,i have dated only her since my divorce.
Favorite childhood memory?
When my Mum bought me my first Green Snickers..
What do you find most romantic?
A kiss to say good morning, A kiss to say welcome, kissing in the kitchen as i prepare us something delicious to eat and

doing things that makes us laugh so hard while tears drops from our eyes.
Do you like things tidy/clean - or are you messy?   (lol)
I like things clean and tidy.
What's your favorite type of house?   (new construction, old/vintage?)
I love old and new houses, they both have their own memories and i love castles as well.
Do you have a bad temper - or are u easy going - mellow, difficult, strict?
I don't have a bad temper and it would take a lot to get me to that point, I am very easy going, laid back, mellow & can be difficult sometimes but not very strict person, who can't be difficult sometimes?...lol
How about possessive, jealous?
I am possessive about things and people i love but not to an extent that drives people crazy, Jealousy....don't think so.
Do you ever curse (say bad words)?   (lol)
No, I don't
Do you like to drive fast/slow?
I drive moderate but fast sometimes, depends on where I am going or my mood
Favorite car?
I have an Audi A5 Sportsback and the new Range Rover Evoque, the Range Rover Evoque is my favorite
Do you like to kiss, hold your woman, hold hands, be affectionate?   How about in public?
My lips is all yours, anytime of the day, night or anywhere, love is life and don't care if somebody is feeling uncomfortable about it cause you don't pick a true love on a road side, so i appreciate it and especially when i know my partner is enjoying it, but wouldn't do things
that will make people think I need to get a room..LOL
What is the most attractive feature on a woman that you like?
As for me, neatness, the eyes and the hands, the hands can do a lot of things...hmmmm
Are you generous to people, helpful?
Very very, i love to assist, give and support.
Do you think you're nurturing - do you take care of someone when they are sick, be by their side?
Very much, thinking of setting foundation program for the less privilege but still looking into it.
Do you worry about things - give an example of something that makes you worry?

The Whole Sordid Story

> I worry about my daughter getting older and someday she will have to be on her own in this world...lol.
> How often do you work, what is a typical day for you?
> When am on a contract, i work 8am to 7pm daily, except Sundays..
> Where do you see yourself in 1 yr from now?
> I see myself in a relationship living happily with someone I love.
> My middle name is Donegal, my daughter is Blessing, middle name Patience
> This are my answers, I hope they make you more interested in me.
> Hugs
> Eamon

And my answers, in hindsight, some very telling critical questions here about my financial capacity in amongst innocuous stuff. Maybe details for him to access my accounts. I am so trusting and naive.

> Beloved Eamon,
> listening to the songs you send have touched me more that you can know. I haven't had anyone wanting to know me in a long time, but it is exactly what I went onto PoF for. I want to explore places I grew up, here in Melbourne, and in other places around Victoria.
> Just a reminder.... I am not a slim blond young thing – I am a buxom mature woman, tending at times on the heavy side. My heart is that 18 year old though, and wants to match your love, moment to moment. I cannot wait to be by your side.
> Some answers...
> > > Do you like to dance? Slow dance or fast?
> I like to move with the music, whether fast or slow, however I haven't done it for a long time, and will need you to lead me at first.
> > > Favourite type of music, groups, band?
> I like many types of music, and hark back to my teenage years, Beatles, the Doors, many of the women singers from that age. One of my favourite albums is a Tapestry revisited one, playing King. Certainly I like ones where you can hear the words. I loved the ones you sent me.
> > > Do you have any close friends in England?
> I have a couple of old friends in England, men I have

shared houses with in the mid 80s. I haven't seen either of them for a long time, though I do connect with them on Facebook and LinkedIn. I also have distant family in England. Both my parents are English, and came out to Australia in 1953. My father died in 1977 though. I think my older brother has links to my father's family in London, and my Uncle has been back several times, researching the family tree, so there are possible connections there, but no-one I have met. Most of my closer relatives came out here.
> > What was the last date you went on - or last relationship you were in?
My last romantic connection was with my mortgage broker. I didn't know it at the time, but he was married. He pursued me a while, but when it was clear that he would not leave his wife I stopped seeing him. If he was going to cheat on his wife, he would eventually cheat on me, and I did not want that. Or to be the person who split him from his wife.
> > Favorite childhood memory?
At home on a Sunday night, cold outside, eating mackerel fish on toast cooked over the heater. I don't know why that's my favourite, but it is
> > What do you find most romantic?
That you send me songs I find very romantic. I'm not use to being romanced.... But I want you to whisper things and blow in my ear....
> Do you like things tidy/clean - or are you messy? (lol)
I like to have a place for everything, but during the week they may not reach that place LOL, but first thing on a Saturday is a clean up and reorganisation so I can enjoy a clean and tidy place when I'm there.... Life is disorganised sometimes....
> > What's your favorite type of house? (new construction, old/vintage?)
Definitely new and passive solar, but old would be OK as long as it could be retrofitted. I built a house (had built by a master builder) about 5 years ago. I still have it, as well as a large mortgage, with tenants in at present. It was by a builder called Phil Anstey, and its in a place called Ocean Shores, just north of Byron Bay in the far north of NSW. It has a large deck looking out to distant ocean view (if the trees have not grown too high). I was living there with my mother for a while, but then she needed more care, and I

had to move away to get work. I would love to live there again someday, but don't know how I could afford it. I expect to have to sell it at some stage, but there is no market at the moment. If I build again, I want another sustainable house, with views of the ocean or some water.
> > Do you have a bad temper - or are u easy going - mellow, difficult, strict?
I am very easy going, very seldom get angry, but you would know it if I did, I would be very cranky! (LOL)
> > How about possessive, jealous?
No, not at all. I believe people need their space, and they need to have their connections with many people, and each will fill different needs. That's not to say I am a swinger – I am definitely **not** that....
> > Do you ever curse (say bad words)? (lol)
I might swear if I am very angry, it will be a clue, but mostly not. There is no need....
> > Do you like to drive fast/slow?
I like to drive at the speed limit, with a good car that will support you if danger arises...
> > Favorite car?
I love the Mazda, and had a Mazda 3, but sold it for my Kia Sportage as I wanted to be able to take my mum out, and she could not get out of the lower Mazda. I would love to get the Mazda 5 or 7, but did not want to spend that much money. I very much appreciate a good car through. I will look yours up on the internet so I have an idea what they look like
> > Do you like to kiss, hold your man, hold hands, be affectionate? How about in public?
Yes, I won't be able to keep my hand off you
(LOL). Already doing this in my dreams. In public is OK as long as its not going to offend others.... The place needs to be right.
> > What is the most attractive feature on a man that you like?
A big strong chest that I can lie against...
> > Are you generous to people, helpful?
Yes I am very generous by nature, sometimes committing myself too much to helping others. I helped my 80 year old neighbour in Brisbane to get a new kitchen, took her around to kitchen places, tile places, designer, and helped her to negotiate what she actually wanted. She would never have done it without me to support her.

\> > Do you think you're nurturing - do you take care of someone when they are sick, be by their side?
I am nurturing by not soppy. I do practical things. I am very motherly, even though I have never been a mother.
\> > Do you worry about things - give an example of something that makes you worry?
No I don't worry, its waisted energy mostly. I make my decisions and do not look back. I'm good at manifesting what I want. The move down here from Brisbane could not have gone better.....
\> > How often do you work, what is a typical day for you?
I'm an office worker – Mon – Friday, 8:30 – 5 ish depending on the work that needs to be done. Sometimes longer if it is needed
\> > Where do you see yourself in 1 yr from now?
One year from now I will have finished my current work contract, so its open from there.... I do feel like I am settling here in Melbourne, and had the idea to buy a house or build here.....
\> > and what's your middle? or let me know what your full names are Just curious...!
Current legal name: Jan , no middle name
Birth Name: Jan Hoare – I changed it by deed poll when I was 17.
Spiritual name (given by Bhagwan Shree Rajneesh in 1982, late known as Osho): Prem Sangam (Sanskrit name meaning sacred place of love)
There's more to that story, but it's a long one.....
\> I hope you like my answers. I find we are very similar. Do you know anything else about your astrology. When and where were you born?

And some questions back to him:

Some questions for you
Do you read newspapers, magazines, books? What do you like?
Have you ever had any pets? Which ones?
What in your life do you think you have excelled at?
Do you do anything creative, artwork, or perhaps make music yourself?
What has been the most joyous moment in your life?
What do you like to cook?
What would you like the place where you live to be like?

The Whole Sordid Story

And later a long session on IM:

E: [8:46:56 PM] Sorry sweetie
E: I stepped away had a phone call
E: I'm here now, are you there?
   J: Yes, I had a phone call too
   J: I sent my questions by email as well.
E: Ok I will respond and send it
E: You'll have it waiting for you when you wake up
E: How was your day?
   J: Ok I look forward to it.
   J: I was preparing information that I have to show to my boss on Monday about what I want to do over the next 10 months
E: Oh ok
E: What kind of information is that?
   J: I did send it off to him, just hope he approves
E: What do you wanna so do for the next 10 months?
   J: A program of work - get the managers trained in how to lead significant change, a qualitative survey of all the business units to see how they will cope with all the change happening
E: Wow
   J: There is a lot of change, it will keep me busy. I am on a 12 month contract
E: I have no doubt that you are very brilliant at what you do
E: So after the contract, you are gonna look for another one?
E: Or you'll renew?
   J: Thank you. There is definitely more work there.... But I will see at the time. I took the job to settle here in Victoria, and then think more widely, but I tend to stay with something once I am there. The last one I took a 6 month contract and stayed there 6 years...
   J: I get attached, and loyal
E: Oh wow...
E: you got yourself another contract
E: to be my lady forever
   J: I like the thought of that one
   J: I'll definitely renew... 😍
E: ahahaahhahahaha
E: You know I always like having an imagination of how you are looking in my head, so please don't get bored if I always ask what you are wearing
   J: Grey jeans, a black grey and white shirt, with a smart red jumper adding some bright color. We have a casual day at work on Fridays...

J: You said early on, on Pof, that you would relocate for the right woman. Do you still think that?
E: Oh ok... I'm wearing a Green V neck T shirt and a black Jeans
E: Sweetie, everything I've said to you, I mean every word
E: Yes I am willing to relocate for you
E: I cannot say for the right woman anymore
E: because I believe I have found her
J: You are such a sweetheart!
E: Guess your next question will be, what happens to my daughter
J: Yes
E: Blessing doesn't want to attend University in Manchester, she says she's been here all her life, so she'd like to further somewhere else to experience a different life and culture
E: So yes, Blessing will be the first to buy the idea
J: What does she want to study
E: Architecture
J: Wonderful
J: I think if I had my life again I would study architecture
J: I think we have some good schools here
E: Good, so that makes it alot easy right ?
E: Where in your house are you right now ?
J: Sitting on my lounge with my ipad
J: The TV is on, but quietly, with Escape to the Country on. I love looking at the English houses
E: hhahaaha
E: The English houses remind you of someone ?
J: I wonder what your houses is like..
E: I lost lots of pictures with my previous computer
E: Will try to take pictures and send to you
J: I looked to see if there was a picture of my house design on line today, but the picture from the designer will not load
J: Did you loose your computer
E: It feel from my hand while I was decending the staircase
E: the screen broke
J: The hard drive should still be ok. Take it to a specialist
E: Ok will try to do that
J: What's you thoughts about coming here for a visit. Could you get work here too?
E: I'm thinking of meeting you any time soon
E: It's already an honor to me that you are communicating with me with such openmindedness even with the distance between us, so I don't wanna force or push anything on you

The Whole Sordid Story

E: but really, sometimes I wish you were just a drive away so I can come see you

J: Soon is good. Just not next weekend, Asa I'm going to Brisbane for a celebration for the project I was on.

E: Yesterday when you were leaving for work and I called twice, that moment I really wish I could kiss you to wish you a good day

J: I want to meet you, to hold you, to love you

J: I hate waiting

E: Me too, me too

E: So what did you have for dinner today ?

J: I want to know for sure that it will work between us, because I'm getting in deep, my heat is opeining g so....

E: I believe for sure that it will

E: I have never felt like this for anyone

J: I just snacked since I was home, on some taramasalata

E: the amazing thing is that, it wasn't my intention to feel this way and I didn't force the feeling

J: Me neither

E: hence it just developed on it's own, I believe it's destiny speaking

J: Ditto, its a surprise to me

E: What time is it there now ?

J: It feels right, and I have to go forward with that

J: 9:30

E: besides chatting with me

E: what are your plans for today ?

J: Tonight?

E: Yea tonight ?

J: No plans, I could not think past chatting with you

E: 😊

E: Plans for the weekend ?

J: 🎱🌸🚐

E: What's that ? 😊

J: Shopping and cleaning tomorrow. Sunday I will go out for a longer bike ride, explore so other parts of Melbourne

J: Just fun stuff..... Sending you lots of fun joy ....

E: We would ride bikes together

E: What is the longest ride you've had

J: That would be wonderful.

E: 30 mins

E: 1 hour

E: 9 hours ?

E: 😛

J: I did a 9 day tour with bicycle victoria, camping in a

45

different place every night -550 kms
E: Really !
E: I'm no match for you then
E: I'm here thinking you'll beg with to turn back
J: In training I did a 100 k ride, but I'm slow, it took me about 8 hours. I'm not in that level of training now though, mor likely a couple of hours is enough, especiallynstoppin g for a coffee on the way
J: We have good bike paths here
J: I love doing active things outdoors
J: I like long walks too
E: I love outdoors too
E: I love public display of affection
E: I hope you don't mind that I can kiss you anywhere
J: I will love that you do that at any time
J: What do you know about australia
E: but don't worry wouldn't do stuff that will make people think we need to get a room
J: Hahahahaha
E: hahaaahhahaha
E: I'm happy to make you laugh
J: Though you will be thinking it though
E: I'm not sure I completely understand your last question sweeie
E: Of course I will be thinking it
J: If you come to visit what would you like to see? I'm assuming you have not been here before, but maybe you have.?
E: One min sweetie
E: phone call
J: Ok
E: Here
J: Hello again
E: there is nothing in mind that I wanna see when I come, I just wanna see you
J: Ok
E: you can take me to see whatever you wanna take me to see
E: Not a problem
E: as long as I am with you
J: Or keep you locked up at home hahaha
E: I don't care
E: As long as I am with you
J: Wonderful
J: What are you doing over the weekend.....?

The Whole Sordid Story

E: We'll go for a movie later tonight
E: don't know what we gonna see yet, the little lady willl choose
E: tomorrow, probably some more shopping
    J: That answered my question
E: You were able to ask what movie I was gonna see ?
    J: Are you looking for another work contract yourself? Do you go through an agency to find work.
    J: Yes
    J: Let me know if the movie is any good
    J: I'm sure Blessing loves to go out with you
E: No I am not yet
E: I don't think I wanna do anymore work this yea
E: the remaining months is for Me, you and Blessing
    J: That's lovely that you have the freedom to not work. I still have to, with the mortgage on my home
E: 😁
    J: Hahahaha
E: You don't work for the mortgage of your home
    J: Yes you do make me laugh
E: You work because you want to
    J: That's partly so, but I would also love to paint.....
E: did I tell you I draw very well ?
E: Oh and also, I can write perfectly well with both hands
    J: No, I would love to see some, take some photod
E: I'll draw a sketch of you when I come to you
    J: I have an image of you using two hands to hold a pen, hahaha
    J: Yes I'd love you to sketch me
E: Just like Titanic
E: 😁
    J: Hahahahaha
    J: Do you draft plans too
E: Yes I do, but because it's not my proffession, I hardly do it
    J: Did you plan your own house?
E: Of course I did
    J: You are very clever, and I like a clever man
    J: I worked for a house builder once, and had to adjust and do quotes from the plans. I really enjoyed that work, though it's not my main profession either
E: 🙂
    J: I'm heading off to bed soon, and will read a little.
    J: I'm reading about Cadel Evans winning the Tour de France
    J: Nothing on tv

    E: Ok sweetie
    E: thanks for all your time
    E: Have sweet dreams ok..
       J: A delight
       J: You have a good day too
       J: :)
    E: You'll have your answers waiting for you and email ok
    E: Mwaaaaaah
       J: [10:20:52 PM] Ok mmmmmmm mwah

The subject of this next email is "Good morning from a heart you have made happy." It's 1st September, just three weeks after our first contact.
He's had enough information on me to check me out fully, and now knows I'm a worthwhile catch.

He reels in the line.

> Good morning dear one,
> I hope you slept well and had sweet dreams. I have answered your questions below it's bed time for me but before I go to sleep, I want to use this opportunity to say thanks for accepting my friendship, making me your friend is the best thing that has ever happen to me in a while, I really enjoy it, and I am enjoying getting to know you more. You are very special and that's why I feel honored to be your friend. Life has been a better place for me since I started communicating with you
> Thank you for giving me your attention , for all the good things you say about me, i will really like to build a more comprehensive intimacy with you because, knowing you has increased my happiness. You are great! With you near by I hardly need anything else. I know I could travel the entire world but I would never find someone as faithful as you if not for destiny.. What thrills me the most about this is that we have an over flooding honesty and a deep connection in such a short while. I trust in that lovely feeling so much considering how much attention you've given me and how good you make me feel, My pretty, you are very sweet, the best I have ever met and the best I have and will like to keep you for ever. I want you to know that you have in a true friend in me, a friend who would never avoid from any sacrifices to make you happy ,to make you feel like a queen that you are, to treat you royal because that is all that

The Whole Sordid Story

> a queen deserves
> Knowing you as proved to me that there's still good women in the world, at some point in life , I thought that I will be single for the rest of my life, but then you came to restore hope to me. You are the best any one can have!! Knowing you has made my faith in the future of living a happy life with a complete family grow, it is all I have ever wanted.
> This fairly recent connection of ours is something I consider to be sacred already. It makes me have faith again in some simple but fundamental human values, which, sometimes, for the lack of practice, we swipe under the carpets of our memories and of our hearts.
> For me, this connection of ours is precious and that's why I intend to keep it till the end of my days. I believe we can achieve that, because I have faith in you and I have more and more faith in life and in the future. Always bear in mind that my affection, love and true friendship will be yours forever, I cant wait for this to grow stronger because i am already falling for you so hard.. SMILE! and stay bless.
> Warm thoughts
> EAMON

A quick response from my iPad. My heart is very much engaged by this time, and feels full, warm, and expansive.

> A quick response for now to say thank you for your words, your friendship and your love and affection. It is very special for me.
> Sleep well, I will send my love to surround you as you sleep, as I feel you doing for me.
> Love always
> Jan

Again, later that day. I am aware of what the time is in Manchester, and thinking about what he might be doing. I check the timing on my iPhone World Clock app. The longing to connect is visceral for me and I am putting that out there.

> Good morning sweetheart. As I have gone through my day each time I have thought of you I have sent you love to wrap you as you sleep.
> I know I don't yet know you well, but somehow there is this deep connection between us. I am surprised also how fast we have connected, and wait eagerly for the next time we

> chat or talk or email. I just wish I was by your side instead of across the other side of the world. I'm impatient to meet, touch, be with the real you.
> Today as well as cleaning and washing, I have been shopping, mostly for work clothes, but with a new glad heart that is awakening to you, like the spring that is starting here today. It gives me much joy. I also never thought I would be with someone again, but now I know different. And I know it will be wonderful, however it unfolds. I have a deep sense that everything will happen as it is meant to happen, and this trust has dropped deep inside my heart.
> I've also been out enjoying the sunshine, and washing my car. It badly needed it, and I love it being clean and shiny.
> Have a lovely day, enjoy the joy that love brings
> Xoxoxo Jan

I send some photos. I want to be sure he sees me in a true light, not placing me on a pedestal or in a fantasy.

> Hi Eamon, working on my laptop, so thought I would send some more photos....
>
> 002: on our way to the 9 day bike ride, Nov 2009, I went with my friend Lynnette. We had trained for it all year.
> 005: me with my bike, a trusty step though, which I have now set up as a trainer in my lounge room
> 0012: me at work in a suit
> 0103: My Kia Sportage, new about a year ago.
> 0075 In my favourite black dress
> xoxoxxoo
> Jan

On Sunday, I am no longer restrained, becoming instead very effusive, responding to my own questions.

> Beloved, all is quiet and I'm missing you
> Some answers from me to the questions I put to you
> do you read newspapers, magazines, books? what do you like? I like to read the newspaper on the weekend, but don't much during the week. I like to read cycling magazines, and property investment magazines.
>   have you ever had any pets? which ones? Until I got

The Whole Sordid Story

Cookie two years ago, I had not had a pet for a long time, though we had them as kids. I was always practical – they don't go with a busy lifestyle sometimes. I am so pleased I got Cookie, as a kitten. He has opened my heart again.

   what in your life do you think you have excelled at? My work over the past years in Brisbane. I could not have done more for them

   do you do anything creative, artwork, or perhaps make music yourself? I paint in oils, and sometimes do crayons, but not enough, mostly when I sign up for a class. I must do that now I am settling in to Melbourne. I like life drawing, and abstract, but need to practice more....

   what has been the most joyous moment in your life? When I was in India at an ashram, opening my heart to the universe

   what do you like to cook? I'll cook anything, but at times when there is just me I am not so motivated, and cook very simply

   You've travelled a lot, what would you like the place where you live to be like? Ideally, I would like somewhere with some land –enough for a nice garden, and not too far from the beach, so I could walk each day and swim in the summer. That could be anywhere though, its more about the people around you ...

Thinking of you

   Jan

On Monday, 3rd September, I get a response to the photos I had sent.

Hello sweet one, the beautiful woman thousands of miles away that makes my heart melt. Thanks for the pictures you send, I love em. I am here missing you so much but I know you are working and I don't wanna distract, so I just thought I'd sit by the computer here and write you thinks about me to enable you know your man better

   Here are some of my favorite things

Color - love Green. I love interior design and also love to be creative. I love a clean and decent environment

     Food - love all foods and they are very delicious with the right person to share them with. There is not to many dishes that I have not tried and cook most really well. Love going to romantic restaurants for a nice dinner (steak, pasta, fish, chicken, rice anything). I also enjoy sea food.

Movie - love action and romantic movies, my favorite is horror movies. Need that special person to go to them with though!

Perfume/Cologne - I love B&G, Given chi play, Armani code.

Gifts to Receive - A hand written note, A beautiful card, flowers, paintings and art work.

Books- Love reading historical books and journals, newspapers and romantic novels when am in the mood.

Poem- I love to write poems or something inspirational in my quiet time but most times am been inspired by those close to my heart.

Style of Clothing - I feel very comfortable on casual dressing but also love to look official sometimes, depending on the event.

Flower - love lilies, roses, lily of the valley, orchids

I think I'm most passionate about finding my soul mate, the one woman out there I have been waiting my whole life for so I can show her all the love and care I can give. To live for nothing else but to be with her and to spend the rest of my life with her in every moment of true love.

I think the three things I am most thankful for would be.

Having the best gift of life (my daughter) and the best mom though she's late

Having my own life, because sleeping and waking up is a miracle

Opportunity to seek that one woman.

I am secure about my self and able to defend myself and my mate, but I think my biggest strength would come from being with and loving my partner. I would always protect her as well as work together with her to solve problems. I am a good listener and understand lots of things told to me and I remember little details that i can someday use to surprise you and make you happy. It is hard for me to get lost when out in the elements and nature, and I try very hard to solve problems.

There are many qualities that I look for in a woman but most important of all is honesty, without honesty there can be no trust, without trust there can not be true love. A relationship without trust is only sexual and can lead to many problems. While with true love there is wonderful love making and sex is great but true love comes from the heart and with that love making love is much better.

The first thing anyone would notice about me other than my appearance is how much I care for the people around me. I think it comes from having too big of a heart. I tend to take on the world's problems and worry too much, and it can make me sad.

Things I can't live without. hmmm..

Love- I have gone without it for so long that it feels like i am not alive. but i want to be alive.

Helping those in need- I believe that what ever you sow you reap.

Good health- Because without that nothing matters and I would have nothing to offer the one I love.

My ideal dream house will be a country home cottage with a fabulous design, big kitchen and a lovely beach view.

Ideal of a perfect date- Letting it flow, Walking hand in hand, romantic dinner, talking for hours and never getting tired of each other

Am a morning person. Love all animals.

Three words best describe me- Loyal, Honest, Big Heart-ed, and Compassionate.

Lately I've been thinking of you, with thoughts of yesterday I had dreams this morning and I woke up smiling. A smile is on my face, because we met so gracefully we orchestrated our own music, like a song with melodies a very harmonic explosion this memory is such sweet bliss. We share some commonalities and with you I always smile at times I wish we were together. I wish that i could make you happy by giving you the world

You in my thought..

Eamon

I can't help but respond from my heart, fully and openly.

Eamon, my lovely, your email has the heart in my chest just about exploding. Thank you for honoring me with all this info about yourself. I feel each one like a caress, knowing that if you were here it would be shared with a caress, and a whisper in my ear. My love is spreading all the way around the world to you.

Over the past days something has changed for me. As we have been getting to know each other over the past weeks,

short weeks, I know I have been reserved and a little wary. What's changed is that, your love has penetrated and reached me at my very core, and a calmness has come over me. Now I feel your love, and know that whatever happens, everything is ok, better than ok.
I want to go to the next level of intimacy with you, and I know it will unfold in due course, and it is not something that can be rushed, we between us have even orchestrated this, somehow connecting across the world. But we have connected from across the world, I don't even understand how, it amazes me.
I know Blessing is also your priority, I won't and can't compete with that, and I have to wait till its right for you to come to me. Now I can wait, though the longing to have you beside me is at times painful.
Meanwhile hearing your voice makes me smile, reading your emails makes me smile, with an inner joy and a fire burns deep within.   I want to get lost with you, and know you will find the way for us.   I want to have problems that only you can solve for us. I want to go to horror movies with you, and will, and I don't even like them, but know you will make me feel safe. I want to drive fast with you, knowing I will feel save and secure with you at the wheel. I want to walk on the beach with you, and run and splash and play..... And so much more.....
Did I write all that? Nooooo....
   Jan

Tuesday, 4th September:

Hi Eamon, I was a bit overwhelmed at the level of my own feeling yesterday, and I wonder how you respond to it.
My turn to answer some of the questions on some of my favorite things
Color - as a Leo I love yellow and gold, but my favorite is a deep dark blue/green, the color of the deep sea, sometimes with a slash of hot pink for contrast.
Food - yes I will eat most anything, and unless there is a special occasion or someone special will mostly cook simple food. I can usually make a tasty meal from whatever there is to hand.   I don't need a recipe to follow, but can if I need to make something special.
movies - I don't get there often enough, I love a good comedy, and one that tells a good story.   I also like to go to

The Whole Sordid Story

the theatre, for drama, or even a good musical.
Perfume, natural oils, lavender, rose geranium,
neroli. Shalimar, by Gerlain. Mostly I like my man natural.
I want to fill myself with the scent of you. I want to breath you in to my being. Even just the thought of it has my juices flowing.....
Gift to receive, something alive- flowers in a pot that will keep flowering, a special occasion, a night out at a performance or theatre, or ever at the tennis.
Books- I buy work books but I don't read them. I like a good mystery thriller, especially with a woman detective. When I am really stressed I love to read a good science fiction or fantasy book, sitting in a comfortable chair, or even a good bath.
Clothing- I don't dress up often, but love to when there is something special on. Mostly I wear bright colors or stones and greys. Oh, and red.
Flowers - daffodils, roses, gingers and day lilies. I grow African violets. The ones I brought down from Brisbane are still adjusting to their new home and haven't flowered again yet. I like to propagate them, and then give them as a gift. I have purple, pink, maroon, and variegated ones.
My cousin Lisa has given me an orchid that was actually grown by my uncle Bram- he has been dead for quite a few years now and she took all his orchids. It has two long sprays of flowers that have just opened this week. They are large yellow flowers, with red spottings on the flower tongues, very lovely. Perhaps when you come you can help me re-pot them, as they haven't been done for years.
Love- I have always wondered why, when I have such a big heart, that a relationship just didn't happen for me. I had given up thinking that anyone would really love me. Moving back to Melbourne, coming back to where I grew up, somehow made me think that at least I could find a friend to explore the old places with. That's one reason I love the song you sent me, about going to all the places I grew up. (i love romantic songs) And now something more than I could ever imagine has happened. Do I dare even put words to it? Now my ideas are totally blown and I don't know what the future will hold, what I can dare hope for......
I had thought that I was just going to be a good friend and daughter......
what I am grateful for- my friend Lynette, who has been a good friend for 10 years, introduced me to cycling again, we

have spent many delightful hours cycling together. She has also been a good friend to my mum, who knew her before me, and regularly takes her out shopping. It makes it possible for me to be down here, knowing someone looks out for Mum. I still talk to Mum every day though, sometimes more.
I'm also grateful for my cat, who has awakened me again to loving unconditionally, showing me I can.
Enough for now, time for bed, dreaming of my head on your chest, breathing in the scent of you..... 😊

Always yours, Jan

On the 6th September he writes:

Hi dearest one, I'm here thinking so much about you and missing you, it's so early in the morning there and I cannot call to wake you up, so I thought I'd imagine you asking me questions and me answering them, just to be able to let you know more about me you've fallen for
Who has been the biggest influence in you life?
My Mom

What kinds of things really make you laugh?
I love to laugh, just anything worth laughing makes me laugh

What's your favorite place in the entire world?
For now, Paris because of the beauty

Who is your best friend? What do you like about him/her?
I don't have a best friend. The woman I have a relationship with next, will be my lover and best friend

Favorite movie of all time? Why so?
City of Angels, it shows how much sacrifice one can make for love

Favorite book? Why so?
The Bible, it's the word of God
What is your favorite way to spend your day off?
Just do anything fun with my daughter, if I have a partner, then I will think of what to do

The Whole Sordid Story

Do you have any pet peeves?
Unnecessary , continuous hooting

What were you like as a child?
I've been gentle all my life, but never scared to do anything, as a kid, I always liked to play games and help my mom

Who was your favorite school teacher or professor? Why?
I loved both my biology teacher in high school. My biology teacher was super nice but tough so some other kids did not like her. But I really felt like she cared about her students and she was passionate about the subjects she taught us about.

When you are just hanging out at home, what are you wearing?
I dress casual, short with T shirt or just some plain jeans with T shirt
I know you enjoy your daughter, but what other things do you do? What kind of entertainment do you like? What about adult things ?
I enjoy going for a dinner with my partner, the drive somewhere to watch the moonlight, I like concerts, I like anything fun

What's the last movie you saw?
The new Batman

Do your daughters friends hang out at your house? Or do they collect somewhere else?
They hangout here sometimes and she goes to them too

Do you like to read? to relax? to learn? for entertainment?
I like to do all

Do you drink? And what is it you drink?
I drink only white wine, red causes me headache, I drink champagne too

When you are having a rough day, how do you relax?
Jump into the pool, when the weather permits, it cold, I chill with a glass of wine in my Jacuzzi
If I'm having a bad day, how do you make me feel

better?
Ok it depends, but let's say you come home from work not looking cheerful, first I will help you take off your coat, collect your hand bag from you, make you sit down then I will get you a glass of whatever you like (I don't know your favorite yet), I will go make water warm in the Jacuzzi, put two glasses of wine there, come back help you take off your cloths and lead you to the jacuzzi and we go in together to relax with the glass of wine in the Jacuzzi, then we can talk about your day

What is your day like when you are not on a contract?
I spend time with my daughter and attend to all my work emails from my house because I have my office here

Do you play or watch sports?
I used to play soccer until I broke my ankle, I am a loyal Manchester United fan, I watch soccer

What is your favorite thing to eat? Are you picky?
My favorite food is Rice with chicken stew, but I am not picky, I like to try new food.

What do you like to do in your spare time?
Play pool , I got a pool table in my house

Have you ever been here? Do you plan on visiting here? Do you have any friends here?
No I have never been there, Yes I plan to visit when it's the right time for us to meet, I don't have friends there

Do you wash dishes, or use the dishwasher? Both
I hope you like what you read..

Kisses
Eamon

It crosses in the night, and I respond on my way to work. We are talking regularly by phone. There are also a couple of photos sent through. One not so good, but one of him in an expensive looking white linen shirt.

My body is responding directly and strongly to him and I am very turned on sexually with my juices flowing.

The Whole Sordid Story

> Good morning again my sweetheart.
> I'm now on the train to work.
> Talking with you last night and this morning was wonderful. My body responds to you very strongly, and I long to have you here in person.
> I think of you often throughout my day. Even though you don't call me at work, and I appreciate that, I am distracted and my body reacts just thinking of you.
> I love reading the things you have written, and will re read it during the day, taking each answer into my picture of you.
> I'll look at some dates for you to come. I have an idea, but will need to check getting some time off.
> Sleep well my darling. 😍 😘

And again later:

> Good morning.
> How was your day ? I hope it went well. Mine has been busy been on a long conference call, I will call you after this email to talk about it with you.
> I have not read any particular books for making relationship grow, but I know that the major things that make relationships grow in a good way is, open-mindedness, honesty, attention , care and respect of the point of view of one another, we don't lack any of these in our relationship, so I believe that it is surely gonna grow. I have been thing thinking of a pet name to give you, i didn't want to call you something common, I don't wanna call you an every day names. I came up with Nectar, it means a beautiful flower with nice fragrance, a sweet liquid secreted by flowers of various plants, consumed by pollinators, such as hummingbirds and gathered by bees for making honey. Nectar are u lonely like I am? like I have felt all night long thinking of u? Before I knew you, I never knew what loneliness was, never felt it, but now i know you , and all of a sudden I feel so alone without you. why is it so hard to get you off my mind? will like to lie close to you, feeling your heart beating. Just want to hold u close till the end of time. I hope you like the pet name, if you don't please don't hesitate to say, there's nothing wrong in that
> Nectar, I've falling so hard for you
> Love, lots of it, Eamon

In a call, Eamon tells me that the teleconference he had was about a work opportunity that has come up in Dubai. He has

59

been asked to do a six to eight week project taking some pipes there and doing some maintenance on an oil refinery. He had previously been asked to do this work, but it had not happened. Now they had come back to him again about doing this.

What I remember about that call is that he promises he is not going to disappear. This is important to me because it has happened to me before. I've had one man disappear, never to be seen or heard from again despite my efforts, and it remains a fear that it will happen again. I have a fear that I am not worthy of a long term relationship.

We also talk about his coming to Australia straight from Dubai, towards the end of October. It begins to feel that this will actually happen, that it will be more than just a fantasy, he is actually coming to meet me.

I don't realise that the 'pet name' is another tool of the professional scammer. I just respond from my heart.

Friday, 7th September:

> Eamon,
> I love it. I am touched so deeply with this beautiful name that you have found for me. So many lovely meanings within it. For me for it to be right I need you to say "my" in front of it, for you to say "my Nectar". For it to be a loving declaration of my belonging to you. I belong to you.
> I don't know where this comes from for me to say this, I have been an independent miss for so long, I can't believe I'm saying it, but it comes from a truth deep within my heart.
>   I want so badly to curl up within your arms, yes I am lonely for the touch that we cannot yet have. I think of you when i wake up, on my way to work, on my way home from work, through the evening, when I go to bed. Especially then when I imagine you touching, caressing, loving me.
> It feels good to know that you are coming, that what is going on between us, this growing love, can become grounded in everyday reality. That will help it grow. I'll hopefully be able to confirm on monday that I can get those days off, nov 2 to 6. You can come earlier and stay later, that's no problem, it's just those days that I will have off work.
>
> As you travel off to Dubai, stay safe. I hold you in my heart.
> Your Nectar xxxxx

The Whole Sordid Story

And from him:

> Good morning Nectar, I hope your having the sweetest dreams of us as I write this mail. I love to sleep with the sound voice. It gives me a very sound sleep and sweet thoughts when I wake up.
>
> What more will be your real effect when you are only inches away? Baby you take my breath away by just the thought of being close to you. My heart has been skipping too many beats these last few days. I can't eat.. can't sleep.. can't stop thinking about you...Your killing me softly. I have being thinking so much about you lately and i must confess that in recent times i have being really happy, i think of you and i smile, just a mere thought of you just lightens everything in me.am so glad knowing that you feel same for me. GOD!!!!! you don't have the slightest idea do you ?
>
> I just fear that am not in this alone, i believe that my feelings for you will be reciprocated as this will give me unending joy..
> You have actually stirred up that which i thought didn't exist again in my life, the ability to love and be loved, the ability to think of a woman and smile.. I love you for that..
>
> Nectar I am so happy to know that I am your sweet heart, I want to be that man to touch your face, hug you , hold your hands, kiss your lips and make love to you for the rest of your life, I am not scared about this at all because I know for sure that this is divinely ordained..
>
> Talk to you in the morning (your time)..
> I LOVE YOU
> EAMON

In another phone conversation Eamon tells me that Blessing has become very upset that he is going to Dubai and leaving her home again, when he had promised to be at home for the rest of the year.

After talking to her teacher, the same one who was with her when she found her mother having sex with another man, he has reluctantly agreed that she can come with him. The teacher is providing suitable school work for her to take and do, and will supervise this.

This will also mean that he won't be able to come straight out to Australia afterwards, but will need to take Blessing home first, then he would come out.

And later, as I board a plane on my way to a work reunion in Brisbane, I write:

> My sweetheart, the hummingbird to my nectar, I hope you had a good night, and that your preparations to go to Dubai go well today. how long is your flight?
> I'm at the airport on my way to Brisbane now. I'll be staying with my friend Dot, who I used to work with, and tomorrow we are going whale watching. That will be a real treat, as it is something I have wanted to do for ages. She is English too, and I think her husband is in England now so she will be thankful for some company.
> Yes I'll still have my cell phone with me.
> I'm keeping my images of our first meeting to myself for now. It's too far off. I'll be nervous though.....
> And I'll just want to take you home, and to bed... And there both our dreams and wants can come true, however they unfold. I'll leave that to destiny....
> Keep safe as you work in Dubai, as I know you will do long hours and days.
> My flight is boarding, have to go. Thinking of you and loving you.
> Jan

A Marriage Dream

The dream of a life together builds.

Still on Friday, 7th:

> Hello Nectar,
> How are you enjoying your time in Brisbane, very well I hope. It was so so nice speaking with you this morning, it really really made my day. My night was so great, it's been so great since the day I met you, you've added so much positivity to my life, I had sweet dreams of us meeting, it was so real in the dream, and I could see all that imagined, I wanted to leave back to England, you didn't want me to go. I am so excited to know that you have me completely, your emails have been wonderful, thanks for sharing alot and being part of me.
> Am so glad to have this feelings that you will be there when I walk through that door and kiss you and make you feel the love that I have through every kiss and touch when I come visit. I think of things we will do together and here are some of them.
> I see us as a family playing a game and eating pizza and having fun and just laughing and sometime during the game I will grab your hand and squeeze, just to let you know that I am so glad to be right there with you.
> I see us making dinner while you tell me about your day.
> I see us cuddled up on the couch under a blanket drinking hot chocolate and just talking as the fireplace crackles.
> I see us sleeping in because when we wake we are all wrapped in each others arms and don't want to move.
> I see me taking your hand and leading you to the bedroom. Candles are lit, soft music is playing and we make passionate love for hours.
> I also have some wants...
> I want to be there when you are sick, I want to take care of you.
> I want to be there when you have had a bad day and just need held or to vent about your day.
> I want to be there when you have had a great day and want to tell me all about it.
> I want laugh and act silly with you.
> I want to go for a walk with you.

> I want to build a happy home with you. (I hope it is not to soon to say this).
> I want to know every inch of you, Kiss every inch of you, Feel every inch of you.
> I love what we are having and building....both of our dreams will come true i know.
> Another song for you expressing my feelings, i prefare the acapela by the Jackson's 5 but i also like Mariah,
> http://www.youtube.com/watch?v=KT-H5eSQ-1U
> http://www.youtube.com/watch?v=52d20PK_Kyk&NR=1
>
> Hope to hear your voice when you wake up.
>
> Your man,
> Eamon....

He has built a picture of my ideal longing and dream, even better than I could imagine myself. A picture of how it might be to share my life with someone. It is a very powerful incantation of my wants and desires, and his ability to fulfil them expressed as his own. I read it again and again. The Michael Jackson video is a good oldie, and reinforces this feeling. The Maria Carey one won't play here in Australia for copyright reasons, so I cannot see this.

I must have the last word of the day...

> Hi beloved,
> I am home at Dots now, have had a good evening connecting with people I have worked with over the past 6 years.
> I love all you have written here, and will savour it as I go to sleep tonight.
> I'm tired now, and going to bed, thinking of you beside be.
> Call me whenever you want or can...

Many of these words are reinforced, repeated and reiterated in our phone conversations, as well as late at night or early in the morning when we are talking or texting. I keep up the frequent contact the next morning, not knowing when I might hear from him again.

The Whole Sordid Story

Saturday, 8th September:

Good morning my darling. I hope your travel has gone well and you and Blessing are settling in to Dubai. Will you be in an appartment there?
I'm shortly heading off whale watching, but will be thinking of you during the day.
Xxxxxx
Jan

Later that evening an email comes through called "ARRIVED!"

My Nectar,
How are you doing? Great I hope, I arrived safely, I missed you so much today because I was wishing I was in the plane flying to you.. Nectar, I really really did miss you so much. You are such a sweet lady ,thanks for sending me safe flight mails ,it was so good to check my email and read something sweet from you, for years I have wished to have a woman who cares to know how my journey went and the progress I am making where I am
   I feel quiet bad right now , Blessing forgot the bag where we had our phones in, my wrist watch, my ipad and her laptop and her game at the Airport, that she needs to keep herself busy while I am working..
When we arrived, the first thing i did was to request for an internet connection and Blessing was smiling at me because she knows the reason am such in a hurry to get connected to the internet , which is because of you, I told her all about you in the plane she is so excited and happy for me.....lol, she said now she sees the reason why I've been acting like a teenager lately...lol, how funny, she is very happy for me. You need to see the way she embarrassed me in the plane, she screamed " daddy's got a girlfriend, daddy's got a girlfriend " every one in the business class looked at us, some laughed, some said " go dad" while some gave me this look. I had to close her mouth with my hands

Romance Scam Survivor

Here is a poem I once read, I dedicate it to you

When I Open My Eyes
To See The Sun Rise
I Think Of You.
When I Hear A Robin Sing
On The First Day Of Spring
I Think Of You.
When I See A Red Rose
On The Bush Where It Grows
I Think Of You.
When I Feel The Summer Heat
On The Sand Beneath My Feet
I Think Of You.
When I Sit On A Beach
Another World Just Out Of Reach
I Think Of You.
When I See The Colored Leaves
Fall To The Ground From A Light Breeze
I Think Of You.
When I Look To The Night Sky
And See The Sparkle Like In Your Eyes
I Think Of You.
When The Snow Is Coming Down
To Softly Blanket The Ground
I Think Of You.
When I Go To Bed At Night
As I Turn Out The Light
I Think Of You.
When I'm Old And Near Death
And I Draw My Last Breath
I'll Think Of You

Love forever
Eamon

I was not as touched by the poem as the songs he had sent. I respond immediately with:

I have been checking the emails every 5 minutes. So happy to hear you are there safe.
    I am out to dinner and will write more later.
    Love love you

The Whole Sordid Story

Then later with:

> Hi my beloved Eamon, I've had a good day today, out with the whales, and it'd been lovely with my friend Dot, but I was also wishing it was you I was sharing it with.
> I had to drive a car back on my own, and I was allowing myself to imagine you touching me. My juices really flow just thinking of you . You don't know what effect you have on me. I just wish you were
> Will you be ably to get your phones etc back, or will you just buy replacements? Maybe it was Blessing subconsciously not wanting to do schoolwork ...?
> I understand how much she would want to be with you and not be left behind in England. Will she be alone while you are out working? That would be hard for a 15 year old I would think.
> I'm pleased you have said something to her about us and that she has taken it well, even if she embarrassed you. Her reaction has been of concern to me, wondering if she will let me get close to you.
> Of course I have been thinking of our little plan to get together after Dubai, and relishing the thought of having you totally to myself for that short few days, however if you want to bring Blessing as well, I know we will somehow make it work. It will just work differently from what we first imagined.
> Would it work any better if I came to you? Longer flights perhaps..... I just want to be with you in whatever way works best.
> I have also begun to tell people about you, saying I am totally smitten (which is an understatement!). Some people warn me about the scammers on the Internet, others are happy that I have connected with someone. Mum asks what is his politics, and religion... ? Straight to the point is my mum lol.
> Beloved I know you will be busy settling in, getting your work underway in the next few days. Know I will be thinking of you, and that it is ok to call me anytime.
> My mobile is below if you have lost it. Home is +███████. I haven't checked the time difference yet, but hopefully it's better for us.
> Dot is taking me down to see Mum tomorrow she is about 1.5 hrs away, then I'll be getting a late flight home tomorrow evening, probably home about 9:30pm. Jan

Romance Scam Survivor

He replies:

Hello Nectar, I'm just about to go to bed now , the time is almost 1 am in the morning here. I've had a very long day. Before I wrote you this morning, I had cleared the pipes from the airport. The man assigned to take me around here, got together for me 20 men to do the manual labor, at 6pm I took them through a safety class, so we are ready for work tomorrow. This may surprise you that I'll be working tomorrow, but here in Dubai Sunday is the first day of work, just like Monday is for us, remember this is an Arabic land, Friday and Saturday is their no work days.

I know that neither one of us had in mind that we would meet someone on the Internet and fall in love but it has happened to me. And for that, I have no regrets. In fact, it is one of the best things that has ever happened to me in years.

For this, and what has happened to us and between us I have you to thank..

Tomorrow's hopes and dreams will never die as long as we believe in one another, follow our hearts and pray. The kindnesses in our hearts will guide us to accomplish many things in life and overcome all challenges and all obstacles. Never give up, always have faith in yourself, and you will gain the greatest gift of all, the gift of hope and love you rightly deserve...

Whatever you may do in the future, never let anyone stand in the way of you pursuing your dreams. Know that you will always have me to rely on whenever you need me. No matter what you may decide to do in life, I will be right there to help, support, and love you.

I know I can't give you the whole world, but I can promise you I will always love you. My heart is yours, and even though I know I¡ll make mistakes, I will never break your heart. I¡ll be right beside you as we chase our dreams together, and you will never have to wonder if I care...

I think about you all day long and when I'm not near you my mind is consumed with thoughts of being close to you...

Just can't wait to see you near me.. I feel like everything in the world is right, and I know I don't have to ask God for anything because as long I have you in my life I have everything I could ever want. All I want to do is spend the rest of my life making you as happy as you have made me. Darling, I went to bed last night with a vision of you next to me. I slept like a baby all night, because I was not feeling

The Whole Sordid Story

> alone. When I awoke this morning to see if it was real or if it was a dream, realty hit me that it was only a dream. Very soon, I know that you will be right next me, and that I will not have to dream of it again because you will be right there so we can hold, hug, kiss and squeeze each other tight.
> Babe, I long to be there with you so I can help build you and support you, so that we can accomplish a whole lot together as one...
> I got me a small phone here that can make and receive calls, the number is +971553796376. Please please call me as soon as you get this, can't call you yet because the international calling hasn't been activated. I miss your voice so much
> My heart belongs to you.. all yours,
> Eamon

We talk on the phone, and he tells me laughingly about the situation with Blessing on the plane, when he told her about me. He was so happy about it. I'm thinking of the future though.

> So So lovely to talk with you just now. And to know I can any time.
> Just a little practical matter.... If you come here to visit me you will need a visa. Here is the
> link //www.immi.gov.au/visawizard/
> Sleep well my darling.
> Xxxx

It seems we are thinking the same things at the same time. Sunday, 9th September:

> Hey Nectar, I'm ready to go start my day, it was so nice to sleep with the sound of your voice, it gave me the sweetest dreams. Thanks for the link about the visa, it shows me how much you are looking forward to seeing me, I already made enquires about it and saw that all I need do is apply for a tourist visa online and I will get a 3 months multiple entry.
> My love, I feel you so near and so distant in the same moment. Every day I find something new in you, something that makes me feel different but sure in one thing you are not only my friend, you are something more, something deeper. Do you feel the same?
> What further words can describe what we have together?

> For us to grow as it has this past times, I took with every beat of my heart. Words can no longer describe it, but rather in feeling and emotion of what we have for each other. You have always had the key to my heart, and you inside my heart has made me more than I can ever be. Though the sea separates us till that special day, I know we take each breath with every beat, and always together.
> I knew that you would hold my heart in your hands and you more than do that because you are honest and trustworthy...you completely own me and every part of me. When I think of you, my heart is so full of love and passion for you that I can hardly contain myself. I think of spending every minute of every day with you and holding you so close to me. Whenever you think of me, please know that no matter how many miles separate us or how much of our lives comes between us, you are and always will be my sunshine and I will never let you down or make you feel bad.. nothing but happiness and true love..
> I am coming for you...I have been here longing to hear the sound of your voice, the touch of your hand, your laughter ever since I first dreamed of you...I have never seen you, but I don't need to. I know that you are perfect for me... We are perfect for each other, in every way. I am torn by the fact that I do not know if I have ever seen you before, or if you are someone I will find later on in my life. I know I will find you, but I find it hard to wait. Every night I dream about you, and every morning you seem to dissolve before my eyes when I first open them... I want you to be the one I wake up in the morning and see next to me, someone who I can take care of and who will also take care of me..
> You give me the most amazing feelings inside, I'll never be able to thank you enough for that... you are the reason I live, breathe, love and laugh. You mean everything to me my sunshine.. Together we can do anything.. I can't imagine where I would be right now without you to think of and and knowing you are there for me.
> Loving you more and more
> Eamon
> P.S Please call anytime

Again, it is everything I wanted to hear, reinforcing the dream that he is coming and will be constant and true with his love and caring for me.

I do call him during the following days. It seems, from the sounds in the background of the calls that he is working.

The Whole Sordid Story

I get texts which confirm:

> **E:** First day at work is going well and I'm thinking about you. Eamon loves Nectar.

And on at least one occasion he could not talk, saying later that he had to work with the men, to make sure what they were doing was safe.

I respond to this email as I fly home from Brisbane.

> My heart is totally open and on the line.
>
> By beloved Eamon, I'm taking some time to write on my iPhone while in airplane mode. I'm hope the email will go once I reconnect.
> To answer your question "do I feel the same way?" YES. I didn't expect to fall in love this way, but I have. There are many levels. One of these is the deepest spiritual level of our beings, that has perhaps gone through lifetimes together, that has waited for the right time in this life. I'm amazed at how soon after I went on POF that we connected. Finally I was ready, and something across the universe let you know. A credit to you that you were there waiting and heard the call..
> And as we connected more and more I felt my heart opening to you, you demanded it of me and any doubts I had were answered. This is the strongest part of our connection. I do believe we are very attuned in our hearts, beating as one across the worlds. And I am amazed at the strength of my feeling for you and I thank you for bringing me to life, to lightness, to a place that is both vulnerable and strong. There can be no one else but you.
> Our friendship is just starting and will grow as we explore how we do things together going forward. I'm not used to being cared for and looked after, yet i feel such a gentleness coming from you, combined with an absolute demand that I let you take care of me. I respond to this with the core of my womanhood and totally respect you for it.
> What was it that I was trying to say about friendship? Oh yes, that I think there is much that we are both interested in, that we can explore together, that we can learn from each other, from the different lives we have led, that will continue to grow and enrich both our lives. I am so looking forward to

playful arguments, sharing our dreams, deciding on one and making it come true together. Playing at the beach or in the pool, holding hands as we go to a special place to watch the sunset, you waking me up because a sunrise is too beautiful to miss. I don't care where, I just want to start now.

I want to know about how you work with your men, to see you work with your own hands, and to have those hands on me, touching me.

On the physical level (finally we got here lol), I'm already so attuned to you I feel like a coiled spring, and you would just have to breath softly on me and I will explode with soft ripples from the inside out. I'm waiting impatiently for that day. You have lit a fire.... All this and we have not even met!

  I don't understand it but I love it.

  I want to have that fire burn, and wake up with you beside me, legs intertwined, hearts intertwined.

  I wish I was flying to you now. My work holds little interest in the face of just wanting to be with you. I've had a lovely time over the past couple of days, and it has shown me the absence of you.

As I have been writing this I have been shaking a little. It could be the cold, but I think it's the depth of my feelings for you and expressing something sacred, that I did not think possible, did not think was for me this lifetime.

I think what we have is sacred. When I say I love you I fill it with the most simple to the most complex meanings and all levels. I love you. And it's forever.

I feel the plane descending

I love you.....

And in the early hours of the next morning on IM, yes, that question came. I have already thought about this, it's been on my mind that I want to be with this man, that I want it to be forever, so the answer is there immediately.

    E: [1:40:28 AM] I love you
        J: Xxxxx I stole your heart
    E: Oh yes you did
    E: I will not get you arrested for it
    E: You are the best theif I've ever seen, because you stole my heart from where it is to where it ought to be
        J: Hahaha
        J: You make me smile and laugh

J: I have no nighty on
E: You've given me a permanent joy my love
E: I really cannot thank you enough
J: Just the Duma wrapped around me as if it was you
E: Awwwwwwwwww
E: Really
E: I so wish I was there right now Nectar
E: You wanna know what I'll be doing to you if I was there ?
J: Mmmmm
E: Mmmmmmm......
E: I'll take you through different levels of orgasms
J: Yeeeessss.....
E: I will make love to you and make love to you and make love you... We'll be making up for all the time we've not made love
J: I want it fast first because I won't be able to wait, then slow....
E: You are the best thing that has ever happened to me in a long long time
E: Oh yes sweetie, you are thinking like me
J: Ditto my love
E: the first day, I wouldn't be able to talk it slow, because I wouldn't be able to control me, but after the first time, then I will take time to explore your body, I will take time to discover all your spots, the ones you know and the ones you don't know
J: Spots... Mmmmmmm
E: Oh yes.... spots
J: That will take a while.....
E: I'm a patient man my love
J: I adore a patient man
E: Sweetie, if you are in love with a man and you are sure he loves you just as much, will you get married to him if he asks ?
J: Yes, this minute!
E: Dancing Dancing Dancing
E: I AM without doubt that you are the woman meant for me
E: we were just away from each other, getting experiences of life to be able to enjoy a beautiful future
J: Getting all we need to be better together
J: Yes yes yes
J: You have made me so happy
E: Do you know why we always agree with each other ?
J: Haha ha
E: It's not because, we have the best thoughts, it's because even in our hearts we are a match and we think alike
E: so whenever you send me an email, if seems like you've

said it all and there's none for me to say
E: feels like you said what I'd have told you if I was to write before you
   J: So true so true
   J: I've been thinking about marriage today, so I already new the answer to that one. You must have been reading my mind
E: Oh there you go !
   J: You put it so beautifully and delicately though
E: I will love to get married again, and lately I've been seeing myself getting married in my dreams
E: I hardly dream Nectar
E: and when I do, I don't remember
E: but when I remember my dreams, it happens
   J: Dreams can be very powerful
   J: You make me so very happy
   J: Did I say that already?
E: You said it already, but I cannot get tired of hearing anything you say
E: Sweetie, I AM so glad that I make you happy
E: A source of joy is what I wanna be to you and nothing less, so If I cannot make you happy then I AM not good enough for you
   J: Ok my hummingbird
E: You are an angel, a beautiful soul, you deserve ONLY the best
   J: You are the best
   J: There can be no other but you
   J: How long is it now since we met?
E: There can be no other but you too
E: The email you wrote make me happy, it gave me goose bumps
   J: I love you
E: just the act of writting me in the plane made me feel honored, because that said you spent most of your time in the plane thinking about me, US
E: I love you so much more
   J: And it is forever
E: 😊😊😊😊
E: Only royal will I treat you because you are a queen, my queen
   J: Ok I'm going to sleep now, sleep with a smile on my face and in my heart
E: and I will NEVER take you for granted
E: go back to sleep my angel and do call me when you wake

The Whole Sordid Story

    up ok
E: Eamon loves Jan... Sooooooo much
      J: IM or call?
E: Good night my love
E: Call sweetie
      J: Ok I love you
      J: Night
E: I love you more
E: Night

The next day on the train to work I write:

> Good morning my beloved. As I go to work this morning I am a new woman. I am not the same person who left work on Friday. Because today I know without a doubt that I am loved by a man. And I am amazed. I wonder if those who look at me can see... See the joy that is bubbling at the wellspring of the heart inside?
> Have a good day ahead my sweetheart.
> Your Nectar

I feel different, that there is now someone there to share my life with. That I am no longer that independent, a lone woman. I notice a willingness to be stronger in my stands at work, to take more risks, knowing that there is support behind me.

It is very different to feel that support.

Romance Scam Survivor

The First Request for Money

This time on IM we try the video call. We struggle to get it working.

10th September:

> **E:** [8:08:42 PM] <ding>
> **J:** i just need to play with the settings a bit to get it working
> **E:** ok
> **E:** do you see any request that asks to accept?
> **E:** here
> **E:** do you see any request here
> **E:** [8:14:43 PM] u see the opton to accept here ?

Outgoing Voice call from dubhlainneamon (8:10:58 PM) Call Ended: 0 hours 4 minutes 42 seconds

> **E:** [8:15:57 PM] Here is where we are gonna accept it
> **J:** are you going to start the call
> **E:** click accept
> **E:** you see me ?
> **J:** no
> **E:** You did not see any invitation that asked you to click accept or ignore ?
> **J:** no
> **E:** do you see anything that says view my webcam, under my name of the yahoo messenger panel ?
> **J:** when I click on that it opens a window but just plays adds, and says its waiting for permission
> E: ok
> **E:** let me try again
> **E:** <ding>
> **E:** can you see me now ?
> **J:** it says I have accepted the invitation to start, but the window is just playing adds
> **E:** really !
> **E:** I'll try again for the last time
> **J:** I have accepted, but just getting adds in the window
> **J:** let me invite you.....
> **E:** Do you see me love ?
> **J:** I saw you for about 3 seconds,
> **E:** you not seeing me again ?
> **E:** Arrrrggggghhhhhhhhhh
> **J:** its says stopped, but at least I'n not getting adds

The Whole Sordid Story

    E: but I see you
    E: it says you are viewing my webcam
        J: just stopped again, I tghink the line is not very good
    E: Yours stopped too
    E: but were you able to see me at least
        J: shall we just do voice?
    E: [8:29:48 PM]ok then

Incoming Voice call from dubhlainneamon (8:30:21 PM) Call Ended: 1 hours 0 minutes 3 seconds

I had seen him for a skerrick of time, and we could not wait to get it working again. It's very frustrating. After this attempt to get a video call working we resorted to using the voice call.
I find out later that it is common for scammers to do this, to not let you see them, or to use something that had been recorded on a chat room earlier. There are reports of where there is actually a digitally manipulated model or avatar. This area is getting increasingly sophisticated.
As we talked, Eamon told me that today the tax people had come to see him. He said they insisted he pay fifty percent of the tax due on his job up front, or else he would not be able to continue to work. They were demanding an amount of $50,000.
Eamon explained this was because he was a foreign company, not a local UAE firm. The difficulty was that he was not able to access his money in his bank in England, because he had recently bought and sold some crude oil, and his bank account had been frozen by the authorities while they checked out that he was not breaching bans on imports from Iran. At the time he had not thought this would be a difficulty, but believed it would be resolved within a couple of days.
He was anxious about now being able to continue to work and complete his contract. He said that the whole contract was for £900,000, and within his contract he would be paid this amount after two weeks of work. At that point he had planned to send me $500,000, so that I could begin to look for a house for us to live in.
Did he ask me specifically for money, or just if there was any way I could help? I don't recall. But it was obviously a request for money.
Could it be a scam? Did my alarm bells go off? Yes, they did.

But I trusted him, loved him, wanted him, wanted the dream he promised, wanted to marry him.

His story was all plausible within this context. On what basis could I make a decision about what to do? When I examined the question, the only basis on which I could make a decision was from my heart. This was my immediate environment. Apart from warnings, there was nothing that screamed, "he is a scammer," at me.
Sadly, those warnings seemed quite distant in the face of the strength of the love I felt.
I told him that I made my decision from my heart, not reason. I knew I had $48,000 savings in my account, and agreed to send him this money by bank transfer the next day, expecting that this would come back to me in a couple of weeks. He had promised to return it many fold.
That it was a bank transfer gave it an air of legitimacy too. I had no idea of the roller coaster that I had just stepped on to.
Did I ever consider saying no, I cannot help financially, and then deal with the consequences that came with that?
No, I did not.
In hindsight, I realise I was totally in the altered state of romantic love. And he was skilled at keeping me there. Here is his response, coming though just before midnight.

I would have read this and been reassured before going to sleep:

> My sweet Nectar,
> my fiancee, thank you very much for accepting me, for believing in me, most importantly for trusting me and giving your heart to me, rest assured it is safe with me and will always keep it where it belongs, very close to my heart. Nectar since I've started this relationship with you, there has been a huge change in my life, there is joy, there is peace in my mind, Nectar you mean a life to me, I feel so lucky and so honored to have you in my life. When things didn't work out in my previous marriage I felt so empty, the feeling was more like seeing a ship it took your entire life building sinking with nothing you can do to stop, but today I feel so filled again, there is happiness in my heart. I feel so revived, back on my feet again, taken out of my old skin to

The Whole Sordid Story

new life.
You are what others strive to be, but will never become, I'm so excited that I found what I have been looking for, I know I'm being too much but understand for years I never felt this way, My soul will only rest when I know that you are aware of the sweetness, purity, and beauty of your heart. You are the gravity that keeps me in reality. You are the sun that illuminates my world. You are more than a best friend to me, more than a lover and more than just a girlfriend to me in other words you are everything I've been longing for. You complete me, you turned my world around, you've given me hope again in life.

Sweetheart, rest assured that I will keep your love in a safe place within my heart. I will cherish my love 4 you and always keep on loving you. I always keep your love in a safe pocket because i can't live without it. I promise to always be there for you, to care and ensuring that you are as well the happiest woman in the world, I'll love you until the day I die, I know this might sound as a joke but yeah till death do us apart, I will repeat this phrase again the day we get married.Hahahahaha, Shocked? Yea I am very optimistic that we will get there

Nectar, my fiancee, sweetheart, my lover and of course, my best friend .....by reading this, I hope you understand that you are the only one for me and always will be, there's only room for one woman in my heart and in my dreams and that's you, this feels like a dream come true , you came as an angel in my heart when giving up was the only word in my mind, Nectar thanks for taking my heart, with you is where I want and permit it to be forver

I love you more than words could ever show
Eamon
Here is the account information
Account name : Gbolahan David A
Bank name   : Dubai Islamic Bank
Acc number   : 067520030888801
Iban   : ae070240067520030888801
Bank address : Sahara center dubai
Swift code   : Duibead

I go to the bank in my lunchtime, transfer the money, and email him a copy of the receipt. It's easy, and no questions were asked.

Romance Scam Survivor

It seems a normal transaction. In the cold light of day ask myself if it is a scam, and know that whether it is or not I don't know, but I have made a decision based on love.

On Tuesday, 11th September he writes:

> Hey love, I just got back into my bedroom, we had a real nice time at the pool, Blessing was really happy that she spoke to you for a few seconds, she said she felt some love in your voice, she says that I should tell you not to worry about her that she wouldn't be jealous even if you take me away that she's had me long enough (I warned you, she talks alot) She also says to ask you if she can send you some of her pictures, she says she has a few in her email
> Sweetie I was thinking about the " a new woman" email you sent me, that really really touched my heart, I am a new man too, I am not the same man who used to travel to work without someone to discuss work problems with, I am not the same man who had just his daughter (who is not matured enough for certain things) to talk to, everything about me is changed, I'm renewed because of you NECTAR, MY FIANCÉE . Oh Nectar ,do you know how much I love you? YES I DO ! I cant wait to be given the opportunity to show you. I want you to spend the rest of your life in my arms, in my heart, in my thoughts, in my dreams ,in my soul.
> I want to be your comfort, you joy, your favorite desert.your favorite hobby .i wanna be your pain pills, i want to be the book you just cant stop reading, I wanna be your favorite beginning and your favorite ending ,i wanna be your favorite smell, your favorite song and your sweet dreams..
> The lord determines who walks into our lives, it's up to us to decide who we lat walk away, or who we let stay or who we refuse to let go. I decide that you stay in my life FOREVER..
> Wherever you go,what ever you do, may an angel follow you
> I love you lots
> Eamon

Reassuring, and reinforcing and promising that the dream will come true.

The Whole Sordid Story

Later, a text comes through:

> Hey beautiful woman, your man is back to work. Why? Because of you, you have no idea how happy this has made me. I love you.

The next morning we connect via IM on my way to work, having missed an early morning connection.

Wednesday, 12th September:

    J: 7:44:21 AM No answer on voice
E: Hey love
    J: Hey
    J: You fill my heart with joy
    J: Just hearing yr voice
E: You fill mine with joy too.
    J: I'll try voice
E: Oh ! I actually hung up the call because I didn't wanna make you talk on phone while in the train.
    J: Ok
E: What are you wearing to work today ?
    J: Grey pants a black striped sheet and red jacket
E: You are beautiful
E: I'm wearing just a white boxer shorts.
    J: What are you wearing to bed?
    J: Lovely
E: You wanna join me sweetie ?
    J: Yes please
E: I'm sorry I kept you waiting ok. I slept while watching the movie.
E: Blessing just woke me up when I called you.
    J: I was wondering
E: I can never keep you waiting my love.
E: I mean. I can never keep you waiting intentionally.
    J: I'm still unsure of you sometimes...
E: Really !!!
E: What are you unsure of my love ?
    J: It's interesting to watch my reactions
    J: Old stories of being left alone
E: Nectar !!!
    J: I so want you
E: I am not chatting with you just because you want to chat with me.. Its because I NEED to chat with you.
    J: You have never given me cause to think you will

> **J:** So I know is not based in reality
> **E:** You are like a survival medicine to me. I always need an intake of you.
> **J:** Me too.
> **E:** Whatever you feel for me Nectar, I feel it for you too... Even MORE
> **J:** I love whn we talk or chat
> **E:** Me too sweetie. Me too.
> **J:** I wait impatientl for these next weeks to pass
> **J:** Go to sleep now
> **E:** I wish I could sleep, wake up and I am done working.
> **J:** Train arriving
> **E:** Oh ok
> **E:** I'll wait till you are about to get out of the train
> **J:** Call or text when you wake up
> **J:** I need to know you are there
> J: Bye
> **E:** Ok my love.
> **E:** I'll call.
> **E:** I love you sooooooooooo much
> **E:** and thank you for loving me.
> **E:** 7:58:13 AM Bye... Signing out now

I update my girlfriend Rosie on progress later that day:

> Hi Rosie,
> I have had on my mind to give you an update on my dalliances over the past few days, finally getting to it now. Well I continued to communicate with Eamon Dubhlainn, the man of "thosesummertimes7". It has gone from emails to chatting to phoning. We have tried to video but haven't succeeded as yet as the connection was not good.
> Through the process we have fallen truly, madly deeply in love. I am amazed at how deep it has gone so very quickly. It has been a process of opening my heart, and we have a very strong heart connection. He is coming out at the beginning of November, or even earlier- he is on a contract in Dubai for 8 weeks.
> I feel we are so matched in our male/female interaction. My spirit is engaged, my heart is engaged, my body is engaged and though there is a lot more to explore, I think we can be great friends too. It's only a month since we 'met' but we are already talking "forever". I'm loving it, feeling very loved and that's very new for me. Can't wait till he gets here....
> I never got to look any further for someone who was local,

> but he's coming here....
> Happy to chat if you want, Jan

It's a month since Eamon and I first connected. He sends me an online greeting card saying, "Happy Anniversary fiancée!, arriving 13th September."
There is also an email from his daughter Blessing, with some photos of a very sexy looking young woman:

> Hello Jan,
> this is Blessing, Eamon's baby. It was so nice speaking 2 u on Monday, u got a very beautiful voice. Dad has told me alot abt u , u indeed make him happy, I've never seem him this way, thank u so much for loving my dad and I luv u 4 loving him. U've never seen my face, u've only heard my voice, so I'm sending u a few pics that are in my email.
> I don't knw what time it is where u are , so I dnt knw if I shld say gud nite or have a good day, but I'm off to bed now
> With so much luv frm ur new daughter
> Blessing

I reply:

> It's good morning from me Blessing, as I am on the train to work. Thank you for the photos. You are lovely. It is great to have them and know what you look like now I have heard your voice.
> I love yr dad very much, of that you can be assured. He has made me happy too, so I know what you must be seeing in him.
> I look forward to meeting you when the time is right. I hope you are enjoying your time in Dubai.
> Including you in the circle of our love.

By this time we are on IM every evening. He can see me, but I cannot see him. Also, before I get up in the morning, about 5:30 am, we are on. And then I will phone as I leave for work. "Call me as you are stepping out," he says. It would be about 1 am his time. I do, loving the connection.
We are also texting a lot in between times professing our love. He tells me how his work is going, and it all seems normal.
My body is increasingly yearning to connect with his, and my sexual juices are spreading just at the thought of it.

He asks me to begin looking for houses to buy, saying he wants something big and spacious. I send him some links, and the following exchange occurs on IM, in between conversations trying to get his webcam working.

14th September:

> **E:** [7:36:12 PM] the two houses are beautiful my love
> **E:** which is your first choice?
> > **J:** the one in eaglemont. I'll go and look tomorrow. but its expensive - how much can we spend.
> > **J:** my money can be included, muy $48k - that was to buy a house
> **E:** Sweetie
> > **J:** 14 Lawrence st
> **E:** I am still old fashioned in certain aspects
> **E:** A man is to provide shelter for his family
> **E:** Not a man and woman
> **E:** Your 48k, yes is our money but it belongs to your account
> **E:** I'm ok with that amount for the house actually... My house is about 100k more expensive than that
> > **J:** I admire you for that.... I just dont know if I'm looking at places outside of our price range
> **E:** it's not outside the price range I had in mind... sweetie, one thing you should know is that we aren't throwing the money away
> **E:** even it it's a 2m house, the money is there
> **E:** if at some point we wanna move to another, we can buy another and sell
> **E:** so we are cool
> > **J:** Its hard for me to even to say "we' might buy it
> **E:** I watched the video of the house, it's magnificent
> **E:** Don't let it be hard for you
> **E:** Don't let it be at all
> > **J:** that are is in a very good area
> > **J:** my uncle lives nearby
> > **J:** I went to school nearby
> > **J:** its big and spacious
> **E:** Sweetie, before I met you, I was already thinking about buying two small houses in Manchester for rent, not really for the rent money but just to have more properties
> > **J:** and the pool is good too,
> **E:** those two small houses were gonna cost be about 1.8m
> > **J:** thats a lot to spend on rental properties
> **E:** so you see, if I'm spending this money on that house, it

seems like an already made budget
E: We can still buy rental houses my love
E: Can I tell you something
    J: you are amazing
E: I wanna enjoy my old age
E: Really!
    J: I want to enjoy it with you
    J: I would love to be in a house like tha
E: My dream for 50s and above, is to be with the best woman, in the best house, driving the best car, traveling to the best places and staying in the best hotels
    J: that sounds like a plan!
E: I've got the best woman.... (that's what was not within my power), hence destiny gave it to me
E: I'll accomplish all that is financially within my power
E: so worry not my love
    J: you are such a sweetie
    J: how did I come across you
    J: saying sweet things will get you everywhere with me
    J: had you noticed?
E: This is not me being a sweetie now, this is me telling you my dream.... So now you know you are a dream come true
E: so give me one reason why I wouldn't treasure you forever
    J: yes
    J: no reason
E: Good
E: 😊
    J: 😊
E: So if you are buying a house there, you are able to pay a down payment of 48k ?
E: I ask because you said the 48k was for a house
E: or you were gonna source some more to add up to it
    J: that would only be a 10%deposit, so something small, more like what I am renting.
    J: I did have more, but went on holidays to the US, and the cost of moving from Brisbane was quite big
E: Oh Oh ok.... I understand now.. Well that's not necessary anymore
    J: ok
    J: so I can look knowing its not just a fantasy that will NOT come true.\
    J: the powere of dreams, very stong my love

> **E:** Sweetie, I will be going out soon ok, the man who takes me around is gonna be here in 10 mins, he just called
> **E:** Yes the power of dreams are very strong
> **E:** that's why we must always dream big, we must always see better days ahead
> **E:** and they'll come true

I love looking at houses, and this is reassuring that this man is serious. He has the capability and intent to provide he and I with a perfect lifestyle.

Yes! The romantic dream of having a man who can provide a high level of financial support and security is very strong.

On more than a couple of occasions over the coming weeks Eamon makes the point that he is not coming to Australia because I want him to, but because he wants to come. He is making that decision for himself, he is not being influenced by me. He makes this point very strongly.

On 15th September he writes:

> Nectar my love,
> we just got back to the guest house now, we really had a fun time out there, we saw alot of things, including a wonderful dancing fountain, we also had dinner in a chinese restaurant in the mall before coming home, I miss you so much but I don't wanna call you, I want you to wake up and find an email waiting for you from me.
> You asked in your text today if your craziness makes me happy, of course it does, it fills my heart with joy because you pour out your feelings to me and I know the craziness is for me and me along.   I dream of hearing our hearts beat and listening to you breathe.   To hold your body close to mine and starring into your eyes.   The first kiss with you is going to be so dreamy, tender, loving and warm.
> I want to go on long walks with you, talk, kiss, and enjoy each other.
> I want to give you a long back massage and have you lay on top of me.
> I want dance with you when you come home from work.
> I want to get caught in a rainstorm with you and get wet.
> I want to listen to you all about your day and smile.
> I just want to hold you, everyday, every moment.
> I want to make love by the fireplace.

The Whole Sordid Story

I want to know your deep secrets.
I want to know you, feel you.
I want to laugh with you.
I want to be your passion.

I am devoted to you!
Love you always
Eamon

He sends me "I Promise", a popular wedding song, as an MP3:

I Promise
Good morning love..
I attached a song and sent to you, please listen to it, all the words I dedicate to you, just imagine me whispering the words in your ears.. I sent an email 3 mins before this, I hope you've received it
I love you
Eamon

Are You Real?

I'm beginning to talk to friends and family about what is happening. In a visit to my uncle I am asked many questions that I cannot answer.

I write Eamon for some details, but in our talking he is encouraging me not to get caught up in other's concerns. He says I can ask him anything, but that others do not have a right to.

There is more to come, as the following SMS sequence shows:

> E: Falling in love with you is the best thing I've ever done. I love you.
> E: How did your day go ? Miss you lots. Mwaaah.
> J: You take my breath away. I love you.
> I went walking around the parklands where I used to go to school.
> But missed you do bad
> J: Talked to some girlfriends tonight. One very concerned I'm vulnerable to being scammed.
> I went numb for a while, but then came to the realization that even though there are many things I don't know about you I do trust you.
> I think I'm crazy
> E: Sweetie, I told you about this things. No one not in this situation will understand what's happening between us.
> J: Yes I'm realizing that
> I'm crazy about you
> E: Are you still at work?
> J: Yes I realized that I have to keep it to myself more
> E: I'm crazy about you too and I'm working. We'll talk when I get to the guest house. Your emotion is too important to me pls take care of it for me.
> E: I don't want you discussing this things with them, they'll ruin your emotions. Be patient and briddle your tongue till I come and you'll show me off in person.
> J: You are so insightful. Yes please call. I'm in bed but phone will be close by. My love.

He reinforces this later, when talking, that those who hadn't experienced this connection and love would not understand what we have between us. They would however never doubt our love when they see us together.

The Whole Sordid Story

17th September:

>E: Hey love.. Pls call....

There is a request for more money, this time to assist with supplies of concrete and water that he miscalculated he would need, as he had not allowed for the temperature and dryness. I am upset he is again asking for money.

I realise he could be a scammer.

As we are talking, I suddenly demand, "Who are you? Are you real?"

He gets angry that I am questioning him. We argue a bit more, unsatisfactorily. I hang up.

The following exchange ensues:

>E: That was a very cool thing to say. Really sorry I asked or mentioned anything, I just felt like an ungrateful man. I love you.
>E: And you hung up on me, I'll never do that to you. I respect you too much for that. Now I'm gonna have sweet dreams ?
>>J: I love you deeply but I just don't know who you are. How can you prove to me you are who you are?
>E: amazing ! Who did you see during our webcam chat ? That wasn't me? You really said your head was gonna take over after you send the 48000 I see now.
>>J: I saw you for 3 seconds. You have my whole life in your hands
>I feel like I'm being made the bad guy because I won't give you the money you need
>E: You know you can't say that, who's talking about money here, you just broke my heart because you said I'm not real even when you've seen me on webcam. Twice.
>E: Saw me for 3 secs ? At least you saw me pulling my shirt because of it. I care too much for your emotions and will say nothing to hurt you. But mine ?
>>J: I have an email address and a phone number and some photos. Yes I have seen you and loved you. But when it comes to the money I need to know more, you already have all

my money.
And you have my heart, which is breaking right now

Because of his righteousness about being questioned, and the continual emotional hooks he throws out, I give up fighting. The following day I send him another $3000, this time via Western Union to his name for his supplies.

On the 20th September, the answers to my questions from our chat on the 15th September come through.

He says:

> Hello my love,
> I just sent answers to your email, I was writing them about 2 hours ago while laying in bed waiting for your morning call and I slept off, just woke up now completed it and sent it..
> I'm sure you are at work now or almost there, I love you so much my darlyn girl. I will always and always do
> EDD !

Also 20th September:

> Hi my Darling, can I have some facts please.
> As I am telling various members of my family and friends about us I get quizzed about you, and I'm often unable to answer basic questions and feel i portray that I don't know much about you. From my perspective I know the important things, that I know your heart, as you know mine, but it would be great to be able to show I knew basic things about you.
>
> When and where we're you born? I'm not even clear how old you are exactly. Do you know the time of your birth too? I would love to have your astrology chart done.
>   April 7 1963
>
> When did you move to Manchester? Have you always lived there? Can I have yr address so I can look at the house you built in google street view please?
> I moved with my mom to England since I waas 3 years old, my address is 7 Carrwood Rd, Wilmslow, Cheshire East SK95DJ Manchester United Kingdom
>
> Where did you go to school, and University if you did?   My

The Whole Sordid Story

uncle who also studied engineering asked this.
I attended the University of Manchester

What year is Blessing in in school?
She is in Grade 10

Will she come to live with us? I'm assuming she will. I know you said she was interested in traveling... I can find out from my sister in law about the good schools. She is an assistant principle at a girls school.
She will live with us, she's looking forward to it, but the will be at the end of her 10th Grade so she can continue from Grade 11 in Australia

I tell my family and friends various things, but mostly that I'm truly madly deeply in love with you, and you are coming at the end of of October. There will be a lot of interest in how it is between us when we finally meet... People are skeptical that we can know what we feel when we haven't even met yet.
Well you are supposed to mind what you say to them until I'm there in person so they don't ruin the joy in your heart

My Mum was a bit shocked when I told her we were talking marriage. She is a feminist from way back and does not like it as an institution very much. she would be happier if we just lived together. I think I have convinced her that you make me happy - she hasn't heard me laugh very much and just talking about you she can hear a difference in me. We talk at least once a day, but I did not tell her about you till about a week ago- probably about the same time you told Blessing.

Are you religious or spiritual? I think you said once that you had been to church..... I think that's a longer conversation......
I go to church yes, but I am not religious

I'm looking forward to finding out many thing about you my love, as our friendship unfolds and we can spend more time together. Long conversations as we have meals together, or lying comfortably in bed together. And looking forward to hearing you say 'really' as you find out things about me....

Hope you've had a good day my love... And that we talk again soon

Jan

I respond:

Beloved Eamon,
I hear you when you say I can ask you anything, but that its not about what other people want to know.
My priorities have been on knowing your heart, your spirit, your being, and you mine, and in that regard I find nothing missing. Nothing missing!
I do want to know all there is to know about you, and know this will unfold with time.   Thank you for answering those few questions.   They may have come from others initially but I am also interested - I want to know everything about you.
Actually as I write that I see it is only partly true – there is a part of me which likes those details and to be able to tell others about you, but really, I do not care – its your heart that I am interested in. I'll leave you to answer those questions of others in your own time and your own way – its not actually my business and you are well able to answer for yourself aren't you.
I have looked at the houses on your street on Google maps – hard to know which one is yours though, but nice to see the area and the type of house you live in.   That is definitely of interest to me.   This information is just between you and me, and I will cherish it, like a secret gift you have given me.
I had started to talk to friends, as I had felt our love was strong and true, and for me this was new.   Now I know that's not quite correct, it IS true, not fragile, but delicate.   And I respect you and what we have tremendously, and will not keep sharing in that way.   I will watch that my emotions are not damaged and that I stay true to the joy that you have awakened there. For both of us.
I want to keep what is between us true, and joyful, and you know just the thought of being with you turns me on till my nectar pours from that special part of me.... And I know our hearts are beating as one.
Loving you so deeply Eamon Donegal Dubhlainn.

The Whole Sordid Story

Nectar pours to EDD

His reply:

Good morning my love,
I hope you had sweet sweet dreams, I'm glad you are happy you have some more information about me, please ask me anything and everything you wanna know about me, because I am you and you should know yourself very well. Our friendship has taken us on a journey to a place where neither one of us every dreamed we could go in such a short time frame. Yes, my love, our desires, commitment, feelings and emotions go deeper and get stronger by the day, and I do feel the same as you.
   Everyday I work hard my job, some days when I am tired, I think of you and smile, knowing you would be there with open arms to listen to my day and unstress me. With great joy I find myself wondering more and more about your day. I wonder what it would be like to be there for you at the end of the day and listen to all that you accomplished and unstress you in so many ways. Being with you, the possibilities are endless.
   At night, my dreams are consumed by you. I feel your presence as I fall asleep and dream about doing everything with you. I want to touch you so tenderly the first time and everytime there after. I want to feel you breathe when I lay next to you and my desire for this grows stronger as time passes. I feel our bond growing stronger and stronger, transcending the vast distance between us, and I know the feelings are mutual.
I have never touched you physically, but yet I feel as if I know more about you know and feel such a deeper love than I thought I would ever feel or experience. My heart and soul belong to you based on the deep feelings I have for you and how devoted I have become for you. I have never been this deeply attracted. I never knew I had these feelings inside of me. NO woman until you has ever cared so passionately for me. I hear it and feel it every time we communicate. As I know more and more about you, you capture more of me and my heart beats for you.
   I am so glad that my path has taken me to you. Would I have changed any part of my road to you, no. If my path did change, I would not have found you. I have always gone deep in my soul and tested my faith as to why the

challenges that were given to me along the way were so difficult and hard, tore me apart and destroyed me at times. As everyone would say – "everything happens for a reason" – and its true, it led me staight to you.

You are my passion. You -- is where I want to always be until my last breath. When I come over, I know it will be awesome because I can feel it and I so know that we will make a couple that other couples will see and look forward to being like

Please give your man a call when you wake up..

I Love you, you are my life

EDD.

My reply to him:

beloved,
I echo everything you have written here! The depth of my feeling for you is nothing I have ever felt before and takes me to places I had no idea about.

And I allow myself to need you, to need to have you fully in my life. I wait impatiently and patiently for you to come over, I need to have you beside me. Only then can my full joy overflow as we complete each other, in whatever and all way our lives unfold from here. You are my very life.
How long had you been on PoF before you connected with me? I know it was 1 day for me...! Existence was waiting for things to come together so we could connect and made sure we did, somehow.
Now I am counting down the days till you come. And looking forward to a long and loving partnership, relationship, love affair, friendship, marriage with you. With all that's both special and ordinary shared together. I love the thought of coming home from work to you, and at other times being at home when you come home. I will kneed your tight muscles, feed you good food, love you.
thinking also of Blessing, I know a good school that I think It would be possible to get her into. Our school year starts in February, so perhaps think of that as a date to work towards....
Also I had a request today for my Brisbane landlady and friend, to come and stay on the 8th and 9th November, when she is in Melbourne for a conference. This is later in the week that I have my holidays and you will be here, so just wanted to let you know, that I have said ok to her.

The Whole Sordid Story

Seeing her and her partner enjoy their life together is part of what made me think I could also perhaps have a partner and enjoy life more than on my own.
Would love to talk more my love. Let me know if you want me to call. I have put some credit on Skype, so am now using that to call you.
Love you my man. More than I can say.

Your Nectar

Hot Sex

The sexual tension has been building for some days.
Twice after our late night IM calls, where he can see me but I can't see him, I am so turned on that I masturbate to relieve myself and to get to sleep, calling his name as I climax.

On the 19th I had written:

> So good to get your SMS just now. I wasn't sure when I did not get anything back if you were getting them. I hope they delighted you, as they did me.. Hmmmm? I try to find something that will make you smile my love, to brighten your day.
> End of October seem so far away..... Longing to touch every part of your body, to taste you, to smell you, to move with you against you slowly and fast. To sleep next to you, to wake next to you and to wake you, to massage you, to scrub your back, to laugh with you, to scream and moan with you, to tingle with you, to pulse with you to buck with you. To nibble you and lick you, to tickle you. To caress you to take you deep inside of me and hold you there feeling the energy flow backwards and forwards between us as the fire burns ever brighter.
> To feel your breath on me, your touch on me, to know my juices flow for you. I've been saving that up for a lifetime for you.
> To have my heart fill with the joy of you. To feel alive with you. To play with you, to laugh with you.
> And then to start it all over again with you. Yum. I will eat you all up! My love.
> When you get this you had better call me, NO DELAYS. whatever time it is! I am forever yours.
> Your Nectar.

I tease him with 'no pyjamas on tonight'. The next night it gets even steamier, and a full-on sex session ensues.
It starts as an IM exchange before we go on to a voice call. There continues to be a 'testing' of the webcam... at least it seems like this.. with no success of me seeing him.

The Whole Sordid Story

22nd September 2012:

    E: [5:16:32 AM] Hey sweetie !
        J: Hey
    E: How is Nectar doing ?
        J: Wide awake and wanting to hear from my man
        J: Missing you
        J: Hot and bothered
    E: Oh wow !
    E: I'm hot and bother too
    E: I need your lips all over my body right now
        J: Yes happy to oblige
        J: But only if you do the same to me!!
    E: Of course I will be doing same to you right now
    E: I missed you soo much today
    E: No
        J: Mmmmmm
    E: We missed you soooo much today
        J: Me too as I was home this evening
        J: It's time we are a family
    E: Yes love it is
    E: What are you wearing ?
        J: My skin
    E: Aweeeessooooommmmmeeeeeee
        J: Haha
    E: Please turn on your webcam
    E: I'm gonna do same
    E: I'm naked right now
    E: Let's get a little naughty tonight
        J: I'm on my iphone
        J: That's different logistics
    E: Well, get on the computer love
        J: But
    E: PLEASEEEEEEEEEEEEEEEEEE
        J: Ok
        J: Hold on

I move onto my laptop:

        J: ok invite me
    E: invite me sweetie
    E: <ding>
        J: are you seeing me?
    E: can you see me ?
        J: no, can you broadcast

E: no you need to accept the wecbam request frm me
E: can you see me ?
    J: your webcam is up but nothing there
E: I can't see you too
E: it's still waiting for you to accept
    J: i aaccepted before - invite again
E: Are you there ?
    J: you seeing me?
    J: im here
    J: hi
E: permission denied ?
    J: it sis you do not support video calls
E: you are clicking decline instead of accept
    J: no
E: why are you declining ?
    J: im not
E: ok read well before you click
E: Your webcam has stopped
E: Send me an invite
E: I can only see your face
E: push your cam down
E: OMG
E: look at that
E: wow
E: why is mine not working
E: trying to figure it out ok
E: You need to see my penis.. sooooo hard
E: push your computer back a little
    J: so you like big breasts?
E: I love big breasts I love you breasts
E: I am sucking them right now
E: OMG
E: Please Please, wait
E: we need to do this together
E: I need you to see me too
    J: they arevery sensitive
    J: and i feel my juices flowing
E: Can I see ?
    J: i want to drape them all over yiu
    J: around yoiur penis
E: Are your fingers In there ?
E: I can see your tongue, are you sucking y penis ?
    J: no too busy holding the pc
E: can you see me ?
E: it says you are viewing my webcam

J: noyhing there....
E: can you see my penis ?
J: no picture
E: really ?
E: hold !
E: Sweetie please push you computer back, let me be seeing you while I'm sorting this out
E: I'm only seeing your too pretty face
E: OK now sweetie you move back
E: leave the computer
E: Just the sight is making me wanna come
E: I am kissing you right now sweetie
E: kissing you all over
E: kissing your lips
E: kissing neck

We are online for another forty-five minutes. He leads me through this, starting with wanting to suck my breasts, together. I squeeze them together, rubbing my nipples. I am already very wet with my clitoral juices, and when he talks about going down on me I position the laptop so that he can see me, and masturbate myself.

I am panting and groaning heavily, excited in a way that I have never been, and easily orgasm. I imagine him large and strong, on top of me and inside of me, reaching to my very core, and once there letting the energy pulse between us without needing to do anything.

He wants to do it doggy style, so I turn over onto elbows and knees, adjusting the computer so he can see what he wants. I can easily imagine what this feels like. He is doing his share of moaning too, and it all seems very mutual.

As we finish this tryst he asks how many times I came. I say five, to which he replies, "when I am with you it will be twenty-five."

He proffers that though he does not have a preferred body type, if he was to have a preference, it would be my body type. This was said with a degree of surprise as to how responsive he was to me, and I hold on to this thought that I am special to him.

Romance Scam Survivor

In the morning I text:

> **J:** "Private message: my body tingles all over and I start to pant and whimper at the thought of what you do to me. Now how am I going to get through the next weeks till you come here? Hmmm?"

The exchange continues:

> **E:** Good morning to you my love. Mwaaa
> Out on my bike burning off some energy....
> **E:** I had the best wake up ever. Wow, last night was awesomely beautiful, I'm trying not to think of it while at work. I soo love you.
> **J:** Good luck trying not to think about it. That's a lost cause.
> **J:** I've just had a long bath, Luxuriating in everything.
> **J:** saying love you doesn't say enough, but you have a good imagination! Love you my sweet.
> **J:** Do take care though my love.
> **E:** Your vagina is so pretty, it's fleshy, I like that, I love that, I'll eat up the flesh, all of it. Ur clits WOW. Pls get out of my head, I need to concentrate.
> **J:** You started it my love!
> **J:** I loved it though. More????
> **J:** I know I'm bad, or maybe I mean good... See what you have awakened in me.
> **J:** I'll shut up now and let you work. Xxxx

I email later the next day about Our Night:

> Beloved,
> well that settles it then, not only are we totally connected through our hearts, and id say our souls, but the sexual energy between us is sparking so bright it's blinding. I already knew you turned me on, got my juices flowing. Now we both know that it goes waaaay beyond that. And I know it's the same for you.
> You blew my socks off!!!!!!!! Thank you for loving me, thank you for loving the real essence of me.
> I'm no longer wondering what it will be like when you come here. We both know.
> Just a warning my love, there has been a flame ignited......
> But I think you are going to keep on fanning that flame and

The Whole Sordid Story

will show me no mercy....
I think it was earlier last night that I said its time for us to be a family, and you agreed. Now it feels even more right. I feel that we are going to have many years of much happiness being together (not that there were doubts before).
My love, hurry up and finish your work in Dubai.
Your Nectar

The Cheque

The next day requests start again via text.

23rd September:

> **E:** I'm so pissed right now sweetie.
> **J:** What's up do you want to talk? Anything I can do?
> I'm here when you want to talk

This time it is that he was paid for his work, paid after two weeks as agreed, but instead of cash, as he expected, they have paid him by cheque, made out so it can only be paid to his bank in England.

He is angry with himself that he has not been clear enough in his contract in specifying that he wanted cash to be paid and locally. It's a group of Saudis who have employed him, and they all need to be there to authorise the cheque being written, which they have done.

Now one of them has died, and they have gone off for a mourning period and will not be coming together again for some time. This means it's not possible to get the cheque rewritten and reauthorised so that he can get cash locally.

He has been advised by his accountant that his account in England has been approved for release of funds, but that he needs to be there in England to complete a legal process, sign documents with the bank, before funds can be released.

In the meantime, he does not have the cash to pay his men, and to get the work to a point where it is able to be suspended whilst he goes to England to free up the money.

What to do is the question?

After talking through some of the options, including any way he can get his account in England opened, we finish our call.

As I am going off to sleep I am still thinking of possibilities though and text:

> **J:** Is there any way you could quickly sell one of your cars? They have places here where you can sell cars for cash.... You would not get the best price, but maybe you would get what you need...

The Whole Sordid Story

> **E:** I thought about that but no one including me and you would buy a car not directly sold by the person who bears the name the car is registered in.
> **E:** Just sleep sweetie, call when you wake up.

In the pre-dawn discussions that followed I agreed to some assistance. I consider myself in partnership with this man, working together to achieve the outcome of us being together. As I have already given him all of my savings, this will need to come from my Master Card Credit account to my savings account.

Over the following day I send him three amounts of $5000 via Western Union:

> **J:** EDD love, $5000 sent. MCTN NO 7573424347 Approx 18,799 AED. Please tell me I'm not crazy. Xxxx
> **E:** Thanks love, you aren't crazy but caring ? I'm on my way to the western union to receive the money. Thank you my love
> **J:** Thanks. Talk later. Xxx
> Spend it wisely my love.

This will not be enough though. I consider making inquiries about extending the limit on my credit card to access more.

The texts continue through the day:

> **E:** Got the money love, I'm working now. Were you able to get inquires from the bank ?
> **J:** I need to work on it when I get home. Too busy at work today.
> **E:** There we go again sending messages same time and you are still unsure of me ? I love you unmeasurably
> **J:** Promise me you'll come
> This is going way beyond my comfort zone

I am having serious doubts.

What am I doing sending all this money?

Maybe it is a scam after all? I don't think scams are this intimate, but I'm still worried. He sees or senses my hesitancy and calls me. He is reassuring, loving, promising to return the money, reaffirming our future together.

I am comforted and re-engaged:

> **J:** Thank you for reassuring me. Love you
> And I will get it done
> **J:** Just got approved for extra $5000 on credit card. Applying for loan now.
> **J:** Ok I have put in for loan, not with my bank but another bank. They say it may take 7 days to process but I don't think it will take that long. Feeling better now. Love you EDD.
> **J:** Darling, sorry I was in such a funk earlier. Thank you for your call. It makes such a difference and you bring me back to reality, and get my juices flowing. Love you.
> **E:** I love my Nectar so much.
> Call me when you are home my love

There is a minor hiccup the next day, 25th September. I am refused permission to send money via Western Union at the Post Office because I do not have a photo identity (ID).
Apparently, the person who had allowed my transaction the day before shouldn't have. I have changed over to a Victorian Driver's License, and the new card has not yet arrived.
I leave, calling Eamon, but later discover that I have my passport in my bag and can use this as a photo ID. Going back, I successfully send another $5000.

> **J:** All ok. I just discovered my passport in my bag. Should be ok
> **E:** Ok Jan Dubhlainn
> **J:** All done. MTCN: 2883242580
> Approx AED 18,748
> **J:** Love you. Sorry to wake you unnecessarily. Just lucky I still had my passport in my bag from when I changed over my car license. Xxxx

We talk again that night, and I wake up the next morning to the following email, on some beautiful email stationary, pink hibiscus on pale green background.

The Whole Sordid Story

26th September:

> Good morning my beautiful Nectar,
> I'm here waiting for you to wake up and call me, I'm missing you so much that I need you right away, my sweet Nectar you are wonderful, amazing, the best, all I've dreamed of and never thought I'd find. You are a fairy tale come to life. You are kind, honest, trustworthy, amazingly sexy and beautiful. Your good heart shines through all that you are. You are the missing piece of my soul, the angel the lord made for me when he made the world, the one I've known across all my lifetimes, who has loved me and who I've loved before. You are my air. You are my heart. You are the reason I love my life. You are my life.
> Nectar, I will love you like you've never been loved. I will make love to you like no one has - I will show you with each kiss, each touch, each caress and with all of me how I love you. How much I want you. You will never have to doubt my desire for you. I promise you all of these things until the end of time. Until the universe reclaims all that I am - and even then from the far reaches of the heavens - even then my love for you will live on and on and you will always know it is there. You my love are now all that I am. You are all of Me. I want so much to look into your eyes and tell you all of this. I want so much to tell you this right now. To hold you and kiss you and love you. Imagine me with you, whispering these words into your ear again and again and loving you and holding you as you fall asleep.
> Ever thine. Ever mine. Ever ours. With all that I am.
> I love you forever Nectar
> EDD

I reply that evening:

> Eamon,
> my sweet, the outpourings of your heart to me ring true with each word. Yes lifetimes together, and yes, promises forever.
> To have you here whispering those things in my ear would be heaven to me. More than I could ever have imagined, or dreamed, but that now I want with a hunger also beyond my imaginings. Our hearts and souls are so intertwined we are one and will be together always. I want to be with you always and forever, as we have promised for lifetimes.
> Loving you so very much it's hard to say in words. I want to

> say it fully with my body. I have already said with my heart and you have heard in a way no one else has.
> All ways, always, from my very depths....
> Your Nectar

We exchange texts over the next few days, and talk evenings and mornings on IM or the phone.

I have applied for two loans. One, with Me Bank, is declined as I am only on probation at my work, and one with HSBC, which is approved. This takes a few days to get my ID verified, and then for the card to be produced before I can take out the $15,000 that they give me.

I had asked for $20,000, but am happy to get $15,000.

In the evening of the 28th September, another email called "My Love!!"

> My love,
> I am the lucky one with the love you share everyday. I cannot even imagine what my life at this point would be like if you did not find me. You make me so happy. You brighten my day. Its hard being here and thinking of you all day, what your doing, if your happy and if you miss me. I am still so taken by you. Everyday I want to be with you more and more. I love you so much, it hurts in such a wonderful way, my heart aches for you and knows that one day I will be with you. You are so caring, and loving of my mind, my body, and my heart. You are so strong. I wish I could just hold you tonight and lean on your shoulder when the pain gets bad. I want hold you. I want to feel you. I want my heart to beat simultaneously with yours. I want to be with you always. I want to make decisions with you based on us sharing everything and holding nothing back. I'm comfortable telling you anything because you are always there.
>
> I had the sweetest dreams of you last night -- you just held me all night long and you never let go. Your love transcends all physical bounds and you love me no matter where I am. When I think of you, my heart races and I have to find something to do to keep my focus, for I have fallen so deeply in love with you, sometimes I do not see straight. For so long, I must have just gone through the motions of living a life, and in the past, thinking I must have

The Whole Sordid Story

been in love. I no longer want to even think of the past, for a future with you is heaven sent. I have never known the love you share with me, until you. Sometimes, like today after my shower, I was breathless thinking of you, for my heart and soul belong to you forever.
Love is where the heart is. And where ever you are, there I am, for your heart is where my home will always be. I love you so much it hurts, and I want to be with you until the end of time. As each day passes, we get closer to each other, sending a tender kiss, a caressing touch, and a warm embrace through the span of time. I have loved you all of my life, just never found you till now. I am praying and hoping this money comes through on Monday so I can leave, I will find you and then our first touch will start the most amazing love affair. I am here for you, wanting you, needing you, and desiring you. I want no one else, for my love for you is strong, never ending, and pure in heart. You are my life and I want to make you so happy. I am so in love with you, I have to go work now outside and swim. I love you so much, it hurts not to be with you.
Missing you like never before
EDD

And on 1st October, subject "Loving you more and more!"

My   baby, because of you I feel like I am the luckiest man in the world and wonder what I did to deserve you in my life. You are the last image before I close my eyes, my dreams come true and my first thought when I open my eyes in the morning. I dream about sharing my life with you....I dream about our future together and the new memories we will be creating together...a new family full of love and support for each other.
The lord has a plan for each one of us and I know that lord found you for me...I didn't know if I was really ready to start dating again but it felt right and led me right to you. I do believe that there was a higher power in our love connection. This was meant to be...we were meant to be...
Words can't not even begin to explain how I feel about you and how much you have become as essential to my being, as life is itself. You make me feel whole, feel loved, feel like a man, feel like I can't exist without you in my life....
My body tingles at the thought of your gentle and

loving caress and eagerly awaits your touch, your kiss. I replay in my mind how I would make love to you on your kitchen counter when you are doing something in the kitchen and we are alone.

How wonderful it would be to come home to you..... your arms, your kiss, our bed.

I want nothing more than you in my life forever. With you I have everything I could ever need or want..."you complete me". I hope you want and feel the same too!

Loving you more and more each day....

Your love for all eternity,

Eamon

I reply:

Darling yes I feel the same way, and I feel blessed by your love. It washes over me, and keeps me true. That is so very special.

Today I was upset that the money hadn't come as its a big responsibility, and I felt powerless. But what to do. There is nothing to do but wait, even if i rail against it. It must be driving you crazy too. At least I can be a bit (just a little) distracted by my work.

My love, I know we are meant to be together, for ever. It's not even worth trying to explain this to someone else. I know i just have to wait till you are here and we get all of this behind us. My joy is there beneath the surface waiting for you to unlock it with the key that only you have, the key to my heart and soul. The key to our future.

Ill make love with you any where you want, any time, you will know how to make me want you, go weak at the knees for you. I long to touch you in those special places that will make you want me, that will show you that I need my man, now.

Soon, soon,

I love you so very much, my love. I love that you want to see me in my early morning disheveled state. I love that my man wants to know when I am leaving the house. I love the daisies on your stationary, flowers picked specially for me.

I'll go to sleep dreaming I am in your arms now. My nectar flows for you.

I'll SMS in the morning, and we can IM chat.

Love you my sweet Eamon.

The Whole Sordid Story

Eventually on 2nd October, the card comes through. I am able to take all the $15,000 cash out, so I immediately send two amounts via Western Union.

On text:
    J: Bank has just called to say the card has arrived. I left my number with them yesterday. Xxxx
    J: Ok. 2 amounts
MTCN: 6079842040
AED: 37,249
MTCN: 9055314192
AED: 18,624

Later:
    J: Is it all OK?
E: Yes my love. I'm so excited. The western union here isn't open until 9:30am, I'll update you soon my love. Thanks soooo much
    J: Ok. Lets just get you both out of there!   Love you.
E: System at western union is down. Got to come back after an hr. I wouldn't go away. I'll hang around. Love you plentyful. Haha you like my self inovated word ?
Xxxx
    J: Darling I have been at company briefing, and having a few drinks after. Now heading to train and home. Love u   Yes good word!
Battery low till I get to my car.
E: I'm on the line now to collect money. My batt is low too, forgot to charge at night.
    J: Ok keep me updated as much as you can. But I won't worry if I don't hear.... Xxxxx

After sending these payments, as I head back to work I still wonder if this is all a scam?
I know there is nothing to say that it is not a scam. But with all our dreams, the passion to be together and all the conversations, I cannot, will not, I don't want to believe that it is a scam.

But that's not the end of it...

More Taxes

About mid evening I get a call, and it is Blessing, Eamon's daughter. She is very upset, probably in tears, and talking very fast. It's hard for me to understand exactly what she is saying, so I ask her to take a deep breath, calm down and tell me slowly.
She says there are men with her dad and they are screaming at each other, sounding violent, and she's very scared. Before I can get a clear picture of why this might be happening, she says she will get her dad to call me, and hangs up.
I am on tenterhooks, wondering what is going on, but there is nothing I can do until I hear again.
I wait by the phone and computer. At night I have my iPhone, telephone landline, iPad and laptop all by my bed, ready for use at a moment's notice.
Eventually, at about 10:40 pm, he comes on IM.

> **J:** Is it okay for you to talk? I had heard there was someone there.
> **E:** Did Blessing call?

When I say yes, he goes off for a minute to check on her to make sure she is okay.

When he comes back to me he explains.

They were police, and the tax department. Back when I had paid the first lot of taxes, it had only been half of what was due, and that the rest was due when I was paid for my contract. I was told back then that if I did not pay the second half within a week after the due date, I would be arrested. They had come to arrest me. It was pretty scary, as it was hard to understand what they were saying, but I had realised I was in the wrong.
The man who he was getting his building supplies off had then arrived, to collect the money owed to him, and he managed to talk to the police on my behalf. He had been able to calm things down enough for the tax department to agree to take the $15,000 cash he was collecting for himself, putting it towards the taxes, and give me some more time to pay them. Now I have to find $40,000 by Friday, or they will come back to arrest me.

The Whole Sordid Story

We talk about how he can get additional funds. He will see if Blessing's nanny in England can help.

We text through the night:

> **E:** [11:10 PM] I'm gonna do my best my love. Pls don't give up on me. I love you and I wish I was with you now.
> **J:** I won't give up on you. I love you. Is there any way the British embassy can help- getting your funds freed up or verifying your signature on papers for the bank?
> Talk to the bank and negotiate with them
> **E:** [3 Oct 2:33 AM] My love is there anyway you can get another credit card. I'll not assure you based on only my word this time. An 100 percent interest loan, anything. I'll pay.
> **J:** I just heard you whispering Sweetie in my ear and woke up
> I don't know
> **E:** When I leave here, we'll not seperate again. You know why ? Because I'm not coming back here.
> **J:** I'm sleeping. Talk in the morning my love.
>
> **E:** [2:45 AM] I slept for about 20mins. I dreamt I told you to make an impossible possible and then I saw myself on a plane. Try my love. It's my last request.
> **E:** Ok talk in the morning, sorry for disturbing your sleep. I love you.

He comes onto IM in the pre-dawn, about 5:15, saying that he knows he cannot ask me to help him just on his word, and he was thinking of what he could do or show me to make me realise he was genuine.
He was thinking to give me his bank account and password so I could access his bank account. That doesn't seem right to me, so I say send me some screen shots.

He emails me two files from NatWest Bank. One shows an online screen for Dubhlainn Constructions LTD, a number of transactions, with a balance of £2,840,509.00! The other is an Account Summary showing the same balance, and that there are 'holds on the account', though I momentarily do wonder about the spelling of the type of account as 'check' rather than 'cheque'.

Still it all seems legitimate, and shows that he does have lots of money, if he could only access it.

I have given him all of my personal savings, and all of the additional credit I have, including the new credit card.

I have no readily available cash left. However, I do have my Self-Managed Super Fund Account. This is not something that is mine to readily draw on, but it is an account linked to my other accounts. As I have just set it up, the funds are all still there, not yet invested.

Though I know I am not meant to, I reluctantly agree to take $40,000 from it to help him. The promise is that once his taxes are paid he will leave Dubai immediately and be able to pay this back to me once he reaches England. This should be in about a week. He agrees to pay me interest too, so I justify to myself that it will be like an investment activity.

I withdraw the money and set about sending it. I take $40,000 cash out of my SMSF account without any query from the bank, and toss up in my mind about trying to send it all to him on one day.

By now I am getting very anxious about all these trips to the post office in my lunch hour to send money via Western Union. I wonder if anyone will notice.

I make a point of going to different counters, and trying to get different people on the counter.

3rd October:

> J: Did you just try to call me? I was just away from my desk for a moment.
> E: No my love. I didn't call. Are you sure it's a good idea sending all that money in a day through western union ?
> J: No but want to get it done if I can. Maybe you are right. It was quite big getting 15000 through yesterday.
> E: I think you should just do 10000 in two transactions, then the rest tomorrow.
> J: Ok my love
> E: Hope your day is going well my love, I just tried calling you. Kisses.
> E: I've not had a wink of sleep all night. I really do miss you, I can't wait to be with you.
> J: Ok only $20000 coming, rest will have to come tomorrow as I reached the daily limit

The Whole Sordid Story

E: Ok my love.
MTCN: 8143483096
AED: 36,903
MCTN: 1544028310
AED: 36,903
J: I have the rest from the bank already, so should be ok tomorrow. Fingers crossed. Love you
E: Love you sweetheart.
E: Sweetie I layed down waiting for 9am and I just opened my eyes, gonna get ready to get money now.
J: Ok I'm pleased you slept a bit at least. Rest of money will come tomorrow. I'm about to leave and head home. Take care love.

And the next day, 4th September:

J: All Ok love. 20,000 coming
MCTN: 4369099705
AED: 36,731
MCTN: 3688452438
AED: 36,731

J: Love. Tried to call. Just let me know when you wake up that you have this. Cxxx
J: Hi love, I'm just going into 2 back to back meetings for next 3.5 hours, so just SMS me once you collect the money. Love you.
E: Good morning my love. Mwaaaah. Xxxx
J: I hope all goes smoothly today. Please be on that plane out.... Cxxxx
E: I need to talk to you ASAP my love.

The latest problem is that he has reached his limit for what he can receive in a month via Western Union, so I will need to change the name on the last transfer I sent though.
He asks me to transfer it to his driver, Mr Waheed. I leave work again, and go back to the Post Office, queue up with the same person, and ask them to change the name on the transfer. This doesn't seem a problem, they just have to call Western Union. She goes off into the back, and takes about ten minutes to get it done.

    E: Hassan Waheed Adisa
        J: Has your man got enough ID?
    Long queue....
    E: Hassan Waheed Adisa
    E: How's it going my love ?
        J: Done. Should be available for you in about 15 minutes.
        J: Please txt when you have it xxxx
        J: I'm frazzled now. Just want no more problems. Xxx
        J: You should be able to get it now.
    E: How's it going my love ?
        J: I'm ok love
        J: Love do you have it?

Frazzled is an understatement. I am shaking and feeling anxious as I head back to work. It took a lot of effort to do this.

I do all this on automatic, without really questioning it.

No-one questions me. If they had I would have gone to pieces.

Robbed

I don't hear anything, and I am worried.
This is not usual. About 11:40 pm, my iPad dings with IM. It is not Eamon though, it is Blessing (B:), and she is worried.

B: <ding>
    J: I'm here
B: Hello Jan.
B: It's Blessing.
    J: Hello
B: Have you heard from dad ?
    J: Hi blessing
    J: No
B: OMG !
    J: Not for some hours
B: We don't know where he is.
    J: When did you last hear from him.
B: Mr Waheed came a couple of hours ago. He said dad left him in the town to go meet the revenue officers because his car developed a problem
    J: His phone is not answering
B: I told him dad isn't back yet and he said dad is probably still at the revenue office
    J: That's a long time
B: He went there only to come back saying the revenue officers said dad didn't come there.
    J: OMG
B: I don't have a phone to call but Mr Waheed says his number isn't going through
    J: Yes I have tried too
B: I'm so worried. I feel something has happened. Dad isn't one to get someone worried.
B: I don't like this place. It's been one bad news or the other for dad since we got here
    J: Yes now I am worried too. He had a lot of money with him
    J: He would not have just left you...
    J: Had he booked flights for you?
B: I don't know.
    J: Ok, let me think
B: I don't think so he said to me that I should be ready before he comes back that we are just gonna go to the airport buy our tickets then wait for the flight as the flight home is @ 8pm

> **J:** I think you need to contact the British Embassy and ask for help. He should be back by now
> **B:** Mr Waheed says he's gonna drive to the airport. He said I should hang in here till he comes back but I'm so worried.
>
> **J:** Your dad would not go to the airport without you
> **B:** I'll just be praying to The Lord till Mr Waheed gets back
> **J:** I've been praying today as well
> **B:** I'm sorry I only contact you for bad news. I didn't know who else to talk to
> **J:** It's fine
> **J:** I would want to know
> **B:** When Mr Waheed gets back. I'll send you a message.
> **B:** If there is no news when he gets back. I'll ask him to take me to the embassy he should know where it is.
> **J:** Is there someone at the guest house who can help you contact the embassy?
> **J:** Ok, mr waheed will help
> **B:** Bye Jan
> **J:** If needed I can try and contact the embassy from here
> **J:** Keep in contact
> **J:** Treat me as your family. I feel as if i am.

Now I am anxious too.
I try and contact her back, but do not get her till after 3am:

> **J:** hi blessing
> **B:** Hello Jan
> **J:** any news
> **J:** is it ok if i come on a voice call with you
> **B:** He came in about an hour ago
> **B:** He refused to say anything
> **B:** He says he just want to sleep
> **J:** at least he's there
> **B:** Ok that will be good. I want to take a quick shower to calm myself
> **B:** I will take the computer to my room after the shower and voice call you.
> **B:** Is that ok Jan ?
> **J:** ok buzz me when you are ready. ill wait
> **B:** I don't like to call you Jan. it sounds disrespectful to me
> **B:** Can I call you mom ?

The Whole Sordid Story

B: If it offends you. I'm sorry
    J: yes thats fine
B: Ok thank you.
B: Bye mom
    J: bye

And later IM, 5th October 2012, 4:12:37am:

B: Hi Mom
    J: Hi there Blessing
B: The option to voice call you is not highlighting.
B: Are you are work ?
    J: No it's 4am here, I'm in bed, but not able to sleep
    J: Turn your volume down a minute and I'll call you
B: 4 am ?
    J: Yes
B: OMG !
B: I'm so sorry. I should let you sleep mom
    J: I'm the other side of the world
    J: That's ok
    J: I want to know about yr dad

Outgoing Voice call from bdubhlainn, 4:06:51 AM:

B: I've never seen him in the mood that he was in when he came in
    J: No the voice is not working
    J: Did he have his things with him, phone etc that you saw?
B: I was scared to talk to him. He just kissed my forehead and said to me that I shouldn't ask any questions yet that he just wanna sleep
B: I didn't see his phone. I looked for it to call you.
B: OMG ! Was he robbed ?
    J: Maybe
    J: I'm thinking I should come there
    J: But it will depend on him
B: I don't like it here anymore. It's been stress for dad since we got here. I'm beginning to feel like it was an error coming here with him
B: All his work travels have been successful but the first time I came for work with him it isn't going well
    J: It's certainly been tough times all around.
B: He didn't want me to come but I insisted

> **J:** It's not anything to do with you
> **B:** Do you think it was selfish of me ?
> **J:** No

IM 5th October 2012, 4:23:16 AM:

> **B:** I just wanted to be with him mom
> **J:** I would have wanted to be with him too
> **J:** We don't know what's happened to him, but it's probably not good.
> **J:** I normally talk to him about 5 am my time, so I'll find out more then
> **J:** If he wakes up and is willing to talk to me
> **J:** It's nothing about you being there, but it's not a good place
> **J:** Are you Ok
> **J:** I want to give you a big hug. It's been a scary day.
> **B:** I'll be fine mom
> **B:** I wish you were here.
> **J:** Ok yes I want to be there too
> **J:** I'll talk to him about that. He's more important to me than my job
> **B:** Ok mom
> **B:** Mom please get some sleep. I'll keep an eye on him
> **J:** I'm going to try and sleep a little now if that's with you. Please feel free to contact me any time.
> **J:** Do you have yr own phone?
> **B:** I'll go ask him for his phone. I'll tell him I want to use it and hear what he says , is that a good idea ?
> **B:** No mom. I lost my iPhone at the airport
> **J:** No let him sleep for now.
> **B:** Ok mom.
> **B:** Bye !
> **J:** I have IM ON MY Phone, but you might need to email me if you want to chat
> **J:** Bye love

Early the next morning, 5th October, I email first:

> Good morning Darling.
> I talked with Blessing and found that you arrive home after 10-11 hours of being missing.   All I can say is that whatever happened is not as bad as the thoughts and imaginings of what might have happened to you.   I could

The Whole Sordid Story

not bear to lose you. I was so relieved to hear you had come home.
I don't care about the money. If need be I will give you more... we'll just wear the loss. I just want to be with you.
If you want I will come to Dubai, get a plane out of here today, be there on your Saturday. And we will get whatever needs to be sorted, together. I don't care about my job, I'll take a week's leave, and come to you. Just say and I will come, and we can be together.
I have IM on my phone too so can chat through that – I tried your phone again and its off the air.
I love you, no matter what. Always all ways
Your Nectar.

I'll be watching my email and IM

Then on IM:

> **E:** [6:20:13 AM] Please send a message when you are awake
>> **J:** I'm awake my love
>> **J:** i just sent you an email
> **E:** I don't think you'll wanna speak to me again
>> **J:** sorry wrong
>> **J:** we said always all ways AND i mean it
>> **J:** if you want i will come to Dubai, get on a plane today
> **E:** No sweetie
>> **J:** make some excuse at work
> **E:** Please don't
> **E:** this place is bad news
>> **J:** yes, but maybe we can sort it together
> **E:** Sweetie, I messed up, I totally blew it... I'm so so stupid, my impatience made me loose 20,000 usd today
>> **J:** its only money
> **E:** I got myself into a taxi, not knowing he's a robber, he drove to a quiet zone, pointed a gun to my head and told me to drop all I have and get out of the car
> **E:** I begged him sweetie
> **E:** I begged him sooooo much
>> **J:** it does not matter
> **E:** I told him to let me go, that the money means so much to me right now
>> **J:** it doesnt mean as much as having you back safely
>> **J:** we can always get more money

J: ive already busted into the super fund, so I will do it again if needed
J: at least you are safe
E: I never should have come here my love
E: what if that bastard shot me today
E: All my life
E: I have never had a gun pointed to my face
E: Mr Waheed asked me to be patient to wait for him to get me a taxi, I didn't listen, I told him to work on his car
J: did he take your passport too
E: No he didn't, he threw it out of the car

IM 5th October 2012, 6:46:41 AM:

J: did you find it?
E: yes
J: good
J: but you should also lok on the british embasy website and get some support for being robbed. i
J: i was looking there when i was imagining you dead in a gutter somewhere
J: darling
J: my love
E: My love !
E: I don't feel like going to the embassy, I don't like getting public
J: at least look at the website then decide
E: What kind of support are they gonna give me ?
E: they aren't gonna give me money to pay the taxes
J: it may help with the revenue guys if you need to prove that you had the money
E: that will definitely take a process love

E: I just wanna be out of here
E: I was a few mins from leaving... I feel cursed at this moment... why did that car get spoilt
J: no understanding what went wrong
J: Blessing thinks its because she came with you that everything is going wrong
E: WHAT ?
J: i talked with her - she was worried about you
J: were you actually bashed, hurt?

> **E:** He hit the booth of the gun on my hand
> **J:** ok, painful, but could have been a lot worse
> **J:** i'm so relieved
> **J:** i had bad feelings when you were getting the money yesterday. i was preying to the masters guides and angels to protect you
> **J:** it seems they did, but they could not save the money
> **E:** You had some bad feelings ? You should have told me, that would have made me more careful
> **J:** thats not important
> **J:** we were too intent on getting it and getting you out...
> **J:** once you got the money I thought it was OK and then relaxed

IM 5th October 2012, 6:54:13 AM:

> **J:** i just want you out of there

We start up a video call (one sided), and I take my laptop with me as I get a cup of tea, go to the shower and prepare for my day.
He does not want to lose contact with me, nor I him. I tell him I have no qualms about using my SMSF money again after all this. I just want to get him out of Dubai, away from all these dangers and back to England where he is safe, and I can get my money back.
To get it all in one day though I will send some via Western Union and the other via MoneyGram.

> **E:** My love
> **E:** if sending money gram it has to be through Mr Waheed

We talk further about the arrangements.
I do all of this, sending money, again. I am even more agitated and exhausted than previously, but drive myself through to get it done. His continued contact and support keeps me going till its completed.

IM 5th October:

> **J:** [12:41:23 PM] Getting money from bank now
> **J:** I'll do 20 western union and 20 money gram to mr Waheef
> **J:** <ding>
> **J:** Hi
> **J:** [1:00:00 PM]<ding>

E: [1:09:37 PM] Hi love
E: 1:11:52 PM <ding>

> **J:** [1:11:57 PM] Battery low. At GPO FOR WESTERN UNION
> **J:** WILL then go to money gram
> **J:** [1:12:29 PM] Hope it all goes through

E: ok love
E: ok

> **J:** I can charge phone back at work
> **J:** For details should I send through to phone as usual or here?
> **J:** So tired

E: here my love

> **J:** Ok

E: onlt gonna get phone later]

> **J:** I'll send the money gram to mr Waheed

E: yes love
E: you done at western union ?

> **J:** No just starting
> **J:** Forgive the question. Are you real my love?
>
> **J:** First one done
> **J:** Sorry just tired
> **J:** MTCN 3649254502
> **J:** 36,824 UAD
> **J:** I LOVE YOU

E: I LOVE YOU

> **J:** or else I'm crazy
> **J:** Please tell me you're real
> **J:** I need you

E: of course I am real

> **J:** Love you

E: Love you

The Whole Sordid Story

IM 5th October 2012, 1:40:27 PM:

    J: Yes
    J: Just counting second !10000
    J: MCTN:
    J: MCTN 9688346773. 36,824. UAD
E: ok love
    J: OK Love off to the next one
E: yhanks alot
E: thanks
    J: <ding>
    J: Stay with me a few more minutes
E: ok my love
E: you look beautiful this morning
    J: What Id will mr Waheed have?
    J: Ok yeah yeah
E: UAE ID
E: passport I mean
    J: Ok
    J: Waiting my turn to get form
    J: Not sure if I need two
E: in money gram already ?
E: use 2 my love
    J: Which is his family name?
E: Hassan

IM 5th October 2012, 2:16:56 pm:

E: [1:59:48 PM] My love !
E: <ding>
E: Is your phone off ?
E: [2:16:56 PM] <ding>

IM 5th October 2012, 2:48:04 pm:

E: [2:28:53 PM] <ding>
    J: [2:36:59 PM] One has gone through. I needed cash for the fees so did not have quite enough for the second yet
    J: Ref no 56987894
    J: 35809
E: Did your battery go off ?
    J: Yes phone went off
E: are you back at work ?
E: ok

J: One gone through
J: I'm back at work, had a meeting
E: Ok my love
E: How did the meeting go ?
J: I'm going to leave, and will do another, but need a little more cash.
J: In 5mins or so
E: I hope you are not gonna get into trouble at work
J: It should be ok
E: Ok my love
J: Stay close
E: ok love
J: Leaving now
E: Ok love

IM 5th October 2012, 3:19:59 pm:

J: [2:52:25 PM] Ok I'm out
E: ok love
J: [2:57:02 PM] Just putting money through. Not quite $10,000. They won't take it, so it's $9711 plus my fees
E: ok
E: ok
E: that's alright
J: Has Mr Waheed turned up?
E: He's on his way
E: he sent me a message on IM about 5 mins ago
E: He should be here in another 5 mins
J: Looks all ok counting money
E: ok
J: Ref no 40396314
E: Thanks love
J: 35,623 AED
J: ALL DONE
J: ok I'm heading home now. Will you be able to pay revenue today?
E: Yes I will be able to do so
E: Mr waheed just got here
E: I wanna insert my sim in the phone he brought
J: Ok STAY SAFE, and get yourself and Blessing on a plane
J: Ok
J: [3:14:41 PM] I'm going to get on atrain shortly and will be out of range while we go thru tunnels for about 5 mins but ill say when

The Whole Sordid Story

    J: [3:18:49 PM] I just hope it all goes ok.

At this time, with his phone back in order, he calls and I say I have put the Western Union money in his name again.
He gets upset, saying he told me he was beyond his limit. He did, but I did not understand it was for the month and he could not have any more in his name.

I am getting more and more frantic, deflated, but know I have to continue, finding the energy from somewhere to fix this:

    E: [3:19:12 PM] I'm sorry love
    E: i didn't know I wasn't clear enough
    E: Sorry !
        J: Ok
        J: I'm just looking at the form

IM 5 Oct 2012, 3:45:21 PM

        J: I'll have to go back to the post office yesterday they just called to change it
        J: I'll go back
    E: Sorry for the stress love
    E: I'm so gonna make it up to you
        J: Do you think you will be able to fly out today?
    E: I'm not sure exactly because of the time I'll get the money.
    E: but I will do my very best
    E: I want to take it easy, I don't wanna try to be extremely fast and end up being more than slow
    E: You understand ?
        J: <ding>
    E: I'm here love
        J: Yes
    E: You buzzed !
        J: Just holding my phone probably shook it walking
        J: Big big line waiting.
    E: Ok love
        J: It might take an hour.
        J: I just want to curl up on your arms and have you hold me
    E: I'm so gonna make all this up to you
        J: Yes
        J: I think I'll get a taxi home after rather than go for the train

E: How is the weather today love ?
E: My love

    J: It's warm hot about 28
    J: Sorry just eating a protein bar I've had no lunch
E: You need it love
E: [3:45:21 PM] and my special protein inside your vagina.

And then after:

    J: At the train station again. I'll call you when I get home
E: Didn't use the taxi ?
    J: I'm just on automatic I think. And my car is at the station. The bar gave me a little energy
E: Ok let me know when you home
    J: Yes, just read yr last IM post. YES

And early the next morning:

    J: 1:58 AM: Darling any news? I can't sleep
E: Got the money love. Paid taxes, can't buy tickets today, ticketing office closed. We'll chat when I get to the guest house.
    J: Ok please
E: Hahahahaah Like minds, I just text you
    J: Love you madly deeply
    J: Love are you awake? im on IM

Paying out the Employer

We get on IM early the next morning, and chat for a while. It is Saturday morning, so it's a bit later than work mornings. 6th October:

> **E:** Good morning love
>   **J:** Goodmorning
>   **J:** I'll open the computer
> **E:** Ok my love

Outgoing Voice call from dubhlainneAM on (6:24:10 am).

Call Ended: 0 hours 8 minutes 37 seconds.

While we chat, he takes a call on his Mobile. I hear the conversation go on for a minute or two. His tone warns me he is not very happy.
He comes back on to me and tells me it was one of the people who employed him, Mr David, and he is coming over to talk to him. He goes off to get ready.

IM 6th October 2012 8:03:07 am:

> **E:** Please call me now love
> **E:** very urgent
> **E:** <ding>
> **E:** I can't get through to you on the phone... I need to talk to you

This time, the story is that Mr David insists that Eamon either completes his work as contracted, or pays back some of the money already given in the payment cheque... or else! It's clear to Eamon that he may not be allowed to leave Dubai, and is threatened with physical injury.
The amount needed to pay them out is $98,000. Eamon wants to find a way to do this, to get finished with it all and get out of Dubai and back to England.
It's what I want too.
With all my heart.
I am already thinking there is no way I have that money. He will have to come up with some from somewhere else, and he

cannot always rely on me to rescue him.
I feel the pressure he puts on me to fix this for him as I have in the past. I still have some in my SMSF, but know I should not take it out. I am beginning to feel I don't want to give any more money to him.
Later I talk with some friends who use Apple Macs about his inability to see me, and they encourage me to get him to use Skype, so I email:

> Hi Darling,
> talking to friends who are Mac specialists this morning and they do not understand why you should not be able to download Skype. They say it should be easy.   Can you try this again for me please, from here....
> http://www.skype.com/intl/en/get-skype/on-your-computer/macosx/ the left side.
> I want to be able to see you please
> I know you said something needed upgrading, but I'm not sure what.
> If you do get an error message again, please take a screen shot (CNTRL+SHIFT+3) and send it to me so they can give some advice.
> Love you

I'm thinking it through overnight, and send him a long email with my thoughts:

> Darling waking up Sunday and there are a number of things on my mind that I want to say, and need some clear space to say it, hence this email.
> Firstly, please really consider your course of action here. I know you just want to get finished with it, but the cost of this is very high- trying to sort all this money out is very complicated. I am very reluctant to give you more money. It doesn't feel right to me. I always believe if something feels right it will happen easily, and this is certainly not the case here. I feel pulled along by your desire to get it sorted.
> You have already had conversations with Mr David that I don't know, but the troubles here with the cheque are really no ones fault. It seems they have contracted with you in good faith, and paid you in good faith, though not as you expected. I am concerned after all your talk about not having access to cash, that if you then manage to get the cash to pay them out it looks bad for you, it's bad karma for

The Whole Sordid Story

you. And though they are honorable about the contract, beyond that I don't know.

Please consider very carefully what are the costs (financial, reputation, psychic, karma) of each option

1. Waiting until the cheque can be changed for cash- just a bit of time, there is plenty of that, and perhaps this is the easiest.
2. Actually finishing the work as contracted to do- good karma, finishing what you started and have all ready been paid for. I think this would clear any bad energy around. You could still decide to do this.
3. Doing all this money manipulation to pay them out- pushing so hard, when it is not easy. There is a phrase, you cannot push the river, and it feels to me that this is what you are trying to do. And this has a lot of cost for me. Is there any real urgency here, apart from what you have in your mind?

My personal concerns are, and I know they are selfish, is that I don't want to do all this money transfer stuff. I've had enough of it. It's not money I should be using at all in the first place and is bad karma for me, and I don't like that.

I'm also concerned that if anything happened to you, I would be left with nothing, and a lot of debt, and no way to rectify the situation. So far I have gone on trust that you will be able to rectify the situation once back in England. After your attack the other night, we know that the unexpected can happen and there is a lot of bad energy around.

I'm not expecting it to, but just looking at the worst case scenario, and it scares me, and I want to put in contingency plans if possible. This is a big ask, but could you write a will with some coverage for me for what I have given you money wise. You are my fiancé, but who knows this? You could also make me Blessing's guardian if you felt ok about this.

Darling it's hard to write this, as I know it's not what you want to hear, but please consider carefully what you are doing. Fast and furious doesn't always win the day.

I want to be with you more than I can say, you know this. But I want you alive and safe more than anything, and I'll happily wait, if this is the safest and easiest course.

Please tune in yourself to what's right, putting your pride aside, and behind that, in your heart what feels right?

You are my man and I will support whatever you decide....

Actually as I write this I had to stop and really check with myself, and In my heart I continue to get a strong NO to

giving you more money...... Si i take it back. If I don't respect myself with this it will damage whatever chance we have to be happy together! I cannot put my love for you above my self respect because I could not expect you to love someone who doesn't respect themselves. It would totally dry up my juices.
Sorry my love but it's becoming clearer to me as I write.... I CANNOT give you more money! I just can't do it. Because it does not feel right in my heart, that is the only true measure I have.
Just wait, this is easiest.... There is no real urgency....
I will be on tender hooks now waiting for you to read and respond to this.
I love you, and I say these things because I love you. I hope you understand.
Your Nectar to EDD

He comes onto IM mid-afternoon. He tells me that he has already organised with Blessing's nanny to pawn his two cars, and the £25,000 is being given as a loan for 21 days only, at 120% interest.

He cannot wait as I suggest, as that would mean he would lose the ability to get his cars back within the allotted time. He says I am just thinking of the worst that could happen, and as it already has, it will all be okay.

I have said my piece, but reluctantly now feel compelled to give in to his drive to get it done and get out of Dubai and keep his cars. I insist though, that I will not do any more Western Union transfers, and that he will have to find a bank for money to go to, so I can transfer it all in one go.

He agrees to ask Mr Waheed if he has an account that it can be sent to.

He tells me that his mother, who was a bit psychic, had once told him that after he was forty-nine years old he should not work outside the country he lived in, implying that bad things would happen. He thought that this was what she was warning against. This little story make it all seem pre-determined, fated, no use arguing against it.

The Whole Sordid Story

Later, on Sunday evening, on text:

E: [9:43 pm] What are you up to my love ?
J: Just finished watching a program on tv. You?
E: I'm at the pool side, waiting for Mr Waheed.
J: Ok remember that there should be an additional bank code or Swift code as well as his account details. He may need to get that from his bank.
J: Sorry telling you what to do again, love you
E: My woman should be able to tell me what to do
J: I've sent a couple of SMS from Skype. Did you get them? How do the sow up from me?
J: You are my man
E: [10:25 AM]: My love, Mr Waheed says the kind of account he has cannot receive a hugh sum.
E: But his fiancee does personal buisness and her account can. What do you think ?
E: Message from skype ? I didn't receive any text not from this number.
J: You have to be certain she can be trusted...
J: I'd still rather do one transaction
J: Did your Skype install?
E: If Mr Waheed can be trusted, then his fiancee can be
J: Ok get the bank details.
E: The mac software is upgrading. It takes lots of hours, about two hours left though, then will install skype.
J: Ok good. Trying to send SMS via Skype as its cheaper, but you don't seem to be getting them.
J: Is mr Waheed still there?
E: Yes love he is.
J: Ok then I won't send you what i would really like to say because its private between you and me, about certain juices that I know you like.....
E: Hahahahahahahahahahahaha...... You bad. Yeees..... Lol
J: And things that need squeezing to get the juice out.
J: And some times I know you like to lick up the juices.....
E: Hey love pls stop, this is torture, I'm by the pool, I'm wearing shorts, it wouldn't be a good sight for my penis to activate here.
J: Hahaha ok ill save it for later just tell me when my love. I'll go back and read my book.... Love you

I go for a walk on the beach and send him some photos.

Romance Scam Survivor

Later he says, delightedly, that he is set up on Skype so I can see him, with nothing on! Blessing, he says, has checked the tests that you can do and it's all working from their end. Excitedly, we try connecting, but despite looking at all of the settings, over and over, it seems I still cannot see him! Very deflating and frustrating! I do not understand and cannot explain it. So disappointing.

He acknowledges the photos I send, in an email overnight:

> Thanks for the beautiful pictures my love, thoughtful of you to share. Was nice hearing your sexy sleepy voice, I hope to skype with you when you wake up
> Here is the Banking information for Mr Waheed's fiancee
> Bank Name : Emirate NBD
> Account Name : Peace Nyerovwo Abolo
> Account number: 1014442343801
> Address :   Union Square Branch
> Swift :   EBILAEAB
> IBAN: AE500260001014442343801
> Thanks so much love, please try to do this in your morning (I'm hoping you don't have lots of meetings) also tell them at the bank that they should make it a fast transfer so it can get here in 24 hours, it may incur some extra charges, but it will make things fast for me. My love , I am so sure that this is the best thing to do and so sure that this is gonna solve and end the drama here that I can say to you with all confidence that IF ANYTHING COMES UP, DON'T EVEN LISTEN TO ME. We are almost there my love, you should take a minute to think, you'll see that there's nothing that can happen anymore. The worse has happened and we've scaled through this, I strongly believe that this is a test of nature and we've passed it. Now it's time to have a wonderful life together, baby I'll so take care of you that, you'll start growing younger instead of older.. Hold me to that word
> I love you,
> EDD

Dutifully I take the money from my SMSF and send the money then next day, $77,000 via bank transfer.

Again, the bank does not query anything that I am doing.

The Whole Sordid Story

7th October:

> **J:** [9:48 AM] Bank transfer done. No way to make it go faster. It goes via an exchange in NY. It still may take a few days to get to you. Do you need a copy of the receipt this time? Love you.
> **J:** [2:53 pm] Hope you slept we'll my love and have woken up refreshed today. Xxxx
> **J:** [5:18 pm] On my way home from work now, but going to my brother's for dinner. Love you EDD
> **E:** [6:54 pm] Love you too. Yes pls send the payment slip to my email
> **J:** Ok will do later, at my brothers now love you
> **E:** Are you having dinner now my love ?
> **J:** A wine, dinner still cooking. Dazz serving up now. .... I'll buzz you once I'm home. Xxxx
> **E:** Glad you are having fun, it's what a beautiful woman with a loving and caring heart deserves. I love you.
> **J:** Thank you my love.
> **J:** Love you madly.
> **E:** Where exactly in the house are you right now ?
> **J:** [8:22 pm] Home now my love. Have just emailed the receipt. Check to see if it is readable.
> **J:** Feeling very vulnerable. You have my heart and all of my money. Now I am totally in your hands!
> **E:** And that's the safest place for you. I love you
> **J:** My first reaction was... And what will you do with those hands?   Sorry I could not resist...
> **E:** No email from you my love
> **J:** Ok I have sent again

I hear from him that the funds are through to him very quickly, and the next day this business is done.

Tickets

And then there was more...

> **J:** I'm here love. Try again

We Skype. Again there is a request for money, this time for paying the accommodation and tickets to fly.
I am exasperated. I turn my head away from him, I do not want to hear it, to face it, it is too much for me to handle.

So he texts to get my attention:

> **E:** [2:20 AM] This is so unfair. Why are you ignoring me ?

I won't argue any more. I say reluctantly that I will do whatever he wants, but my tone is resigned and unenthusiastic. He says he doesn't want it like that, seemingly arguing against me giving him money.
Is he that principled, I ask myself?
He makes the point, as he has before, that he is not coming to be with me because I want him to. It is because he chooses and decides to come.
Would a scammer argue like this, I ask myself? He says that I am being unfair to him and we argue in circles, seemingly at cross purposes, until I agree to see if I can find more money.

Later I text him some ideas:

> **J:** [3:15 AM] Maybe I can increase the credit limit on my credit card again.
> **J:** Please check again to see how I can buy yr tickets love

This to see if there is any way I can buy tickets for him on my Amex charge card, but he says they insist on seeing the credit card before they will let you fly. I don't know if that's true or not, as it seems wrong to me, but I accept it.

> **J:** If I can increase my credit limit by $5000 I can do it. I think that will be ok. You owe me BIG TIME EDD.
> **J:** [4:20 AM] I want that happy playful man back. I've missed him so much these last days. Xxx

The Whole Sordid Story

> **J:** [5:20 AM] I'm awake love. Skype me

I don't remember what we talked about. I was probably asking how much money was needed. I go to the city, but before I go to work I call my bank to ask for more credit. They give it, unquestioningly. I have a good credit rating and a good job.
I am totally strung out and shaky, but do it anyway. I feel close to breaking point, but I'm good at covering it up.

I go into my online banking and consolidate all my now available funds, and later send another $10,000 via Western Union, to Blessing's name this time:

> **J:** [8:13 AM] Additional credit approved but will take a couple of hours to be applied. That should be ok. Love you.
>
> **J:** [12:36 PM] All done. Western Union for Blessing
> MTCN: 2929505403
> AED: 36, 734
>
> **J:** Please let this be ok and the end of it. I am very stressed.
>
> **J:** [5:17 PM] Hi love, I'm hoping all is going well with your plans to leave today. I'm heading home from work. Should be there on about an hour. Love you
>
> **J:** [8:01 PM] Darling, I want to know but I don't want to know. I'm so scared you are going to say something else has come up and you need more money. Please don't tell me that. Please get on a plane today. I won't be able to relax until then. I'm wound up like a coiled spring.

I don't hear anything. The loving, playful man has disappeared, and I notice.

10th October:

> **E:** [5:47 AM]: Couldn't get flights for today. Booked for tomorrow 8pm, the price for tomorrow morning and tonight was outrageous
>
> **J:** Ok my love. I have been so anxious. Love you. Stay safe.
>
> **J:** You are my man, and totally precious to me.
>
> **J:** What time do you arrive in England? Do you still have your old phone for there or was that lost?

135

No response to these queries. We Skyped a little later.
When we talk I ask about Mr Waheed, the driver. There has been no talk about money for him. Eamon has talked to him he says, and all he is asking for is $1000 to have his car fixed, and is okay to get more later. This man has been a stalwart for Eamon in Dubai, and if he does not notice, I do.

I find I have additional cash in my purse which I did not realise was there. I had probably gotten it out earlier to send to Eamon .

In my generosity, I send it for Mr Waheed, via MoneyGram:

> **J:** Money for Mr Waheed
> Ref no: 95426193
> AED 2923
> Please thank him from me for all the support he has given you my fiancé.
> **J:** Love, today feeling much calmer. Love you and take care. Xxxx
> **J:** Good morning my sweets. Hope you slept well   cxxx
> **J:** Just on train heading home. wish I was rushing home to you. Love you

There is a brief phone call:

> **J:** 8:14 pm: So good to hear your voice my love. It's like balm for my soul.
> **J:** Darling I am going to doze now. Please text when you leave for the airport. And if you can as you are boarding. Keep safe, a let me know when you are home my love. Love you so much.

In the early hours:

> **E:** [11 Oct 1:32 AM] Leaving for the airport now my love. Don't call because my matt is low. I wanna be able to call you when sitted in the plane. I love you bunches.
> **J:** OK my love xxxxxx

And later, when I hear nothing:

> **J:** Did you get away?

The Whole Sordid Story

I wait impatiently to hear that he has managed to leave Dubai, that awful place. I get more and more concerned that I have not heard anything.

I don't sleep well through the early hours:

> **J:** Are you there? I am desperate to hear from you my love.

Car Accident

I do not hear that he has boarded, or arrived. Initially I think that his phone battery has run out. I hope he has gone, managed to get to England.
Hoping beyond hope.
Early on the morning of the 12th October I get a call. It's a woman saying she is a nurse, and asking me several questions about who I was in relation to Eamon and Blessing, to which I reply that I am his fiancé.
She tells me that he has been in a car accident, and that he asked her to let me know by calling the last number called on his phone. The driver was killed, but Eamon is okay, just under sedation. Blessing is under sedation and they are waiting for her to come around. The accent is strange, and I do not catch the woman's name or the name of the hospital.
She calls me again later to say that Blessing has woken up.
I'm both relieved and reassured that I have heard and he has found a way to contact me and let me know. But at the same time aghast at what has happened.
I am frantic about what I can do to help, so call the British embassy to see if they can assist. They politely tell me that it is probably a scam, that there are many like this. They look up their names, but do not find them. They even call the phone, but there is no response at the other end.
I justify to myself, reasoning that they wouldn't understand, and that I think their passports are Irish, not British. I don't want to believe what they tell me.
I get a call some time later from Eamon himself, but he is so faint it's difficult to understand what he is saying. Finally, I realise he is saying that Mr Waheed, his driver, was killed. He says he has to rest and will call again later.
The next time his voice is a bit stronger, but still not normal.
He tells me he has a damaged hand and a cut on his head. Again, we don't talk for long, as he is still weak. He says when he realised he survived the accident he could only think that he was given a chance of being with me, that this was his whole purpose now.
We are able to talk on the phone more and more over the coming days, as he gets stronger. I begin to text him regularly, so he knows I am thinking about him, but do not get a

The Whole Sordid Story

response until 15th October.

I know he has no money, and eventually I get a call from a woman saying she is his doctor. She talks about the fees that need to be paid. Although I do not understand exactly what she says, it's about 46,000 Dinas (AED).

The call is cut short as she has to go off and do something, and she realises I do not fully understand.

I call Eamon, upset of course that this woman is calling me. He says to give him thirty minutes and he will go and talk to her about what is going on.

We talk again a little later and Eamon says the doctor called me because she did not want to worry him. He says he has explained that I do not have any money, and he has access to no money. She is apparently understanding, but needs the fees to be paid.

Over the next couple of days the conversations continue, with the doctor saying that she cannot rely on anything being paid once he gets back to England. At the very least, what needs to be paid is the pharmaceuticals used. She has had to buy them from a pharmacy, and she cannot let her reputation with them be sullied, as it will impact her ability to do work in future.

Eamon tries to talk to the pharmacist directly, but he happens to have gone on holidays for a week. The doctor then comes back and says that she has some credit, and with this taken into account the amount that needs to be paid is (Eamon has converted for me) $5000. I protest that I have no money left, and cannot help with this.

I ask what will happen if he doesn't pay? He does not know.

My fortnightly pay of $3500 goes into my account the next day. I offer to give him $1500, as I know I have rent and food to pay with this money.

He says he will not take this money just for the sake of it, but will see if it will make a difference. He does not want to leave me short of money for food.

He manages to get some more money via Blessing's nannie, and I agree to send him some, expecting that by the following week I will have it all back once he has reached England. That way I will be able to eat and pay my bills.

I send him $3800, my pay and a bit more of the last dollars I have across various accounts.

It is to go in the name of the doctor's secretary, Alhena Boulos, as she will collect it from Western Union.

Then I realise that some money has gone into my retirement fund, so I text him:

> **J:** More money has gone into retirement fund. If you personally need $1000 I can send it. Just let me know best way to send it. Love you.
> **J:** Love, if you want me to send you money today I need to know in the next 1/2 hour, to be able to do it before I leave the CBD. Let me know. Xxxx
> **E:** Hey love. I've given the info, they've gone to get the money I think. You can send the 1000 through same person. Thanks so much love.
> **J:** Are you sure they won't just keep it?
> **E:** No ways my love, the doctor is too nice to do that
> **J:** Ok. I'll go and do this now.
> **E:** Ok thanks love, no reason not to fly
> **J:** I'll call once I'm home, in about an hour and a half.
> **E:** Ok my love. Pls do

So I send another $1000 before I leave the city, then head straight home.

Later that evening I get a call. Apparently the ID of Alhena Boulos was out of date and cannot be used. Instead he gives me the name of Carla Moss. I do not question who this is, in my mind it's just another person from the hospital. I call Western Union and manage to change the name on the transactions to Carla Moss over the phone.

With this all done, he is now free to leave the hospital. He has told me he still has the tickets that he was going to fly on when he had the accident, and he expects to be able to use them. It's not that simple though, and when he goes to get tickets the next day he finds that because he had confirmed and booked in the previous week, he will need to pay additional money.

After much negotiating, pleading and so on, he is offered thirty percent off this, now a cost of $2400. He books for the following day regardless, and goes back to a cheap hotel close by the airport, costing $150 a night. He will need to be able to pay for this too.

Again, I offer to put the tickets on my Amex card, but he says he has checked again and they will not allow this without seeing the card itself.

The Whole Sordid Story

He says he has asked Blessing's nanny if she can borrow money from a friend to help. It's now getting quite desperate to get the necessary money together.

We are still trying to see if I can access money on the Amex charge card:

> **E:** Sweetie I was told that western union can be sent online if it's less than 1000,can you try with your credit card and see if some miracle will make it go through.
> **J:** How much?
> **E:** 900 or 950. Send through Carla
> Its late afternoon, so I go online at work and set up an account with Western Union, but have problems
> **J:** Trying - wont accept amex.
> **J:** Would $500 help? My cards will bounce, but should be able to recover next week
> **E:** My love at this point, anything is a plus to me.
> **J:** Do you want it in Dina's or us $$$?
> **E:** The money I told you I need is in usd, but you can send it whichever way. They'll still give it to me in their currency.
> **J:** It's not allowing me to send online. I think a problem with visa Internet password   Ill try again
> **J:** Trying again
> **J:** I've checked password and its still rejecting me. I'm going to go home and try again from there. It should be working....

Whilst heading home on the train I get an invitation to my brother's house for dinner.
At this point I still think he has tickets, but they want him to pay extra:

> **J:** Just tried to call. I am not going to try and send money again. I thing they will let you fly but probably won't make a decision till later. Just keep your cool, keep saying you have a valid ticket, that. $700 is all you have and if you have to wait till tomorrow you will have even less. They will want to have their seats full. Just keep faith that they will let you fly.
> I've just been invited to go to my brothers for dinner.
> Love you. I clearly believe you will be flying today.

At my brother's I get a text:

> **E:** I'm pretty sure you are forgetting that I'm in some pain still.

> Anyways enjoy your evening.
> **J:** Yes you have not told me about your pain, so I am forgetting that. I'm sure you will fly.... I'll call when I get home. I love you always and you know that. Xxx

I call when I get home. He makes it clear that he has had to buy new tickets.

I complain about all of the money I have given him, over $200,000, and the connection is cut off. Whether deliberately or not, I do not know.

I go onto the computer to try again to send him the money via Western Union, and this time it goes through. I send him the details.

Another $500 that I have managed to cobble together of small bits left across my accounts. The measuring bar for what I have left in my accounts has come down over the past weeks. After this I have $210 left in my account, with all my other accounts under $20:

> **J:** $500 on MCTN:9907194523 for Carla moss. Yes I am in pain too
> **J:** Please find a way to fly out if there. Please

This is not acknowledged. When I talk to him then next morning, 20th October, I ask if he received it, and he doesn't know about it.

He goes off his mobile to check his messages, and then confirms back that the detail is there.

I rack my brains for what else I can do to raise money, I'm so desperate to get him out of Dubai. I offer to pawn some jewellery I have, though its' not much.

He says no, it does not feel right for 'his woman' to be pawning her things. At least he has some concern and respect for me, I think.

Later in the day he calls me, all very chirpy, saying he has tickets to fly that night. I am very excited, and so relieved.

Only three more calls and he will be in England, he says, one as he leaves, another once he is seated on board, and then he will be in England. He doesn't want to use his phone time as it is limited, but keep it for this, so I allow him to disconnect.

I don't know how he has managed to get the money together, and assume Blessing's nanny has helped. I am so pleased he is

The Whole Sordid Story

finally leaving Dubai, and can't wait till he is back in England. I'm happy for him, and that my money will soon be returned. I stay awake through my early hours, waiting for his 8 pm time, as I remember this is the flight time given earlier for daily flight departures.

I expect him to call, but at 2:20 am I get a text, not the call from the plane that I was expecting and anticipating:

> **E:** Boarding the plane my love.... I love you sooo much and thanks for everything.

I text back:
> **J:** You and Blessing have a good flight. Xxxxx

The Realisation

Though I think the second part of his last text is a bit dismissive, I think this must just mean all I have done for him in Dubai, and expect that I will hear as soon as he lands, the third call that is promised.
I know he has no phone in England, as it was left at the airport on the way to Dubai. His Dubai phone will probably not work in England, and his computer is broken. Thus I am not surprised when I don't hear anything immediately at the time I am expecting him to land in England, about 7 pm Saturday night.
I don't worry too much the next day either. I know he needs to get to the bank on Monday to be able to open up his account, and after this would be able to buy another phone.
That day I am watching the clock, waiting through various deadlines in my mind, and regularly checking my bank account to see if any money has come in.
The deadlines pass, first a couple of hours after the banks open, and I receive no calls. Why has he not gone and immediately bought a phone and called me?
No money appears in my account.
The only contact I have is via email. I email him my back account details, just in case he has lost them. I had given them to him after the first bank transfer was made to him, expecting money would come back to me then.
It never did.

My emails are getting more desperate as time goes by. This one as I travel home Tuesday evening:

> I'm heading home from work as you wake up today my love. I hope it is going to be a good one. I love you and feel you loving me out there. Missing you though.
> Whatever the situation please let me know what is happening my love. I'd prefer bad news to no news at all.
> Love you.

The Whole Sordid Story

And Tuesday night, I check my bank account again:

> Hi love,
> I've just checked my bank and two of my accounts have now gone into negative. Have you been able to transfer any money to me to take care of things? I'm relying on you now.
> Hope all is going well. what's my man up to?
> Love you heaps, hoping to hear from you soon,
> Your Nectar

Through the day, my Wednesday, his Tuesday, I begin to realise there can be no excuse now. If he was going to do it, call me, or pay money, he would have by now.

Wednesday morning, I email:

> Good morning my love. I'm wondering why you are not in touch. Are you throwing me over? Were you scamming me after all? Even now I am finding that hard to believe, but maybe I am just still in denial.
> Please do me the courtesy of letting me know what is going on. Truth is better than the not knowing. You owe me at least that.
> My love hasn't ceased. I will love you always, as promised. What's happened to your promises?
> What's happened?
> Always yours
> Nectar

Slowly through the day, I realise he is not going to.

My only conclusion is that I have been scammed.

It was all a big con!

I had always known this was an option, but hadn't believed it was the case. It's not a surprise when it dawns. But it is a huge shock that I will not get my money back, that I had given away ALL of my money, over $250,000, and all of my superannuation money.
How could I possibly explain that? I cannot, at least not in any way that is rational.

Romance Scam Survivor

I realise I am in desperate financial circumstances, and cannot even pay my bills due over the next two weeks, let alone have money to buy food. I have food in the fridge and my cupboard, so I know I will not starve, even if I cannot buy food. But there are a number of key bills due this week that need to be paid.
My Mum is the first one to call, and I do that Wednesday evening. She goes into shock and cannot understand. What can she say? Nothing worse than what I thought myself. But I know she will always love me regardless. It will have direct implications for her, as some of the money I have given away is hers, and she will need it to move to Melbourne when the time comes.

I write to Eamon:

> I have realised today that you are not going to return my money are you.   That "thank you for everything" was a last dismissive good bye.
> You would leave the woman you love with not enough money to buy food. That's how short of funds I am right now and you knew it would come to this.
> I wouldn't let you go without but you would let me.   I guess that's my fault though, for choosing love over money.
> I'm in shock of course, haven't yet allowed myself to feel.   The loss of your love will be the most painful, because I know, even if you scammed and manipulated me, that you loved me too. I know that, because I felt your heart with mine. And you confirmed it in your last message.
> Part of me hopes you will just turn up on my doorstep, surprise me, make it all alright, and we can be together the way we'd promised each other, forever. Deluding myself again.....
> Was any of what happened true, or was it all a manipulation.   I certainly believed it, you made it so believable.   I guess I will never know.
> Who are you, are you real?   I still believe you are. More fool me.
> If I have it wrong, please get in touch.   If I have it right, please get in touch.
> Otherwise I guess I draw my own conclusions, broken heart and all.
> I am your woman, always, all ways.   Now we have to wait another lifetime to complete this bonding, promised to each

> other for lifetimes past.
> I know in your eyes all of this must sound pitiful, you are probably laughing at me, at how easy I was to manipulate, but I know my love was honest and true, full and generous, and sexy, and I stand strong with that.
> With an open invitation – turn up on my doorstep some time....
> Back to you..... I love you sooo much. Thank you for everything.

I didn't expect a reply. I didn't know if he is even reading them. In Skype his details were offline.
Thursday, I manage to get through the day at work, but I know I have shut down my feelings, compartmentalised parts of myself so I can function.
That evening I contact Rosie, who was warning me to be careful, and tell her the news. I took the easy way and emailed:

> Hi Rosie,
> you were right with your warnings to me. The only problem was that I was already hooked.
> And I have now been comprehensively and completely scammed.
> Despite your and other's warning I went ahead and made a decision to give money, which has led me into a situation that I had no reasonable control over, I see now.
> I'm still very much in shock about it all, though I take full responsibility for the decisions I at least initially consciously made.

I contact another close friend who had been concerned. She agreed to loan me $5000 to get through the next month, though she needed the money back after this.

Part 2: Aftermath

Reactions - Mine and Others

Immediate Aftermath

That first week was dominated by a multitude of thoughts, emotions, realisations and numbing shock. This chapter includes the interactive journal of my feelings at the time, post the scamming.
On the one hand, I at least intellectually understood that I had been scammed. But not yet emotionally.
I had to let key people know, even though that was admitting I had been wrong, been a fool, made a mistake. I did not understand how. I kept the exact amount of money to myself. But I kept myself from feeling, so I did not have to deal with theirs or my reactions of incredulousness.
I accepted the consequences were mine and that gave me the strength to go forward. I had always had a philosophy of making the best of things and going forward. I'm good at putting on a brave face, not letting my feelings show, not feeling or showing my vulnerability.
On the other hand, I was still very much thinking of him. I wanted to be in touch with him and say, "whoever you are, you owe me. I stayed to the end, loving to the end and giving all my money to the end. I had played the role of willing victim to the end. You owe it back to me five-fold, as you promised, because I played your game."
I fulfilled my part of the contract of this game of scam, I demanded to the universe. Promises were sacrosanct in my mind, though obviously not to the scammer. I railed against the injustice of those promises being broken. I had entered the game naively, trustingly, not knowing the true nature of the game, and believing it to be something else. The scammer, my scammer, played a false game, deliberately using and abusing my mistaken view.
Though intellectually I was beginning to realise this, I could not yet emotionally accept that the promises had all been lies, that the dreams had been lies, that the man I thought I had loved was a lie.
At another time, I wonder how the scammers feel being showered by love. It cannot NOT have an effect on them, I

thought. Love is powerful, so I believed.

Or do they just shut off from it, playing the game? I hung on to his comment that he was surprised by his reaction to me, at least sexually. In order to retain a modicum of self-esteem, in my mind, I want to believe that there had been something between us, that it was not all lies.

I ask myself, why did I never see it as a scam and get out? Many times I looked at the situation, knowing it could be a scam, but I was too invested in the intimacy and personal nature of the relationship.

I never considered the question that, if it was a scam, what could I or would I do? There was always something that allowed me to keep on with the justifications that a scammer wouldn't say this, wouldn't be this intimate or personal with me.

In my Journal

Following weekend, about ten days after.

Saturday, 3rd November:
I still cannot believe that this person wasn't truthful, wasn't what they promised. Still 'hope', 'fantasise' that he, or he and his daughter will just turn up at my front door... somehow intrigued by what took place... I want this even if it is not the person in the photo. It is the person I was relating to. I still want the promised sex and companionship, and have a burning desire to have this fulfilled. I would forgive everything.
A family member said this was not one person, but a factory line of people doing different roles. This hard for me to believe... it was in my experience one person I was speaking to every night and morning.

Monday, 5th November:
I do not relinquish the promises he made because he robbed me. I believe words have energy and power, particularly when it's a promise. His last email he says:

The worse has happened and we've scaled through this, I strongly believe that this is a test of nature and we've passed it. Now it's time to have a wonderful life together, baby I'll so take care of you that, you'll start growing younger instead of older. Hold me to that word.

"Hold me to that word" he says... I do hold him to that. I will be looking out for him to appear one day, as there is unfinished business here... whoever he is, he owes me.
He took me on this journey, and I went with him...

Tuesday, 6th November:
Spent the rest of the day yesterday looking at sites on scamming, seeing more the reality of it, though I still cannot quite believe the Nigerian model was in play in my case. But maybe there is a Russian model – I will explore that more... I find other examples of Dubai as a place of scams... But what does Dubai have to do with Nigeria?

Wednesday, 7th November:
Realising that he had stopped me thinking about the reality of the relationship by the constant contact, giving me no time, no space, no chance to question what was happening and what I was doing.
I need to look at what happened with my uncle, my reaction to being thought not worthwhile, not good enough to have a lover, a good provider. Why had this caused a reaction and made me so rebellious? Maybe there were links to my reactions to my long-lost father here, and perhaps some hidden learnings.

Sunday, 11th November:
I have had a call from my bank. There may be some possibility to get some money back...
I've done more reporting to scam sites online...
Feeling very alone, lonely, wanting a man in my life, still cannot believe the promises will not be fulfilled.... Starting to get a little angry about this.

Tuesday, 13th November:
I have a counselling session today that I organised for myself through the Employer Assistance Program. I needed to do something for myself, to come to terms with my emotions, and do this in a way that does not impact my work. Feeling much stronger, and know I need to look after myself so I don't go totally to pieces. I cannot let this happen at work, as it is the only stability that I have.
In the conversation I acknowledged some of the positives... that I have opened up to that part of me that can connect intimately with a man, and the love I have to share in that relationship. That there is a possibility that I can be in a relationship....
But the counsellor is aghast that I comment that it is an 'interesting' experience, and questions my lack of emotion and my distancing from it all. She cannot understand why I am not more angry. How can I be angry when I did it all myself? It's my fault. I believed. I gave the money away. And its done now. Anger does not help.

The Aftermath

Gradually over the past 3 weeks I have been able to tell some other friends and some family. It's not easy and I have mostly kept the exact amount of money involved to myself.

I did, after some encouragement, report it to the police, but that was only to a Constable taking my statement at the local station. I go through the information mechanically with her, and without emotion. She photocopies all the relevant information. I know it has been forwarded on to a detective, but at this stage have not heard anything more, and do not expect to.

What can they do? I am resigned, from the reading I have done online, that I will not get my money back.

Only in the last two weeks have I been able to look more at the information on the internet, and I have placed reports on some sites. See the details in the relevant chapters below.

The main Australian site is Scamwatch, a website run by the Australian Competition and Consumer Commission (ACCC). Scamwatch provides information to consumers and small businesses about how to recognise, avoid and report scams.

I'm disappointed to see that they say on their site that there might be a long wait if you want to phone them, and that they may not respond to your report. I know I filled in the on-screen form. It is designed to fit all types of scams, which does not make it easy to complete, but I have a feeling that I did not hit the submit button on this form, feeling hopeless and helpless after reading their comments.

Only by doing this research on scams have I been able to realise that scammers are professionals. I am not alone in being caught this way, there is a whole process that they go through to catch you in the scam and to keep you in it. I do believe it is my fault, that I have been complicit and colluded, that I am not a true victim because I have given the money willingly. But there was a big hook. I was caught in needing to get him out of Dubai in order to get my money back. And that hook just kept getting deeper and deeper the more money I gave him.

I replayed in my mind the times he said to me that he was not coming to Australia because I wanted him to, that it was because he wanted to come, to meet me, to be with me. He was not reacting to me, he was actively choosing this course for himself. This always seemed to me to have a high degree of integrity, but maybe, I now thought, it was part of the 'strong man' game. This keeps the power on his side, and makes sure I am not able to influence him.

From inside you cannot see what is going on, I now realised. There were those times when I wondered if it was a scam, but could not confirm if it was or wasn't, and decided it was not. Even towards the end, when there was more evidence it was a scam, I would find a way to not believe this and give more money.

In hindsight, I understood that he was playing an archetypal game, and as such it was not personal. It was a formula that was played out, and I responded exactly as the formula expected. The formula was a good looking and successful male provider seeks female partner to love and look after, a very 'romantic' notion.

One of my ways of trying to understand what had happened was to write the scam diary.

I started on the 26th October, the same week of my realisation that I had been scammed. It took me several months to put the whole scam diary together, mostly on weekends and holidays. I took information from my emails, messages, and other records. It was an attempt to understand where the hook got in, and why I had not realised it was a scam.

I had thought I would get it published, and talk publicly about it. By late October, I had even put the idea out to a publishing agency, but they came back saying it was not for them.

At this point I found I did not want to look at it again. It would be several years later, when more healing had been done, that I would be ready to publish.

Reactions of Family and Friends

I told my mother first about what had happened. I did not tell her how much as I knew that would just cause more upset. I did indicate that it was a lot though. She did not know what to say. What can you say? It was done. She told me later she had spoken to a number of her friends, simply because she needed to talk about it to someone too.
Most people were shocked. And many of them had to educate themselves. In the following days I received a number of emails and messages with links to news reports, scam sites or articles on scamming. We all increased our knowledge about the topic.

More specific responses from friends and family included:
- How could they do that, take advantage of you like that?
  (This was usually accompanied by anger towards the scammer on my behalf.)
- Who can you contact to get action against the perpetrators? Police, federal police, political representative, press... surely there must be someone who can do something?
- How could you be so naive to send money to someone you have never met?
  (But in my mind, I had met them.)
- How could you not be more discriminating, more cautious, warier?
- How can you get the money back?
  (You can't.)
- We tried to warn you. How did you reject all the warnings you were given?

I was unable to answer many of these. I was just resigned to my situation – numb and powerless. I asked all these questions of myself, and had few answers.
I understood that I had made a decision to go with love, and now had to deal with the consequences. I was not doing this very well, but I was doing the best I could by focussing on what I could do.
I felt pressured to do something, but only at my own pace.

Initially I pushed back, refusing, but did make small steps. I did report the scam to the police, and put reports onto the various scam websites once I was able to face looking at them. Some more distant family members I did not tell, or only told the briefest of information.

In the early stages of the aftermath, I had a close friend and her husband come and stay. I could not tell her at all what had happened. This meant that through this period I was very closed to others, and largely agoraphobic. I kept very much to myself, using the writing of the book as an excuse as I went through the emotions, thoughts and feelings on my own. For most of the following year I experienced low level depression I realised in hindsight.

My key support people, particularly close family and close friends, were a constant source of support, emotionally and financially. If I did go out it would be to my brother and his partner, and there I was able to unburden myself and get some nourishing friendship. At this stage my mother was not nearby, but in a different state, but I spoke to her daily on the phone.

I write to a friend in the early aftermath, 11th November:

> I'm doing OK with it all. I had 5 days off last weekend, and spent most of it writing/compiling my diary. That felt good, and it is not far off being finished. Then is the process of somehow getting it out there. I'm not sure how just yet.
> I have got used to the idea that I have been scammed, and that I am now poor, with very little discretionary income for now, though I can cover my Bills if I manage tightly.
> The hardest part for now at least is dealing with the longing for an intimate and long term partner, which I was promised, had a taste of, but now don't have. Still dealing with that one.

A great source of comfort was my cat. He was always there, another living being who needed me, and I needed him. He would come onto my bed, lie on my chest as I rubbed behind his ears and under his chin. Just as I was drifting off to sleep he would hop down. Sometimes he did this in the morning too.

At least I knew someone loved me.

The Aftermath

Dating Continues

It wasn't until early November that I felt able to go onto the Plenty of Fish dating site again to make a report on my scam situation.

They came back a week later with a form letter response:

> Thank you for taking the time to email POF.com.
> We have received your report and assure you that it will be looked into immediately.
> As we do not disclose confidential details about our users, we will be unable to inform you of any actions taken.
> In the future, you can report a user by clicking on the Report User link at the bottom of their profile page.
> When a user is reported our team carefully investigates their account for suspicious activity. All reports are anonymous and confidential.
> We appreciate your co-operation.

As a result of the scam however, my sexual energy was very much awakened, and seeking some expression and outlet. I check out the dating site RSVP, and see that they have more education and concern for scams, so think this is a reasonable site to join.
This time I am much more determined that they be a local person, and check out any photos that are remotely suspicious with a google reverse image search.

I prepare my profile, being deliberately provocative:

> I always have a positive outlook on life, I trust, perhaps too easily, I am generous and have a huge heart that wants to share with someone, be close to someone, long term.
> I've newly returned to Melbourne, and there is much to explore across Victoria, hopefully with someone at my side, including live theatre, art galleries, wonderful food and wine, cycling the rail trails, walking great beaches. You will have some ideas too and I'm open to new ideas and experiences.
> With good conversations, and the right chemistry between us, I'll be keen to make up for being on my own, so I hope you are sensual and romantic too. You will be interested in

a woman of voluptuous bumps and curves, no slim or average here. I'll be more than a handful in many ways. It's time for life to be an adventure, maybe even create some dreams together, and create synergy.

I do get a response via the RSVP Mailbox from someone called Marcos (name changed) a few weeks later, on 6th December. He has a rugged face and blue eyes.
I check out his profile and Google his photo but find nothing untoward. He is a middle European immigrant to Australia, so English is not his first language.

This explains his poor written English:

> From: Royal15 To: Beautiful Lady -Time4adventures- Ok, I think it's worth a little bit of effort, Because of your Beauty. First (1) How do I get your Attention? What makes me different from the others man's? What to say here about me? What do you want, or need to know about me? Where do I start? I'm finding a bit difficult, it is not easy talking about myself...... Believe me what a difficult it is to give self description, and value of it if any? I will try my best and I Hope you will Forgive to me if I failing. Mmmmmm.....Well, just looking.... This is hard bit. Ok! Well!! Yes!!! As you know I read your profile in detail, and Seriously I Like and Love it. Perfect Also your photo is, and you a Very Beautiful and Very Special Lady
> Want to know more? If yes, take the time Please to read me now and to get to know me bit. A bit of Adventurous (of course in young age, not now) Lover of Peace and Harmony (in old age, now) I think of myself I am little bit shy, with finest Manners and Character. (most of time's) Values of Morals man of bit of sense of Chivalry, and Good old fashioned manners. (Old fashion Values stil count's with me, but not in the extreme's, of course with some modern Attributes) I am not afraid of Expressing my thoughts and Feelings, Compassionate, Passionate, Protective, Loyal, Honest, Supportive, Optimistic, Acknowledging and Respecting Differences. Respectful of those I Love in big and small what life's ofer's, and would like to share the up's and down's with support each other, because isn't that what life's about?
> I think life, and Relationship is what -two- people make it to be isn't? (not manipulative) Have a good sense of humour genuine, straith man down to earth. Kind and warm- sharing, Considerate, Mature-caring Trustworthy, Forgiving, Thoughtful

The Aftermath

Affectionate, Huggable, also Romantic (sweet) And......? Oh! Yes!! Adore, Enjoying and Loving A Hugs, Cuddling, Warm-embraces Slow-Kisses!!! Lovvvvvvvvvvve it!!! (How sad not to have that) Oh! That's right! I do believe in never going to bed on bed feelings, rather to go to bed with a Chocolate treat, and light a fire inside heart and make feel Special. A Hearth that never hardens, a temper that never tires, a touch that never hurts. Exuse-me (no-joke) but among other's
Love too many to mention, but truth-as-above. Very important my Apologies, Please, no misunderstand and don't take this wrong way, Non-judgmental, good communicator who doesn't like arguments, but rather Lives a good discussion-Peacemaker and Happy to admit when I'm wrong. Communication is very important to me, and I think an ability to listen is essential, without that it is hard to connect well in a relationship and Respect my partner's independence too, and Compromise. Wise Acnowledge tell to us relationship are something what two-people willing them to be. Thre things are require for Happines I know it the Happines are: Something to do, Something to Hope for, Something or Someone to Love. (of course in Love return) Truth, Trust, Honesty, Faith, Hope and Love. But also not like too much dreams, fantasies and illusion's (no good to anyone) Prefer realistic to be honest down-to-earth unpretenitious. Conventional Wisdom tells us that people don't like to be deceived (but because our wickenes) it is Actually, they do that is way so many of us end up being so easily misled. We enjoy being fooled-especially if this allows us to feel that several of our -favorite fantasies- are being confirmed as "probably true". What we don't like is to be undeceived. We don't enjoy being told the truth or forced to face some uncomfortable fact. We must be Brave enough to accept that this can only be beneficial (to us) Most often we do not see things as thy are, we see them as we are so we hawe be carefully not to project our judgments onto others. So all in all I'm a positive person, Well I think I am an easy-going man. It is me! And little bit of who I am. So what is unique about me? Maybe nothing.....and then again... Maybe everything. Guess that's up to you.
Thanks for reading. Yes I would Like to know more of You and would Like and Love to meet you. Please! Coffee? Or Dinner? And some Wine? (of course on my expense) Whenever suit you, let me know Please.
Typing about myself just does not seem natural., It's so much easier talk in person. Please if you a comfortable to using the telephone it will be easier for me to express myself more

> clearly and find out your interest and questions.
> My phoneno is: ▮▮▮▮▮▮▮▮ Please feel free to call me I leave it to you and Trust in you. I Greatly Regret and Deeply Sorry if I have upset or hurt you in any way Hope you accept my Apologies. A note from you would give me Great Pleasure. Hope to hearing from you. Most Kind Regards ▮▮▮▮▮▮
> (enough from me for now? And a bit who I am.)
> PS: There are only -2- mistake one can make along the road to Truth and Honesty Not going all the way and Not starting at all. To me Life is about, Living, Loving, Forgiving, Giving and Winning. Learn from yesterday Love for Today and Hope for Tomorrow Cheers!

(Redacted information includes local details, a workplace and email address.)

We connect on the phone, and he is well able to hold up a conversation, even if his written English is not good.

We begin to have quite flirty, provocative and even sexually explicit conversations on the phone. This is a part of me I have not expressed before, and it is a lot of fun. We seem well matched with this. He is someone who openly prefers a larger woman's body. We talk for about an hour the first time.

He wants a photo and put an additional one on my RSVP profile.

8th December, 6:45 pm:

> **M:** Thank You Jan
> I did get photo it is
> Very Beautiful
> Marcos xxx
> **J:** Thank you. It is nice to be appreciated. Jan xxx

9th December, 1:57 pm:

> **J:** Sorry I missed your call.
> I've been out walking.
> I'm home now if you wish
> to call again. I'd love to
> hear from you. Jan xxx

We talk again that night. I am up front about what has happened with me. We both enjoy the sexual interplay and I

The Aftermath

know I am responding to him.
I am turned on by the idea that someone could find me attractive and want to be with me, even if only in a playful way.

11th December, 9:33 am:
M: Good-morning Jan
Thank You for
Last-night Please no
misunderstood and don't
take me wrongly. It all
Just helps to us to get
More close and relxst
With each other and yes
Also it fells good to joke
And playing that way
Well I think it helps me to
Failing in Love too with
You
Jan My Love To You xxxx
J: Hi Marcos, we covered a lot of
ground last night, and as you
said, doing this on the phone
was a good way to do this and
will make it easier when we do meet.
I am a straight forward person
and I don't take things the wrong
way- I will ask if I have concerns.
Thank you for your message.
I look forward to talking more
tonight. Xxxx Jan
M: Oh Yes Jan!
Thank You! Love You
Marcos xxxxx
J: Now you understand how
it's possible to fall in love
without even meeting them in person... Xxxxx☺
M: Yes I do and yes it is
Very possible because
Love caber lot ground
We all need Love in the
First place that is our
body programed? We all
Conceived in the Love!
Love You Marcos xxxxxx
Ps:

Go back to work we talk
To-night xxxxxx
Xxxx
And from me Marcos to You
Jan xxxxxxxxxxxxxxxxxx

 J: Good morning Marcos. Now is my turn to say don't misunderstand me. When I talk about wanting a deep physical and spiritual connection, I think this is something you work towards together. It is not something that is there in the beginning, but grows as you/we get closer, more intimate. Please don't think I expect this of you immediately. We have to take our time learning about each other. And to have fun doing it!
This is too serious a conversation just need to have fun together and the rest will take care of itself. Xxxx Jan

12th December, 11:33 am:
M: Good-morning Jan
Thank you! Yes I though
This myself too I did
Understand you you just
Seed this in very nice way
Ok! Then it is -2- more
Things you must to know
About me (and it is little
Bit scary!??)
Can be serious and don't
Heave to be it depend of
Person and personality I
Love You Jan
 Marcos xxxxxx
 J: That's good. Look forward
to talking more tonight!
Love u xxxx
M: Well because you a very
Polite and didn't asked
More questions I would be
telling to you but
Because it is not pleasant
To telling I didn't
Ok to not too guessing
It is of my health
 Marcos xxxxxxxxxx
 J: Marcos, Health is important, sorry I did not ask, I was

The Aftermath

confused by your message,
unsure if you were wanting
to share more things, or
 if you were meaning being
serious and not serious. Do
 you want to tell me in
messages, or on the phone?
If this is easier, then tell me.
Xxxx
M: Did I put you off?
It needs more explanation
 Marcos xxxxx
M: I would like to tell last-
-night that way I went a
bit silent I was thinking a
Way how to tell you in the
first place I think I am bit
Chicken?? Don't you
Think some?
Anyway Love You Jan
 Marcos xxxxx
        J: It is hard talking about
personal matters I know.
I also have health issues.
No need to be chicken
we are both adults and
know that life (and health)
is not always simple,
particularly at our age.
It is important we share
these things, find ways
to talk about them. So,
tonight I will be all ears.....
Xxxxx
M: Jan I Love You! Marcos xxx
      J: Thank You for your
Understanding again
M: Love to you you a Very
Nice Lady xxxxxxxxxx
Xxxx

When we talk more that night he tells me about his bad arthritis. I'm familiar with this because my mother has it. I do not think too much more about it. I tell him about my melanoma. We are both of an age where these things are likely to be issues more and more. Despite the seriousness, we still have fun provocatively jousting together.

13th December, 10:11 am:

> **M:** Hot hot hot too HOT!
> Good-morning Beautiful
> Lady how are you? Are
> You hot? Or angry from
> From last-night? With me
> Marcos xxxxxx
> **J:** In cool air conditioning
> learning all about the
> superannuation industry.
> All ok. Jan xxxxx

13th December, 2:29 pm:

> **M:** Panadol OSTEO.
> Is the one I using
> M.xxx
> **J:** Yes that's what my mother
> uses too, with occasionally
> something stronger.
> MOBIC I think it is.
> Xxxx

He missed calling the next night, so I send him a prompter.
13th December, 10:18 pm:

> **J:** Pleasant dreams love xxxx

14th December, 9:41 am:

> **M:** Sorry I failed a sleeping !!!
> It is cooler weder I don't
> Know how to spelling a
> -weder-
> Love you Marcos xxxxxx
> Weather. Ok I was a little worried. Sleep well. Xxxxx
>
> 14th December, 9:41 am:
>
> **M:** Good-morning Jan!

The Aftermath

Thanks God for cooler-
Weather much beater today
Ps:
Xxxxx
Hey! I noticed you a very
Affectioned! I do no is it
Wright way to spell. Hope
You know what I meant
Afecttion is exposing of
Love
Love you Jan Marcos xxxx
    J: I'm in a training course again this morning. Just on tea break. I think you mean 'affectionate'.
Are you working today? Xxxx Jan
M: Yes I do working
Yes I think you a right
This way is right spelling
Well you know you self
The best way
 Marcos xxxxxx
    J: Xxxx

14th December, 1:31 pm:

M: And -2- more things we
Wave to talk
1) my financial position
Wich you all ready know
A bit (I am not rich)
2) and satisfactory Well on
This hew to be working on
Too-getter? (of corse)
 Marcos xxxxxx
    J: Hi Marcos, I don't understand what you are trying to say in 2). Please say another way.... Or else we can talk tonight. Jan xxxx
M: We talk tonight
Satisfactory In sex, Love
And things what going in
Bed-time!?
(I'm trying to be gentlemen and don't won't to using bed words)
 Marcos xxxxxxxxxxx
    J: Oooh! haha. Ok. Tonight then..... Xxxxxxx

The exchanges continue in this vein.

Romance Scam Survivor

Now Marcos is suggesting we meet. I want to, but I am nervous. He has raised several issues with me that he thinks might be a concern. He is just a pensioner, so has no way to support me. He lives in community housing, but still works sometimes at a magazine collator/distributor. He is a sometime smoker. The fact that he is discussing these things is an indication that he wants to get a lot more serious.
I do too.

14th December, 9:11 pm:

M: Just by joking and talk I
Falling in Love with you
I think!? Some how you a
Very powerful in this sennce
bus coming I haw to go
Love Marcos xxxx
    J: I'd noticed, and its a bit scary.
Xxxxx
M: Way?
Not too worry you will
Haw your freedom I
Promise it is Onlly way
Expressing my Love to
You because you Very
Nice Lady maybe it is
Beter that way
 Marcos xxxxxxx
    J: Don't get me wrong you
know I am enjoying our
connection and want
to explore it further.
I don't know yet how
strong my feelings are
or are going to get,
and I don't want to feel
obligated. It's still early days. Xxxxxx
I love that you are expressing your feelings to me. I am very responsive in my body to you. Jan xxxx
M: All this is Exellent so not
Too wory all is going be
Ok! I think it is just some
Sort of attraction probably
Should be that way I do no but just nice fealing

The Aftermath

And yes we didn't yet meet!!! But we alredy
Know a lot of each-other!
Anyway I do Love You
Jan!
 Marcos xxxxxxx
I think it is the BEST ever
Message I recived
Thank you
Wen ever I'm going be
seed or unhappy I will
Re-red this
Love you Jan Marcos xxxxx

15th December, 9:27 pm:

Because he seriously wants to meet, he gives me all of his personal details as a token of his honesty. I reciprocate. We exchange further details, and plan to meet at Jimmy Watson's wine bar. I haven't been there for years.
I am nervous about meeting him. We both have enjoyed our connection immensely, and want this to work out. We are both envisaging having a lovely time together. I am even wearing a dress, which I don't often do, and have made a special effort to dress up.
He is a little late, and when he arrives is wearing a bright, shiny royal blue suit and tie. I love blue, so even if it's a little extreme, I love it. He has flowers and chocolates for me. He is obviously nervous too, and wants to make a good impression. He has a tall but very bent body.
We go into Jimmy Watsons and have a drink to begin. We chat, but we are both too nervous to eat so decide to go for a walk. As we go out and cross the road, he lumbers along. We check out the movies at the Nova, perhaps we will come back here later. We wander down the road, down to an Italian restaurant down one of the laneways, and order some gnocchi. Afterwards, Marcos goes out for a smoke.
Initially, I don't know why, but I find I am closing off to him. Despite this, we go off to the movies.
I had not realised it, but he saw this as a willingness on my part for him to feel me up. I had to push his hand away. That was not what I wanted. I am sometimes slow to understand even my own feelings.

Afterwards we sat on a seat on the street, so I could explain. I realise I could not see myself being with him and have to tell him so. His arthritis was too great and he reminded me too much of my mother. I could not see us doing active things together, and I would just end up taking care of him. I already had someone to take care of, my mother.
I could not do it. I was devastated and heartbroken for what might have been, and I expected he was too.
We went our own ways. A day or so later I went back onto RSVP, as that is where we had first connected, and wrote him a letter of apology and sorrow, for what I had done to him, for what we might have been. He does not see it immediately.
When he finally sees it he contacts me, just before Christmas and suggests a drink. We met up. I had wanted to, thinking of him many Friday nights on my way home from work, but was very withdrawn still, and did not know how to relate to him now.
It was not a comfortable night.
After this experience my ardour cools a little, and though I occasionally go on to RSVP I am not really taken with anyone, and am very suspicious of photos. I found at least one profile that was an obvious scam, and found similar wording on romancescams.com. I reported it to RSVP and it was not visible the next day. They at least were doing their checking.
Very little attracted me. Many of the profiles were similar, and of course, many wanted slim women. I had put on weight since the scamming, and by six months afterwards had gained ten kilos, which did not help my self-esteem, or my wardrobe.
In March the next year I did get approached by another man, in a very respectful way. He was sixty-five, and a retired computer programmer on a pension. We went out a few times, for a bushwalk and picnic, to a movie, but whilst it was comfortable talking and doing things together, there was little chemistry.

The Aftermath

I had been fairly reserved, taking quite a passive role, but there was no connection when we hugged goodbye. We went to dinner one night and he spent some time going through all the financial difficulties for two people on a pension, and what he would lose if it was found we were living together (he was looking for a long term partner).

The following week I got a message that he did not want to see me again, because of the financial difficulties. I thought it might be that he was not physically attracted to me. As I had not built this up in my mind to be anything that it was not, I was comfortable with this and not too concerned. Obviously I was still attracting someone with money issues, though the opposite end of the spectrum this time.

I resigned myself again to never having a partner, to not giving any energy to looking for someone to share my life with, and made my profile invisible on RSVP. I stopped looking for potential matches. Whilst I actively felt the 'I don't have anyone to do things with' loneliness, I reconciled myself to this.

By late January 2013, with the financial help of family to pay for airfares and removal costs, I moved my mother from 'up north' to an aged care placement in Victoria. This meant that much more of my time, at least a day on each weekend, was taken up with her, taking her out somewhere, or sorting chores for her. It also meant that I did not, except for late at night, have to think too much about being alone.

I did for a while join one group on Meet-up, for forty to fifty-year-olds, Left of Centre. I went to a few of their events, but after turning sixty I didn't feel I could go any longer. I went on a cycling Meet-up and had a good time, but did not go on more as we moved into winter.

It Wasn't Personal

I began to explore the information that was available on scams and scammers on the internet. It was a gradual process, but proved fruitful with some of the resources I discovered. One of the best sites I found was:
http://www.romancescam.com
(different from http://www.romancescams.org)

I started by looking at photos of known scammers. What I was shocked to find is that no matter what age or sex, the perpetrator was a young, black and presumably Nigerian man. How they got those photos I do not know.
I did begin to realise that my Eamon, the person in my photo, was not real. This realisation finally began to land deep in my belly.
There are links on this sight to other sites (Spokeo) which purport to search the email address to find hidden profiles, but this revealed nothing for me. I tried to check the IP address, but kept getting results that it was a Californian site.

I found information on how to do a search on the photo in Google from:

http://www.scamdigger.com/picsearch.php
(a tab in romancescam.com)

> "Suspicious of somebody? Want to check if their pictures were used in scams before? Your first stop should be Google Image Search. Click on a little camera icon in the search box and upload a picture - either from your computer or from the Internet. You will see if that picture belongs to somebody else, was used by somebody else, already scamlisted, etc."

I did this, using all of the photos I had of Eamon. I found the photos used on ten sites, all different!

I could not believe it.

Some examples of information on *my scammer* found on these ten sites

The Aftermath

1. http://www.bestdatingnow.com/braveman_1.html
   A 55 year old Englishman living in Germany, self employed with a daughter.

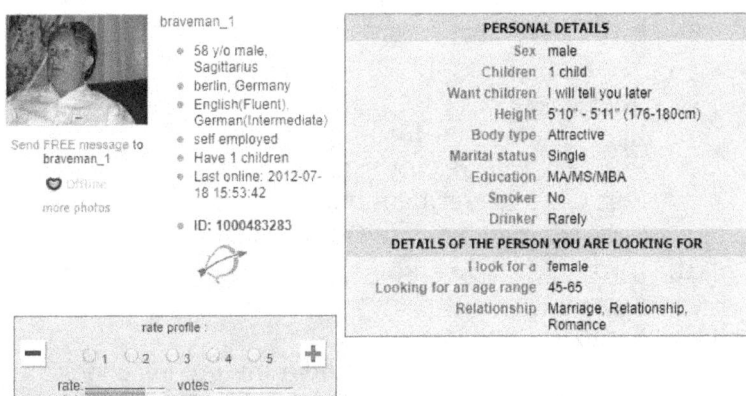

2. http://www.fishmeetfish.com/profile/glennjohnson
   A forty-one year old native American living in Missouri.

3. http://www.blackplanet.com/marcozlarry/
   A fifty-six year old living in New York.

4. http://myphsclass.ning.com/profile/marksmith?xg_source=activity
   A graduate of Parkview High School in 1976.

5. http://community.justlanded.com/en/profile/William-Wilberforce
   Living in Denmark.

6. A number of other pages that I saved at the time which will no longer load, the profile has most likely been taken down.

7. Other scam sites with people of other names and ages, using the same group of photos such as:
   a. http://taglisted.creatingforum.com/t1876-david-b
   b. https://www.scamwarners.com/forum/viewtopic.php?f=13&p=202518
   c. http://anti-scam-forum.net/cgi-bin/yabb2/YaBB.pl?action=print;num=1330341183 Sorry, it's in German, but you can read his profile, a Scottish man living in Germany.
   d. http://scampicsandmessages.weebly.com/seniorpeoplemeet-pic-p1.html - Scammers found on Seniorpeoplemeet.
8. I'm sure at the time I found him on Facebook, and LinkedIn, but with very little detail/history/profile there and not coming up now.

9. Doing a new search now (October 2014) using the various photos I have:
10. On Google +
    a. https://plus.google.com/108527097728032132388#108527097728032132388/posts Johnson Bernd
    b. http://www.meetup.com/singles-2431/
       A speed dating meet-up site in Long Island NY. Could not find photo.
    c. https://www.scamwarners.com/forum/viewtopic.php?f=13&p=215409
       Another warning of stolen photos.
    d. http://mysocial-eyessite.com/members/MichaelHanderson
       Michael is making many friends.

Going back to www.romancescam.com , I searched through the lists of pictures used by mail scammers and found additional entries for Phillip Moore (Self employed from East Sussex) and Allyn Lasut, (Lives in San Francisco, Zulia,

The Aftermath

Venuzuela.

Romancescam.com comments on this picture that:

> "The real man on these pictures is unknown. His pictures are used by scammers quite often. These pictures are stolen, and the person in the pictures is a victim of identity theft."

My search on Eamon's picture provided a link to:

http://romancescam.com/forum/viewtopic.php?f=3&t=50379, a listing for Phillip Moore, philipmoore121@hotmail.com, and two other names being used by scammers.

The other photos I had were here. And I could see that postings were actively moderated by site admin.
There were more pictures here than I had, linked to multiple names, not just Phillip Moore. I took the chance and signed up to the website. Posting this conversation, I asked if I should let all the other sites know there were scammers on their site.

The response was:

> "As for other sites, there is no point of reporting him, even if they boot him (which is not a fact), he will immediately re-register with another name and fresh picture. Better if people google his details and pics (like you did) and realize they are being scammed."

Seeing that people were posting whole profiles and interactions, I began searching on text from my interactions with him, firstly 'Blessing,' no luck, too many of those. Then 'Blessing Patience'.

What I discovered was amazing. In a listing for Donegal Ayden Cosgrove, donsgrove@yahoo.com, I found a story with MANY similarities to mine.

- The first name was my scammer's second name.
- Daughter's name in reversed order.
- The location and story was similar. In U.S., back to Manchester, then on to another place, South Africa (not Dubai).
- Used the music Rascall Flatts.

I added an entry with a link to the Phillip Moore thread. When I came back to this at a later date, there was another entry from someone scammed after me, by a man who called himself Donegal Ayden Lyons. Their story was the same as mine but the photos were not the same.

All the photos connected to EDD were under the original thread of John Holland/Phillip Moore. I searched on Rascal Flatts and found five or six references to this song being used. This could not be a coincidence, I realised.

I loved that Rascall Flatts song, and loved him for sending it to me. It seemed to reflect exactly my state of mind at that time. It had a very special meaning for me. At times I still replay it.

However, more and more my images of a handsome man who treated me as someone special and wanted to be with me were being broken down to being similar to many others.

One more thing though. I wanted more on the email and IP, so went back to the thread on Phillip Moore. I posted an email header there. They stripped out what was not needed, and commented on the IP address:

> "that's OC3 Networks, bad IP, proxy, used in scams a LOT."

No doubt now. Not that there wasn't before, but I could not hold on to the fragment of belief that I was different, special, that I meant something to him. Whoever 'he' was.

No, he did not love me, I now fully comprehended. It had ALL been a lie, an act, put on to get my money. An act performed time and time again with different women. It was not personal. It was nothing about me, except my money.

How could I have been so deluded, so incredibly wrong, to the extent that it had cost me all of my money and more? I felt so

The Aftermath

ashamed. I had wanted so much to be in love that I jumped at the first offering of it.

I still couldn't tell if he was Nigerian, but it seemed likely. If the reporting was right, there may have been more than one, beyond the daughter, as part of the scam. If you count the nurse and the doctor, then there definitely was.

Was it a call centre team? I couldn't say. I began to do more research on the other names and photos I had.

The photos of his 'daughter' were revealed to be stolen from a model, Josie Anne Miller:
http://www.scamsurvivors.com/forum/viewtopic.php?f=11&t=77&start=120#p18802

Clarification about who the real Josie Anne Miller was:
https://answers.yahoo.com/question/index?qid=20131115204604AAbI7LG .

Reading this last one again now, it is followed by many that have been lured in by this woman's picture and had been scammed or had been the victim of an attempted scammed.

And when I check out other sites:

https://www.scamwarners.com/forum/viewtopic.php?f=4&t=4038 has some sample fake documents used by scammers, which are very convincing, unless you know better.

Of all the other names used with me, none of the names except Carla Moss responded with anything meaningful on Google. Carla Moss was found in a similar scam activity:

http://www.justanswer.com/fraud-examiner/74sjf-verifying-identity-simon-xxxxx-xxxxx-london-age-55.htm l (a similar story to the one used with me, needing money to get out of Dubai).

As I read about scams I also read about the Red Flags, things so commonly done or used by scammers that they have become a checklist for scammer identification. Many of them applied to my scam, but I did not see them at the time, or did

175

not want to see them. How many did you see as you read through Part one?

When I read this list it again confirmed that what had happened to me was a scam. But it doesn't help to know afterwards, and reading it later reinforced the feeling that I should have realised that it was a scam, and that I only had myself to blame.

Typical Characteristics of Scammers

Here is a list, many of which occurred in my scam, and a few that did not. I have included this here as I want to paint the clearest picture I can for you, so you are better equipped to recognise a scam and not get caught up in one in the first place.

Transcribed from http://www.romancescams.org/redflags/

While reading the following, if you answer "YES" to three (3) or more, you are involved and in contact with a scammer.
When Contact is First Made
- They immediately want to get off the web site and onto Yahoo IM or MSN IM
- Their profile seems to disappear off the web site immediately after conversation begins
- They claim it was destiny or fate and you are meant to be together
- They immediately ask for your picture and they send you a picture of themselves
- They immediately want your address so as to send you flowers, candy, and teddy bears, often purchased with stolen credit cards
- They claim to love you either immediately or within 24-48 hours
- They immediately start using pet names with you: hon/hun baby/babe sweety/sweetie
- They claim God brought you to him/her
- They typically claim to be from the US (or your local region) but they are overseas, or going overseas mainly to Nigeria, sometimes the UK for business or family matters

Communication Skills
- Their spelling is atrocious
- Their grammar is not consistent with how Americans speak, French speak etc.
- They appear uneducated with their speaking/writing skills
- They over-use emotions
- They are notorious for using BUZZ
- They are notorious for using "i" instead of "I"
- They consistently use web speak or abbreviations; u r ur cos pls/plz ma sry brb div
- They often mix up their phrases: "i" will like to heer from you soonest, I am kool, Do you have any man you care to meet, Do you have any man you planning to meet, Looking for someone to love and care for in life, Am cheerfull in life, I will like to meet someone that is careing and loveing for real in life, "i" am too young for my age if you don't know, Ok so how will you feel if i says i dont mind you, i will like you to be my best friend, You are so pretty for my likeness
- They misunderstand our slang or comparisons such as night owl/early bird, poker face

Their Habits
- They are not usually around on the weekends to IM
- They IM at unusual hours for your time zone
- There are times they are gone from the conversation for a length of time and will sometimes come back at you with a different name, they're usually conversing with more than one person at a time
- If you ask them a question they don't know they will usually be offline for a length of time so they can go look up the answer on the internet always claiming they had a phone call or had to go to the bathroom etc.
- They like to send you poems or love letters, most of which can be traced back to lovingyou.com. Sometimes they even forget to change the name in the poem or letter to match your name
- They send you flowers, teddy bears, and candy within the first few weeks of talking

- They typically ask you to get on your web cam yet they never seem to have a web cam of their own
- They ask for your phone number but when they call you can barely understand a word they say because of their accent and back ground noise
- They may give you a phone number but it's typically a calling card or a call center, you can rarely get them on the phone
- They do not like to answer personal questions about themselves and tend to ignore questions
- They often do not know the correct time difference between where you are and where they claim to be
- They often claim to have one parent that is of African descent
- A majority of them claim to have lost a spouse/child/parent in a horrific traffic accident or airplane accident or any of the above are sick or in the hospital
- They have no close family or friend or business associates to turn to, even the US embassy, instead they can only rely on a stranger they picked off the internet
- To them love equals financial assistance…if you do not send them money or help them out with what they ask, you do not love them
- If you deny them or question them they become verbally abusive and will resort to threats
- They will insist you keep the relationship a secret until "they" come to you live with you
- Above all, if you call them a scammer they are highly offended and some will start throwing words at you in their native language

Their Inconsistencies
- The details they give you on IM are often different that what was stated on their profiles, one of the more common ones they give different answers to is their birth date, height/weight, and age etc.
- If you catch them on an inconsistency they will claim a friend or relative must've been using their id to chat with you, they will always try to come up with a cover-up and

The Aftermath

of course, you are always wrong or mistaken
- They often misspell the cities/towns they claim they are from and are unfamiliar with any of the local landmarks and attractions
- They do not know common questions that every US citizen would know the answer to

Trying to Find the Trail

Money Trail

From the moment of realising that I had been scammed, I was resigned that I would not get any of the money back. I had not believed this was a scam because as far as I was concerned, this had gone to a person who presumably would have had to use a legitimate passport to access the money. As some money was going to a bank, this seemed secure.

This email I received from D.C., the Police Officer at the local station that was handling my case, again confirmed that the money had gone to Nigeria, and reinforced that it was a scam. Our knowledge of how Western Union works in terms of money collection authentication is poor. Both Police Officer D.C. and I were surprised to get this information,:

> **From:** DC
> **Sent:** Wednesday, 28 November 2012 4:05 PM
> **To:** 'Jan Marshall'
> **Subject:** RE: Update on Dubhlainn Romance Scam
>
> Hi Jan,
> I received the relevant information from Western Union - re the payee names and Payee Addresses they appear to be correct however the Payee ID location is Nigeria on each occasion? Im a little confused - I can only assume that the money has ended up being picked up in Dubai then transferred to Nigeria - from my experience the majority of these scams somehow relate back to Nigeria - is there any thing else that you can assist me with - obviously I have let Western Union know about the Investigation and they are well aware of the relevant names etc....
>
> If you could get back to me;
>
> Many Thanks,
> DC

There was little I could provide.

The Aftermath

Bank Trail
Though I did not originally contact the bank, being too much in shock, one day I received an unexpected phone call from someone in my bank, querying the purpose of the second large transaction I made by telegraphic transfer.
They said they had received a query from the bank in Dubai, who were checking to see if the money had been involved in money laundering. I advised that this was the money that had been paid as a result of a scam and should not be paid out if it has not been paid so far, and if possible, the money should be returned.
I was so surprised and shocked that unfortunately I did not take the caller's details. I was buoyed by the possibility of getting nearly $80,000 back. I even told friends and family this might be a possibility.
I waited a week to hear more, then realised that I needed to actively follow it up myself.
Originally, I contacted the fraud investigation office of the bank, then spoke to someone in the local bank who eventually connected me to the International Operations section.
They supposedly contacted the bank in Dubai about it.
I did not hear anything again, so followed up in a week, and then again, a week later. Each time International Operations said they would phone the bank in Dubai.

Eventually when I followed up again, I received the following response:

> Thank you for your kind patience. We have attempted to phone several departments within the overseas bank with no such assistance. We strongly suggest that you liaise with the beneficiary to recall funds as we have exhausted all avenues at this point of time.

It was a dead end! I was now resigned to the awful truth that I would not be getting any money returned to me.

International Trail
I looked for organisations in Dubai that I could engage directly and on the web found the Dubai Financial Service Authority (www.dfsa.ae).
I posted a complaint on their website (see Appendix, Item 1).

Their response (see Appendix, Item 2) was that they could 'take no further action', but suggested I take my concerns to the Central Bank, the Emirates Securities and Commodities Authority or Dubai Police.

I duly contacted the Dubai Police, the Economic Crimes Combating Department, receiving this back from them:

> Dear ▮,
> Thanks to connected with alameen service which is player in the integration of security and cooperation among members of the community in the country, it develops self-responsibility, including participation in the protection of the community in which they live.
> We would like to inform you that your mail was received, and regarding your complaint, you should go to police station of your area.
> Accept our deepest thanks and respect, and we are always happy to meet your proposals and inquiries dealing with for the better.
> For further inquiry, please contact: Alameen Service
> Tel 800 4 888   Fax (04) 209 77 77   Sms 4444
> E-mail alameen@eim.ae website www.alameen.ae
> United Arab Emirates. Dubai

I contacted Emirates NBD, with a similar response from them:

> Customer Care - Retail Clients, Division
> <customercare@emiratesnbd.com>
> Dear Mr. ▮
> We request you to kindly take this matter with your local authorities, and they shall do the needful.
> We wish you a nice day.
> Regards,
> Hamed Alredha
> Group Service Quality / Tamayyuz

Finally, I contacted UAE Embassy, but have no saved response from them. It was close to Christmas, so it is possible I did receive another negative reply and did not save it.

The Aftermath

After all this, I had misgivings about the efficacy of following up on the other links, and on review of their websites did not see that they had any jurisdiction over my issues and were most likely unable to help.

No help from that trail at all.

Surviving

Directly after the scam, to help my own understanding of what had happened, I spent some time saving and compiling all of the communications I had in the relationship with Eamon. This included as much as I could remember of what was not recorded, and is now the diary in Part 1 of this book.

Having done that, I had to put it aside. I found it difficult to re-read this material, to re-live it, to see the red flags that I now know were there but that I had not seen at the time. To realise how emotionally engaged I was, to my detriment. It was hard to acknowledge my responsibility in all of this.

I wrote Parts 2 and 3 some years later, without re-reading that earlier material.

At various times since the scam I had undertaken intensive research sessions on the internet. Much of my findings are listed in the chapter 'It Wasn't Personal.' It was easy to get links to news articles, and over the following months there were a number of television programs and reports highlighting the issues. A Google and YouTube search will find these for you if you are interested. Links to some of these and others were sent to me by close friends that I had let know about my circumstances. Everyone was trying to understand for themselves, as well as being concerned for me.

Many of my friends ask, "Can't you do something?" Or, "Can't someone do something?"

Even though I had contacted the Victorian Police, there was little expectation that they would be able to do anything. There was much anger expressed by friends at what had happened to me, that people could do such a callous and dastardly thing. There were other suggestions of people to contact, including my local member (state or federal parliamentarian), the federal police, international police. I felt unable to tackle any of these for a variety of reasons. I was terribly embarrassed, and was still in shock and coming to terms with it myself, leaving me feeling resigned to my fate.

It also took time and energy, and I needed all I had just to maintain myself in some semblance of balance in order to maintain my job. This wasn't so easy. Partly because I felt it was all my fault, a 'you've made your bed, now lay in it' approach, and I had to fully wear the consequences of my actions. Logistically it was difficult to find the time and energy outside of work to even think of making contact and following this through.

In the very early days, when some of these suggestions were coming, I was still fantasizing that he, my scammer, would turn up at my door and all would be okay.

I did not want to do anything that would confirm that this could not be true.

I was fully resigned that no-one would be able to do anything, and this was reinforced by the absence of any stories of things being able to be done, of money being recovered.

I now saw all the messages of caution and warnings on the various sites of what scammers do. All of which I had had no idea of before. Even when I was directly warned by my friends, I did not take it in somehow. Even though I looked, I concluded it did not fit with my situation and circumstances.

My friends were surprised that I was not angrier, not grieving more for my loss. It wasn't there on the outside, and I have never been one to be regretful for actions I have taken, I look forward, not back. But it was there on the inside.

I never cried about it, never pitied myself for what had happened. I had lost a lot of money, but all sorts of people lose lots of money. I have friends who have lost thousands of dollars in property deals. Every day people lose money in share market crashes, others have lost money in investment companies that went bust, with hundreds of people losing their life savings. I put myself on a par with these people. I made a risky *investment,* and it had gone wrong. I tried to put it behind me and get on with my life.

But looking back now, I know that for most of the following year I experienced a low-grade depression. After an initial period of continued searching for a partner, I stopped. For the rest of the year I kept very much to myself. I saw few people, apart from my mother, brother and family, and I spoke with interstate girlfriends on the phone. Just getting through work and these few things was about all I could manage.

I wasn't able to put it out of sight totally. I still had to deal with the consequences, managing my finances being a big one of these. And that wasn't straightforward. More on this later.

Being an emotional eater, I put on ten kilos in weight over the following six months. In about February 2013 I joined a gym, and in April, signed up for a twelve-week program. This had me going to the gym at six am every morning, doing a session with a trainer each week, and a group session every Saturday morning. I joined the RPM spin cycle class as I got stronger, and the weights class, as I did not have spare money for training.

I quite enjoyed it, and got to experience that exercise buzz that people talk about. However as much as I tried to watch what I was eating, I did not want to go extreme with this, as I know it just causes you to yoyo with your weight. Or at least that is what has happened in the past. As a consequence, I only lost two kilos over the twelve weeks, and was very demoralised after all the effort I had put in.

Though I might have continued less rigorously after the twelve weeks, towards the end I had a very sore left knee. A physio gave me exercises, which I did for several weeks, until I went away for holidays in September. I had increasing pain in my left shoulder, arm and neck. When the osteopath was unable to provide much improvement, I was diagnosed with a chronically inflamed shoulder. Though I was meant to have a cortisone injection in it, I never did. I was distracted by moving house.

The sore shoulder is still there.

Financial Management

Immediately upon realising I had been scammed I knew I was in dire straits financially.
I had given away most of my last pay packet, my bank accounts had gone into negative and I had about $4000 in monthly bills that I needed to pay.
I did not have enough money left even to buy food for myself. I was in a bad way. This was another shock on top of the others, but did make me focus not on what had happened, but on the future and my day to day survival.
One of my good friends that I had told about the scam offered to lend me some money, which I gratefully accepted. Thus, within a day or so I had $5000 back in my bank. She helped me survive that terrible first month. I knew she would need this back in the not too distant future, as she was planning to buy a house, but at that stage I had no idea how I would pay it back.
When I looked at my finances, I realised that I had no other financial reserves. I also had an additional $39,000 to pay in credit card debt on two accounts at the highest cash withdrawal rates of interest.
The lack of reserves was brought home in early January 2013 when my cat Cookie became ill. I took him to the local Animal Hospital late at night because he was so lethargic, and not eating or drinking. I was so worried about him, and could not stand the thought of waiting through the night, and for some reason him not surviving.
They could not find anything specific that was wrong, but wanted to put him on a drip and antibiotics overnight, and do X-Rays, more blood tests, medications and examinations next day. Unfortunately, before the Animal Hospital will release your pet you are required to settle your treatment bills. By the time more tests were done, although they found nothing specific, the outstanding amount had ballooned out to $800.
That was $800 that I did not have. All I could do was defer the payment, hoping that by next month I would be able to pay with my regular wages coming in. So, I put it on my Amex card, and thankfully was able to take my cat home.
As Amex is not a credit card, I knew I would have to find the money within the month to pay the card. I just did not know

how I would do it. By this time, I was juggling my cash flow day by day. Although I had another pay packet come in, I still had to closely watch what was going out to make up the ground of the overdrawn accounts.

I was planning to move my mother from a residential care facility in Mullumbimby, New South Wales, to one in Victoria. That meant that I would fly up, pack up her things and get them on a truck, including her electric wheelchair, and bring her back down on the plane. The Victorian residential care placement came up in late January, when I was already struggling to make up the vet bill, and you have to physically take the place within a week.

My brother and sister-in-law, who had been a great support during this time, paid for my airfare. My aunt paid for the removal fees for her things from northern NSW to Victoria. I did the heavy lifting by going up, packing everything and bringing her down. Coming down on the plane was a saga in itself, but that's the stuff of another book. Suffice to say that this would not have been possible without the support, especially financially, from my family.

During those first few months there were several times when payments were not made on time because I did not have the money, and I had to quickly follow-up and request or grovel to the respective company for the payment to be made at a later date. I had to regularly move money between bank accounts and take further cash payments on my credit cards to make as many regular payments as possible.

All of this was constant stress on me, although my family did not know the full details of this financial juggling. I knew, with my steady work pay packet, I would gradually get on top of things. Later I would jokingly talk about my 'creative accounting' from this time. Having work not only provided the regular balance and routine that I needed at this time, but enabled me to keep moving forward.

I kept myself in a positive frame of mind by frequently reminding myself that in **that** moment I had a good place to live, a good job, a car, good food to eat and life was on an even keel. It never got worse than that, so basically, I was okay. I was not homeless or out in the gutter.

In my mind I put my financial losses in the context of anyone who loses money through investment, so justified that what had happened was not unique.

I convinced myself I was no different from many others who may have been even worse off. In this way I avoided feeling sorry for myself and was able to keep on going.

One of the other strategies I used to improve things was to review all of my outgoings and look at where I could reduce them. This included:

- Reducing the level of health insurance I had, from the top level to the most basic level, although I did keep my extras cover.
- I then took quotes on car insurance, and was able to reduce this by moving to another company.
- I moved a number of payments which had previously been going onto my credit card and been paid off each month, to be paid instead through my bank account, month by month, as I did not want to increase my debt.
- With a significant amount of credit card debt, I looked around for a new one which would include a zero interest twelve-month period and transferred the existing debt to that one. My goal was to clear that credit card, and I was able to do this and reduce interest expenses.

Later in the year I moved my car out of my company, which I was not using because I was an employee now, and into my own name. Whilst there was some stamp duty from the transfer, I was able to get a loan that reduced my costs by $150 per month, and get cheaper insurance.

In total, with all the changes, I had reduced my expenses by about $500 a month, and my credit card interest by about $300 a month. I was pleased with my achievement, and surprised at how much can be done when you set your mind to it.

Any spare money I had went into my credit cards, and I mostly managed to pay the equivalent or more than I had debited that month. I was making some small progress but it gave me a renewed sense of being in control of at least something in my life.

In April 2013 I received a large tax return payment. I used this to repay the loan of $5,000 from my friend, pay some bills I had, and put the rest towards my credit card debt, reducing it by about $10,000. At this time it was a real boon and made me feel I was able to make some headway into my debt. I had come through the initial crisis and could breathe again.

I should have moved house at this time, as I was paying $440 a week for a three bedroom house just for myself. It would have been the rational financial thing to do.

I could not do it though. It would have caused too much stress when I needed some stability. As things settled, I was able to manage this and still reduce my debt gradually. Over a year later, in early 2014, I finally made this step and found somewhere cheaper to live by moving out a few more suburbs.

The Aftermath

Part 3: Survivor

Dealing with the Consequences, and Recovery

Non-compliant Superannuation Access:

Step 1 – Making an Undertaking

In Australia it is compulsory for employers to pay 9.5% of wages into a retirement account, which we call Superannuation. There are legal rules around this, which include that this money cannot be accessed until you are age sixty, at which point you can cease work and retire. Mostly the money is put into secure investment funds, which manage the access and eventual payouts. It is possible, however, to set up a Self-Managed Superannuation Fund (SMSF), and personally manage the fund investment process and the returns that you can get from this money.
Early in 2012 I had gone through the process of setting up an SMSF, and transferred money from a general superannuation fund into my own fund. I had done this for the purpose of purchasing property, from which I intended to gather rental income and capital gains on the property value, and thus leverage my retirement funds through a property mortgage.
I had chosen this strategy after participating in a year-long property investment training course, so it was not done lightly. I was confident I could make a good choice of property as a consequence of the training I had received and the ongoing support I would receive from the training company. Setting up the fund meant that to facilitate purchasing a property, I had personal control of the bank account where the superannuation funds were held.
An SMSF has some legal restrictions on how and when to access these funds and the reporting that was required, and I had completed training in how to be compliant with these legalities.

Romance Scam Survivor

The actual step of selecting and investing in a property was delayed due to my decision to move from Brisbane to Melbourne, and the starting of a new job in Melbourne. In the interim I organised for my new employer superannuation contributions to be paid into my SMSF.

I had accessed and withdrawn all $166,000 of these funds as a result of the scam, and sent it to Eamon, believing his entreaties for the money and his promise that I would get the money back, and tenfold.

Having realised this would not now happen, I understood I should advise the relevant authorities that I had taken and used these funds. I decided it would be better to do this actively, rather than wait till later and then be discovered.

Throughout my life I had always taken the view that if I made a mistake it was better to not have any regrets, better to look forward and make the best of it.

I contacted my SMSF specialist on December 13th, 2014:

> Unfortunately I have some bad news and I may need your help.
>
> I was recently caught up in an internet romance scam and I have financially compromised myself. I have given away all of my personal savings, taken further credit and given away all of my super funds in my SMSF.
>
> I know I have acted in-compliantly, and that I should report this, and wonder if you could help me with the best way to do this so that I have the least likelihood of being charged for my actions.
>
> I have reported the matter to the police and ACCC (Scamwatch), but they are not able to do much, except monitor the growing amount of this problem generally.
>
> For your reference I am including links to a couple of articles that were in last weekend's Sunday Age here is Melbourne.
>
> http://www.theage.com.au/national/no-fairytale-ending-for-this-online-romance-20121208-2b2tl.html

Survivor

> http://www.theage.com.au/digital-life/consumer-security/online-daters-lose-millions-in-scams-20121208-2b2fl.html
>
> These people are very skilled and once I was involved I had little ability to act rationally, and was compliant with their requests for money. I believe I was in an altered state when I did this.
>
> As well as how best to report this, there is the question of if I should close the fund down, given there is very little in there now, except the super I am being paid in my current job. (current balance is under $2000).
>
> I'd appreciate your thoughts.
>
> PS I also have little ability left to pay you so please take this into account when considering what is best for me to do.
>
> Many thanks

December was not a good time with Christmas holidays coming up and my regular SMSF specialist being unavailable, so I was referred on to someone else that had helped in the initial SMSF set-up process, with the following advice:

> I am truly very sorry for your predicament. I know that this problem is just all too common, and the consequences disastrous.
>
> In regards your super, the problem is that you have accessed your superannuation before you are eligible to, which is termed 'early access'. Normally the ATO takes a strong stance against this sort of thing, but I'm pretty sure that, given you have reported this to the police, and under the circumstances, etc, that they will take a gentle approach.
>
> Also, you are almost 60 and have resigned from an employment position you were in until recently, so you are so close to being allowed to withdraw your super anyway (if you reach age 60 and THEN resign from an employment position, even if you take up another position, then your super is accessible at that point). However technically you were not eligible at the time you withdrew it.

Jan, what I would do would be to contact the ATO, explain all of the circumstances, add in the police report if you have it, and ask them for 'mercy'. Put it all in writing. If you contact them before they contact you, then they are much more lenient.

That's all I can really recommend. I feel for you Jan.

In a further correspondence I requested advice on whether I should close the fund, as there was no money left there.
As the fund Trustee, I wrote to the Australian Tax Office, as advised, on January 5th, 2013:

To whom it May Concern

In March 2012 I set up my Superfund and transferred funds to it, with the intention of investing in residential rental property.

In October 2012 I became engaged in an internet romance scam, though I did not know it at the time.

As a consequence of this I removed funds from my SMSF account, and paid them to the scammer. I felt compelled to do so, though I knew it was not appropriate. I believed that the funds would be returned within a very short time, with interest.

The amount removed from the fund was $165,000, the full amount in the fund at the time. I also paid a further $100,000 of personal savings and freshly borrowed credit card funds to the scammer. I have since reported the activity of the scam to the Victorian Police, and the funds are unlikely to be recovered. If you wish to confirm this, contact Detective Constable DC, at the Preston Police Station (DC@police.vic.gov.au).

In hindsight I realise all of this was a mistake, irrational, and grossly inappropriate. It has left me financially and emotionally compromised in many ways. I greatly regret what I have done.

As there are now minimal funds in the fund account, apart

from recent super payments from my current employment, I will take steps to wind up the fund. I believe my accountant will undertake the appropriate auditing of the fund.
I understand that I may be liable for penalties for acting as I did, but respectfully ask for a lenient consideration of this, given my self-reporting of this matter, and that I have little ability to pay any financial penalty.

Other factors to consider:

My date of birth is ▉▉▉▉▉ I have reached preservation age, and am 59 years old.

I did, as of 30 June 2012, leave gainful employment as a contractor paid through my own company Sangam Enterprises Pty Ltd, working for the Queensland Government in Brisbane.

I have since returned to work as an employee working on a fixed term employment contract in Melbourne, and through this, continue to contribute superannuation payments to the fund.

Please advise any additional documentation that you require.

I respectfully ask for your due consideration of these matters.

Yours sincerely,

The ATO (Australian Taxation Office) responded to this, and a call on January 10th (confirming the content), that I had been caught in an internet romance scam. They advised that I should not do anything further as the matter had been referred for review. (See section in in Appendix: Item 3: ATO/SMSF Documentation).
I did not have too long to wait, and received the response via my accountant in mid-February.
They requested a great deal of documentation about the fund, the amounts paid out, any documentation of loans made, and if any rectification of errors had been made, a statement in writing detailing what had been done so far, and any supporting evidence.

They did not request any evidence in relation to the scam. Some of the items I could provide, some my accountant could provide, and others were not at all applicable for my situation. It was obviously a pro forma request letter used for fund reviews. (See Number 2 in in Appendix: Item 3: ATO/SMSF Documentation).

As well as providing the relevant copies of banks statements, I completed an in-depth 'statement in writing' (See Number 3 in in Appendix: Item 3: ATO/SMSF Documentation).

In mid-May I was asked to provide further information, and attached more details on the scam and scammer, including copies of the bank statements he had provided to me (See Number 4 in in Appendix: Item 3: ATO/SMSF Documentation).

It was May when I had a further response from the ATO, and it was not good news! (See Number 5 in in Appendix: Item 3: ATO/SMSF Documentation).

My case was being escalated to audit, as they had determined that I had contravened superannuation law in my role as Trustee of the SMSF. It was verified that I had contravened the Early Access of Benefits, as I had taken the money out before I was eligible, and contravened the Sole Purpose Test.

They "*allowed me the opportunity*" to provide a written undertaking, setting out my commitment to winding up the fund. Undertaking to close down the fund was acceptable to me, as I already had decided to do this.

The reasons why were another thing altogether. Rather than put it all in, here are some highlights from the six page and 101 paragraph legally argued Position Document.

I have selected parts of the document as it is largely what you already know, and tedious to read as a legal document.

The early part of the paper serves to rephrase the details of all the information I had provided them, including full records of what was paid to whom and when.

Of the scamming they note:

> 29. You advise the monies withdrawn and loaned to the member Ms Jan Marshall were transferred to an internet romance identity to which the member believed she was engaged to be married to but later

was revealed to be an internet scammer.
30. You advise that the member expected the payment of funds to promptly facilitate the ability of the person to return to England, where his funds would become available for repayment. He had a significant payment for his work by cheque which he was unable to cash while in Dubai.
31. You advise that he provided a number of urgent reasons why he needed additional money sent.
32. You advise the member had already provided $81,000 comprising personal cash funds and additional approved credit card funds and had no access to other personal funds.
33. You advise that during this period the member became increasingly anxious to do what was necessary to get him out of Dubai and back to England to remove him from a dangerous situation, as well as to be able to refund her the loans.
34. It was only after he had advised he was on a plane to England and she was unable to make contact and she realised it had been a scam.
35. You advise that the scammers are professionals at personal manipulation.
36. You advise the member Ms Jan Marshall is unable to repay any monies to the fund you have allowed to be withdrawn inappropriately.

Conclusion on "Loan to Member" (ie from SMSF to me):

55. You state that this money was provided to the member Ms Jan Marshall as a loan and that the member then transferred the monies provided to a third party internet romance scam.
56. Fund bank statements and the member's personal bank statements confirm that the amounts were provided to the member from the fund.
57. You have indicated that the amounts were supposed to be loans to Ms Jan Marshall. You have provided no documentation that indicates the amounts are loans. In addition you have not treated the amounts as loans. You have no loan agreement, no interest has been

accrued or paid and no repayments have been made. There have been no steps taken by you to recover the money from the member, though it is acknowledged that the member has reported the internet scam to the Victorian Police.
58. It is therefore considered that you have forgone your right to these amounts and they were benefit payments to the member Ms Jan Marshall.

Survivor

59. From the information provided it is considered that you have not made a loan to the member and therefore have not contravened secion 65 of the SISA.

Contravention – Early Access

Because I had continued to pay in money from my new employer, even though I had left a previous employer, it was:

" therefore considered that at the time the fund monies were provided to the member (me), she was gainfully employed and the condition of release under retirement had not been met."

That much logic I followed, even though they had made an error in saying that I had work through my company with my current employer. Because I had taken more than ten percent of the fund, the release could not be considered as 'transition to retirement'.
So, I had failed to comply with the regulations, and contravened section 34 of the Superannuation Industry (Supervision) Act 1993 (SISA). Because this means I had contravened the sole purpose of superannuation, to provide bencfits for members in their retirement, this contravention, they say *"is considered especially serious."*

Contravention – Sole Purpose

88. Paragraph 6 of Self managed superannuation funds ruling 2008/2 (SMSFR 2008/2) states that a trustee must maintain an SMSF in a manner that complies with the sole purpose test at all times, including investing, employing and using fund assets. You are therefore required to invest, employ and use fund money in accordance with the sole purpose test. Paragraph 7 of SMSFR 2008/2 specifies that the sole purpose test requires exclusivity of purpose.

91. You have stated that you used the money from the fund as a loan to the member Ms Jan Marshall who then used the accessed funds as she saw fit. Ms Marshall has stated that she transferred the monies to an internet

romance scam and the unfortunate nature of these circumstances is acknowledged.
92. It is considered that you have provided the member Ms Jan Marshall with benefit payments without meeting a condition of release. These circumstances clearly show that these actions were made for the current benefit of the member and not for the benefit of the member in retirement.
93. Such actions clearly display a lack of due diligence on your part to adhere to both the core and ancillary purposes of section 62 of the SISA and as such you are considered to have contravened that section.

Seriousness
94. The Commissioner considers that a contravention of the sole purpose test under section 62 of the SISA to be of a serious nature as the intent of the legislation is to ensure that the retirement income objective is paramount. The sole purpose test and the associated standards prohibit the use of concessional taxed superannuation savings for purposes such as providing pre-retirement benefits.
95. You have provided current day benefit payments to the member without them having met a condition of release. Your actions as trustee of the fund have restricted the fund's ability to meet the member's retirement objectives and therefore the contravention of the sole purpose test is considered especially serious.

Not being a lawyer, all of this seems to follow logically. From a personal perspective however, I had not separated me the member and me the fund, and to me, the lay person, had separated these two entities to the advantage of their argument.
This means they were able to discount any interaction by me and the scammer with regard to a loan to him, except to acknowledge the "unfortunate nature of these circumstances". Instead, they have argued that the loan was from the fund to me, leaving me accountable in both circumstances.
Their final conclusion is that I should not be a trustee of a self-

managed superannuation fund and the fund should be wound up. I was happy to do this, and began to write up an undertaking using the template provided.
I completed a final version dated 16th June 2013, allowing all matters to be finalised by the end of the next quarter.

This included:

1. Finalising all tax returns, including for the following years.
2. Closing the legal entities that made up the funds.
3. Notify the ATO in writing, within 28 days of the SMSF being wound up.
4. There were fees to pay for all of this too, which went on to the credit card.

Each time I had to write one of these letters, provide information or deal with a response, I had to generate significant energy to do so. This was mainly done on weekends, leaving little time for rest.
During this period I wanted to put the whole matter behind me, get back to living 'normally.' Each time I had to respond to the ATO I had to reconnect with the scam event.
Those who knew me would have seen me as dealing competently with all of this, however underneath the capable exterior I was suffering a low level of depression. This was manifest in behaviours such as me staying home, except when I needed to do something with my mother, and otherwise being generally reticent when I was out socially.
I think they knew I wasn't really there to connect with them, but there was little they could do.
It was my journey.

Step 2 – Closing the Fund

I had assumed that winding up the superannuation fund would be the end of it, however in mid-September 2013 the reply from the ATO that my undertaking had been accepted included a shock.

The money taken from the fund would need to be included as personal taxable income for that financial year. My accountant had rung me with the news about the letter from the ATO, and advised this meant that it would be taxed at the top level, at 46.5%.

That meant that I would have a tax bill of $77,260! The statement from the ATO was clear and threatening:

> *"If Jan Marshall does not report this income, penalties may be applied."*

I was devastated. There was no way I could pay that amount of money. I still had about $30,000 in credit card debt. It was a double whammy. First I was scammed and lost all that money. Now I had to pay what felt like a huge fine to my own government because of it.

The financial future looked bleak.

Realistically, I believed that I would be able to make arrangements with the ATO to pay off the amount. But even if I took it over the remainder of my working life, that is up to age sixty-five, or even if I planned to work till seventy, it would keep me poor for all that time, and beyond.

This meant I would have no opportunity to put anything aside for my retirement, apart from what might be paid by employers as part of the employment guarantee, currently 9.5%. It also meant that paying down my credit card debt would be delayed, and more interest would be applied, keeping me in debt for longer.

My accountant suggested, however, that I could get a legal opinion with regard to my rights to dispute the inclusion. And he had the name of a lawyer who had worked at the ATO.

Survivor

I decide to call the person who had been handling my situation at the ATO in the first instance, but find she is on leave. I write back to my accountant:

> "I'm sure those guys at the ATO get schooled in how **not** to be sympathetic – and they just follow processes. Do you have any sense that they can be compassionate at all – is it worth the effort? I don't expect they have any discretion over these matters do they?"
>
> I know I feel like I have been penalised, fined for being scammed, but they just see that I took the money out of the SMSF when I shouldn't have, and now have to deal with my actions.
>
> Not much different than if I had put my money into an investment fund that had gone bust with no recourse.... And there are enough of those.
>
> Its just a bummer as it will keep me poor in the long run and mean that I will not recover the level of super I could if I did not have to pay this. It will come back on them when I have to go on the aged pension because I don't have enough super....
>
> I'm happy if you call the lawyer at to briefly to get a sense if something could be done, but given we did not dispute their earlier findings I would suspect I don't have much recourse now the undertaking is in place. So I would not want to incur huge legal fees for nothing. Also what are the penalties if I do not report it on my tax return?"

My accountant did talk to the lawyers, and he received the following back from them:

> Hi ▮
>
> In our meeting this week we discussed another matter that you have with the ATO.
>
> Your client has withdrawn funds from her self-managed superannuation fund without meeting a condition of release. The funds were sent overseas to a fraudster who took advantage of your client. Your client did not receive any of

205

the funds herself.

The ATO have audited the fund and directed that the monies taken from super be included in your client's tax return for the relevant year(s).

Under section 304-10(4) of the 1997 Act, if the Commissioner considers it is unreasonable to do so, you do not need to include amounts taken from super in breach of a legislative requirement in your assessable income.

The cases on section 304-10 are varied in their results, because each case turns on the facts and evidence.

Based on the cases we have read, there may be grounds to argue successfully that 304-10(4) should be applied and no amount should be included in your client's assessable income. If we can show:
your client did not obtain the benefit of using the funds (in the sense that she lost the funds, and the imposition of tax is in addition to the economic loss);
your client was defrauded, including police statements, emails etc;
the amended assessment would cause financial hardship (not necessarily within the meaning in the *SIS Act*); and
your client was not in a rational state of mind at the time;
then there may be grounds for a successful application.

However, as you can appreciate we cannot guarantee that the Commissioner will accept our submissions, but depending on the tax involved it may be worth asking the question.

Our fees to meet with your client and draft the letter to the ATO would be approximately $2,500 + GST.

Please let me know if your client is interested and I will prepare an engagement agreement.

Hope. It seemed it might be possible to do *something*, and there were grounds for this. Though I did not have the $2,500 + tax it would cost, it seemed worth putting this on my credit card if it meant I did not have to pay the $80,000 (I had rounded the amount up in my mind).

I had the agreement drawn up and agreed to go ahead with the lawyers. My accountant sent them the relevant details and correspondence with the ATO.

On Sunday, 3rd November 2013, I write a letter to the lawyer, addressing the possible grounds he has put:

> I wanted to provide additional information to assist with possible grounds to argue successfully that 304-10(4) should be applied and no amount should be included in my assessable income causing a tax liability.
>
> You have indicated that possible grounds could include:
> - I did not obtain the benefit of using the funds (in the sense that she lost the funds, and the imposition of tax is in addition to the economic loss);
> - I was defrauded, including police statements, emails etc;
> - the amended assessment would cause financial hardship (not necessarily within the meaning in the *SIS Act*); and
> - I was not in a rational state of mind at the time.
>
> I will address each one in turn, as best I can.
>
> I did not obtain benefit from the funds:
> - I have documented evidence of the removal of funds from the SMSF, their payment into my personal account, then the transfer or payment of those funds overseas, either via bank transfer or Western Union transfer to persons or accounts provided by my 'scammer'. None of the money remained with me.
> - As well as removal of funds from the SMSF, this include payment of personal savings or income of approx. $37,600 and additional credit card funds of approximately $39,000, through extension of credit on a current card and the acquiring of a new card of $15,000.
> - None of these funds were used to purchase personal items or activities for a personal use, and records of transfer of all funds overseas of $259,322 including fees is available. This information was provided also to Victoria Police.

- I was fully defrauded of these funds.

I was defrauded, including police statements, emails etc;
- Once I realised I had been scammed, I reported this incident to the Victorian Police, at the Preston Police Station, providing records of all my transfers and a summary of the story.
- Their records are Inc No: 120328842, Sub-Inc No: 120437875
- Contact Officer D.C. .
- I made also several contacts with agencies in Dubai, where I believed the scammer to be located to see if they could take any action. They referred me back to local police agencies.
- I also asked my bank to see if funds provided by bank transfer could be returned.
- See Appendices A through D for copies of emails (embedded files – let me know if these cannot be accessed) received from these agencies and my bank.

The amended assessment would cause financial hardship:
- Current savings are nil, as a result of the scam. I had to ask for personal loans and gifts from friends and relatives to get over the initial impact of the scam.
- Current remaining credit card amounts are
- St George Mastercard – $9,964.03 Some inroads to the Master card were made due to a tax return which enabled some credit to be paid down. Current minimum balance payment would take 34.5 years to pay off and incur $12,381 additional interest
- ANZ Visa Card - $11,938. The ANZ visa card is being paid off at $300 per month, minimally over the minimum payment amount. This is on zero interest for 9 months, and ceases 10/11/13, after which time it will incur a normal interest rate. The Minimum payment warning on the credit card statement indicates that at a minimum payment rate, this will take 26 years and 2 months, and incur and additional $13,039.32 interest.

Survivor

- Total remaining credit card debt is $21,902, plus, if paid off at minimum balance, an additional $25,420, totalling $47,322.35 to be paid over 35 years.
- As I am already 60, and can only be expected to work another 5 – 7 years, maybe 10 years, paying off these credit cards is already likely to cause financial hardship into the future beyond that 10 years.
- Whilst I have a property at 103 Orana Road, Ocean Shores, the current mortgage on this property is $520,000, however over the past several years due to the GFC and its effect on property, especially rural property prices, this is valued by RP Data at between $500,000 and $550,000. It is uncertain when and if property prices will increase, so a sale of the property will not currently and may not eventually generate any profits that might enabling paying off any debt. Current rental returns do currently pay a major portion of the mortgage, and there is no market for properties at present in this area (average days on the market 365 days). I had hoped this property would assist me with my retirement, however it looks like this will not be the case.
- I have no other property, so in my retirement will be at the whim of the private rental market, which is known to not provide sufficient properties for low income earners (as I would most likely be on an old age pension).
- Whilst in my remaining years as a wage earner, some additional funds can be paid into superannuation, this is unlikely to be sufficient for a lengthy retirement period, so more than likely I would require an old age pension to support me.
- In this context, to have to find another approx. $70,000 - 80,000 to pay a tax bill that means that I would have $80,000 less to support me in my retirement, and I would be likely to be more reliant on the aged pension and stricken to a life in poverty. This would be the case even if allowance was made to pay it off, as I cannot see myself being able to do this within my remaining working life.
- I have already been defrauded of $260,000. To

209

have to pay another large amount of tax feels like I am being fined and punished for being a victim of this fraud. This does not seem in any way fair.

I was not in a rational state of mind at the time.
- The fact that I allowed myself to be scammed to such an extent shows that I was not in a rational state of mind at the time, as a rational person would not have done this.
- Scammers are skilled and experience manipulators of people's emotional state, and I was sufficiently 'hooked' by this scammer to override warnings from close friends, warnings on Western Union literature, common sense hints that things were not as they seemed. In hindsight I can see these things, but at the time I disregarded these hints and provided money anyway believing it to be a loan. This was not rational given the hints that were there.
- In all other ways I would be regarded by friends and colleagues as a successful profession person, a good money manager.
- I sought counselling services via the EAP service of free counselling via my workplace. I undertook two sessions. See Appendix E for confirmation of one appointment.
- Whilst I have not sought medical support, I have suffered depressions over the past months. Only my ongoing work situation has kept me in a stable situation.

If you require further documentation on any of the matters listed above, or matters in other correspondence please ask.

Errors in ATO assessment
There were at least two errors in the ATO assessment of my situation, though of minor detail. If this is of any use, please let me know and I will provide further detail.

Background on scamming
I have kept a watch on Romancescam.com, and there has been further activity of the person who scammed me...
http://www.romancescam.com/forum/viewtopic.php?f=3&t=55151&p=289015

If you read all the posts for this one, you will see the similarity and the history. If you search this site for Phillip More, you will see the photos that the scammer used with me.

I did a photo search on the photos that I was provided with by the scammer as him, and found them in use on 10 different sites, all under different names, all very different...

By Wednesday, 27th November, 2013, I receive back from the lawyer two draft files for review. One is the draft letter, the other is a statement of my circumstances, with some requests for clarification on a couple of points to flesh out the statement and background circumstances. My accountant receives these, and has a few considerations.

He writes:
> Per your point 2 – please note that [my] personal income tax return has not been lodged as yet for the financial year ended 30 June 2013. We have only received correspondence (refer attached) from the ATO stating that $166,150 is to be reported in her personal tax return for the financial year ended 30 June 2013.
> Per your point 9 – please refer to the attached document stating the purpose of the fund.
> Per your point 14 and 15(d) – our concern is that if the fund is treated as non-complying then the ATO is entitled to tax the income (not significant) at 46.5% and also the assets of the fund at 46.5% and the ATO may deem the assets of the fund to include the loan to the member of $166,500. So we don't want to suggest to the ATO to disregard the withdrawal in [my] personal income tax return for them to then tax it under the fund and seek payment from the director of the trustee company.
> Per your point 17 – no assessment has been issued as yet, as the 30 June 2013 has not been lodged with the ATO.
> Please refer to ATO correspondence attached.

I did not fully understand what he was saying, but got the gist of his concern that I might be taxed twice if the issue was not handled carefully.

Romance Scam Survivor

The lawyer drafts a separate letter to the ATO and advises:

> Our intention is to get the ATO to confirm, in writing, that other than seeking undertakings (which you have already given), they will not be taking any further action against the fund. This should eliminate any risk of penalty tax in the fund.

Advice comes back from the ATO. They could not guarantee anything until the winding up of the fund was confirmed.

In the background, all that needed to be done to wind up the superannuation fund was progressing, with the closing of the bank account, finalisation of tax documentation and auditing and closing of all of the fund structures.

I had asked for a fixed quote on all of this work and had prepaid before the bank account was closed, with money again taken from my credit card. Documentation to the ATO confirming the fund had been closed and the undertaking had been complied with was completed by the end of November 2013.

There was further signing of documents, and all was completed in the relevant timeframes. A notice was received back from the ATO dated 4th February 2014, that based on the information provided:

> *"...you have complied with all the undertakings and rectified the conventions of the SISDA. According, the Commissioner has decided not to take further actions".*

This whole issue had now been ongoing for over a year since the scamming. No getting away from it all with the constant need to review, rewrite, reconsider, deal with the lawyer, accountant, and ATO. No opportunity to push it all into the background and get on with life.

For most of this year I had been emotionally and energetically shut down, with all spare energy going into my work, the main foundation of my stability during this time.

On the surface, to my friends and family who knew what was going on, I seemed stoic, and resilient, getting on with life, but it wasn't much of a life. Underneath, healing was happening.

Step 3 - Asking for Discretion From the ATO

It was in early 2014 that I felt emotionally strong enough to face the world again. As a new year's resolution to get out more, I booked into some College of Adult Education (CAE) classes to nourish myself and do something I enjoyed.
I did introduction to Watercolour, and Basics of Acting as a form of self-expression. I selected classes held in the city after work, so it was easy to go there from work, then home on the train afterwards. Conveniently for me, the station was just across the road from the college.
I chose watercolour painting because even though I had done oil, pastels and drawing before, I felt starting a new one would be a good way to gently easy myself back in. I also had all of my mother's watercolour equipment available, so did not have to spend much money on equipment.
Now that the fund was closed, and the undertaking completed, the lawyers could go ahead and submit their letter. It was in typical legalese. The section below is section 16. (See Appendix: ATO/SMSF Documentation, for full transcript).

After all the legal references, the gist of the letter says:

We draw the following facts to the Commissioner's attention:
  a) The policy intent of parliament by establishing the self-managed superannuation scheme will not be undermined by excluding the amounts from Ms Marshall's assessable income.
There is no suggestion that Ms Marshall deliberately abused the self-managed superannuation regime as by her own admission, she was under the genuine belief that:
   - the Fund would be repaid with interest; and
   - she had no choice to save the scammer's life except to loan the amounts.
  b) There was no 'fraudulent enterprise' or any suggestions of impropriety by Ms Marshall.
In the case of Brazil v Federal Commissioner of Taxation [2012] AATA 192, the Senior Member affirmed the Commissioner's decision to include the amounts taken from the AON Master Trust (an APRA regulated fund) because of the overwhelming evidence of a 'fraudulent enterprise' (at paragraph [25]).
There are no such suggestions in this instance.

c) Ms Marshall did not receive the benefit of the money taken from the Fund, nor does she have any likely prospects of the money being returned to her. There is clearly no tax avoidance purpose in this case.

While Ms Marshall always had sole effective control of the Fund (see Mason v Federal Commissioner of Taxation [2012] AATA 133), this case can be distinguished from the facts in the Mason case because Ms Marshall never received the use of, or benefit from, the money withdrawn from the Fund (unlike Mr Mason) as the money was all sent to the scam artist.

d) On this basis, it is unreasonable to include the amounts in Ms Marshall assessable income because she did not receive the benefit of those funds.

e) The non-complying status of the superannuation fund is more than a sufficient fiscal penalty for Ms Marshall, together with the fact that she has been forced to return to work to start saving again. She has not obtained any 'excessive benefit', or any benefit at all, from the withdrawal of the funds. In addition, she has suffered emotional distress and embarrassment.

She has also incurred professional fees to rectify these matters.

Based on the above facts, we request that the Commissioner exercise discretion to exclude the superannuation amounts from Ms Marshall's assessable income under section 304-10(4).

Requested action

We ask that the Commissioner exercise discretion to exclude the amount of $166,150 (the amount of superannuation benefits accessed form the Fund) from Ms Marshall's assessable income under section 304-10(4) after she lodges her 2013 income tax return.

This was accompanied by my statement, a summary of the facts in the first person, explaining what happened, remedial action taken and the long term financial consequences for me. You've seen most of it before, so see the Appendix: ATO/SMSF Documentation for full transcript.

This was in effect asking for a Private Ruling on my special circumstances. It was finalised and sent off to the ATO on February 6th, 2014.

I wasn't sure what the response would be. I thought the moral high ground was on my side, but did not fully understand the legal detail of the matter.

I spent the waiting time hopeful, but not too expectant.

The response came back two months later, via email on April

2nd, 2014. Here is the short version, summarised by the lawyer:

> We attach the decision received from the ATO for your matter.
>
> Unfortunately, the ATO have refused to exclude the early access benefits from your assessable income. What this means is that you will be taxed on the amount of the benefits ($166,150) at your marginal rates.
>
> The ATO have denied the application for 2 principal reasons (at paragraphs 43 to 48):
> "The Fund was not made non-complying... and the inclusion of the superannuation benefits would not in addition to other taxation consequences".
> "It is also clear the breaches did not arise in circumstances beyond [your] effective control".

This was devastating and distressing. How would I ever find that amount of money to pay the tax? And now I have added $2,500 additional money to my credit card to pay the legal fees. Not good!
It confirmed in my mind that the legal imperative to provide for superannuation was one way only, it was on the head of the trustee, but did not equally rest on the head of the ATO or government. They had no consideration of the financial impact on me into the future, or the additional expense of an aged pension that may eventually land on the government in order to support a much poorer me.
There are six pages of restatement of the facts and legal argument for the decision in the document. The option to object to the decision, if this is done within sixty days is also explained. When I asked my lawyer about this option, he advised that it would cost further money for the legal work required to write an objection to the private ruling. This was money I did not have.
He explained that the ATO must apply the law 'as it is written,' so they cannot do other than go through each potential legal issue. They are not concerned with the person behind it at all. To the uninitiated, discretion can appear to mean exercise compassion and understanding. But this is not what it means in the legal sense, and certainly not in this case, I realised.

Romance Scam Survivor

To see the full detail of the Private Ruling, see the *Register of Private Binding Rulings* on the ATO website, and search on Authorisation Number 1012608950334.

Writing my Objection, Becoming a Survivor

As I let the response settle with me, reading through it again, I realise that the parts that I have objections to are not the legal arguments or reasoning, but rather, they are the parts that reflect directly on an assessment of me.

Applying the law to the facts:

27. From the information provided, it has been stated that the monies had been intended to be a loan to the member who then used the accessed funds to send to a third party. The unfortunate nature of these circumstances is noted.
28. However, the total amount of the withdrawals ($166,150) represented almost the entire member account balance at the time including employer contributions which were accepted by the Fund during this period. Therefore the circumstances clearly show that the payment of benefits were not made for the benefit of the member in retirement.
29. Such actions clearly display a lack of due diligence on the Trustee's part to adhere to section 62 of the SISA and as such, the actions taken by the Trustee have contravened that section.

At the end of para 27 above is the only mention of the scamming – "*The unfortunate nature of these circumstances is noted*". I am disgusted and angry that what happened to me is regarded as 'unfortunate'!
In par 29 above, "*Such actions clearly display a lack of due diligence on the Trustee's part...*". This, in combination with the conclusion in para 44 below, clearly show that they do not understand the effect of a scam on a person.

44. It is also clear the breaches did not arise in circumstances beyond the effective control of the recipient of the benefits (your client) who was the sole member and sole director of the corporate trustee of the Fund (the Trustee).

Contrary to their view, my assessment of the effect of the scam on me is that I was not in effective control.

In para 42, the legal requirements for the Commissioner to consider discretion are spelt out, and I am struck in particular by the last bullet point:

> 42. Therefore, having regard to the legislative history and the context of the subsection 304-10(4) discretion as provided by the EM to Tax Laws Amendment (Simplified Superannuation) Bill 2006, and the use of the word 'unreasonable' in the corresponding discretionary provisions of former section 26AFA and 26AFB of the ITAA 1936 (as above), it becomes evident the discretion would be exercised only in the circumstances where the Commissioner considered it 'unreasonable' to include superannuation benefits paid in breach of legislative requirements in a person's assessable income where:
> - it would be in addition to other taxation consequences and
> - the breach arose in circumstances beyond the effective control of the recipient.

As it is their assessment of me to which I object, including the understanding of what happens when you are scammed, and the impact of this, I decide to write the objection myself rather than continue with legal help and incur further legal fees. This will allow me to have my say more directly. I know this is a long shot, as it means I might not sufficiently address the legal issues, however the more I think about it the more determined I am to do this.

I had already done a lot of research on scamming. Now I set out to do more.

A couple of days before, on April 1st, there had been a very good SBS Insight program on the topic of internet romance scams called 'Love Bait.' As well as a number of female and male victims of scams, there were comments from Detective Superintendent Brian Hay from the Queensland Police and Detective Senior Sargent Dom Blackshaw from Project

Sunbird in WA, commenting on how difficult it was to deal with the perpetrators, but how disbelieving the victims sometimes were.
See http://www.sbs.com.au/news/insight/tvepisode/love-bait to watch it or retrieve the transcript. This just added to the growing information out there.
I talked to my close girlfriends about it, and they offered to write letters in support of the effect on me if that would help. I wasn't sure if it would, but as I planned to call the ATO I would put this question to them.

My lawyer made it clear that if I did write and submit an objection, I would not have other options to object:

The ATO is correct that you can lodge your tax return and then object to the ATO's assessment (whatever it may be). You generally have 2 years to object to an assessment after the assessment is made. Objecting to a tax assessment is different to objecting to a private ruling as there are further evidentiary issues you will need to satisfy. We can provide advice or assistance drafting the objection to your tax assessment if you wish but there will be a fee for this work.

On the other hand, if you decide to proceed with the current objection to the private ruling and the ATO deny the objection, then there is a general rule that you cannot then object to your income tax assessment about the same issue ruled in the objection (section 14ZVA of the Taxation Administration Act). This means that if you do not get a favourable outcome at objection then you must appeal to the AAT or the Federal Court to overturn the decision – there are no other appeal rights; the matter will be considered to have been ruled on.

This is a complicated area of the tax law (i.e. review and appeal rights to private ruling decisions). There has recently been a case in the AAT highlighting these issues (The Public Servant and Commissioner of Taxation [2014] AATA 247).

Complicated, yes. If I lost I would close off any further options to take action, as I understood it. I had no faith that the lawyers could change anything though, so I may as well try. I was determined to have my say.

As I wrote the objection a number of things became increasingly clear to me:
- Firstly, that scams are in fact fraud, and in this case, internet romance scams are professional fraud.
- Secondly, that the grooming and emotional manipulation that takes place makes it very difficult to act rationally.
- Thirdly, that whilst I accepted the well-intentioned arguments of my accountant and lawyer to argue my case on the facts, that in accepting this I was colluding with an assumption that it was a rational and considered act, but in the wrong circumstances. I now considered this the wrong approach.

After a few attempts, and incorporating feedback from my lawyer and my girlfriends, this is what came together, using the legal template provided. It is included in full here as it details my developing understanding:

I requested an assessment private ruling on the inclusion of funds taken from my SMSF, ▓▓▓▓▓▓▓▓ in my assessable tax income for the 2013 financial year, having been advised that there was some possibility of discretion by the Commissioner to be made in "instances where there are no tax avoidance implications and where the excessive benefit arose fortuitously or in other circumstances beyond the effective control of the recipient or the employer". This discretion is provided to the Commissioner under section 304-10(4) of the Income Tax Assessment Act 1997.

The private ruling has determined that the actions that led to the early release of funds from the SMSF
  i. Were a result of *lack of due diligence* (para 29)
  ii. Did not arise in circumstances beyond the effective control of the recipient of the benefits (client)(par 44)

Given the potential financial impact of the private ruling, I am unable to access further legal advice on this issue.

I submit the decision of the Commissioner in the private ruling is incorrect for the following reasons:

The gravity of the situation affecting me was not understood or appreciated by the Commissioner. The statement in par 27 of the Reasons for Decision simply states "The unfortunate nature of these circumstances is noted."

　　i. **I was not in "effective control" as claimed by you,** when I undertook these actions, as I was caught in the midst of a fraudulent engagement.
　　ii. **I demonstrated a high level of due diligence** in relation to the administration of the fund, when in effective control, both prior to and subsequently when effective control was returned, I self reported the breach, then undertook the necessary actions to wind up the fund in a fully compliant manner.
　　iii. The future financial impact on me (and indeed on the Australian Taxpayers of the future) has not been fully taken into account when exercising discretion.
　　iv. There is increasing **information in the public domain** about the effect of relationship fraud and scamming, including from Australian Police jurisdictions. (some information is included below.)
　　v. As a result the Commissioner failed to give due weight to all relevant facts and if had done so may have exercised the discretion differently.

I will now explain what I mean by each of the above grounds for Objection:

The gravity of the situation affecting me was not understood or given due weight.
I was not a wilful and considered plunderer of funds from a personal superannuation fund; I am the VICTIM of a sophisticated international FRAUD. I reported the matter to my Bank as well as to the Victorian police, who did not advance the case. Neither was able to obtain any redress or return of funds.

The word "unfortunate" cannot describe the result of being targeted and becoming the victim in such a fraud. It is devastating. This decision in the private ruling is inadequate and has led to further erroneous conclusions by the ATO, including that I was in effective control of what I undertook (see following section for further explanation).

This type of fraud is now a known process and is clearly explained on the government's Scamwatch website. (see

Romance Scam Survivor

http://www.scamwatch.gov.au/content/index.phtml/tag/DatingRomanceScams). It affects many people across Australia and results in millions of dollars leaving Australia every year.

The prevalence and impact of such frauds is so severe that at least two police jurisdictions, Western Australia (Project Sunbird), and Queensland, have established a task force, or a dedicated area to address the situation. Unfortunately the Victorian police were not responsive to this type of fraud at that time; it is an international crime reaching our shores in Australia relatively recently. Even with police intervention, there is little recourse and most efforts by these police groups are in prevention, by making contact with people making unexplained transmissions of large amounts of money overseas and warning them of the possibility of fraud. In only one recent instance have they been able to achieve the partial return of funds (WA April 14).

This fraud took place over several months and was undertaken by a **skilled emotionally manipulative professional** whose sole purpose was to separate me from **any and all money I could provide to him**, whatever the source, and without any consideration of its effect on me.

Until recently, due to the shame and devastation that I faced emotionally and financially, I also thought that the responsibility was purely my own, and as a consequence engaged legal assistance to put potentially 'reasonable' justifications to my early access of the superannuation funds. This included early release, expectations of investment returns from the 'loan' I had made to the scammer, etc. This has led to unfavourable assessments of my actions which I seek to redress in this Objection.

The action of trying to justify what happened is similar to that of an abuse victim feeling responsible for causing the abuse when they have done nothing to incite it. I now better understand that I am the VICTIM of a FRAUD, and was not responsible for the actions that were perpetrated on me as part of that fraud, and that I undertook whilst within that fraudulent engagement.

Police Bulletin 347 reports on a research project conducted by the Queensland Police Service. The project, a joint initiative between Community Safety and Crime Prevention Branch and the Fraud and Corporate Crime Group, is being conducted by research analyst Dr Cassandra Cross, and is based around the issue of seniors and online fraud.

Survivor

http://www.police.qld.gov.au/Resources/Internet/services/reportsPublications/bulletin/347/documents/internet%20scams.pdf.
The Bulletin states,
"After the initial contact via email, the scammer builds a relationship with the victims over the telephone or face-to-face, and this **contributes to their inability to recognise their experiences as fraudulent**." (my emphasis)

A recent SBS Insight program on 1 April 2014 with Jenny Brockie profiled romance scams on a program called Love Bait. The program can be seen here
http://www.sbs.com.au/insight/episode/overview/604/Love-Bait.
The transcript is attached for reference.

A member of WA Project Sunbird is willing to provide verbal explanation of what happens in many similar scams/frauds. Please call 1300 304054 and ask for Project Sunbird, or call directly to Adam Edwards on (08) 92820994.

When I undertook these actions I was not in effective control
The effect of the fraud was to capture me in a 'thrall' (a state of slavery or bondage, of moral or mental servitude). I was bound to do what was asked, believing it was required for the safety of my (imagined) life partner. It may also be described as a hypnotic state. As stated below, people caught in such frauds refuse to believe it is a scam even when contacted by the police. This indicates how powerful the "thrall" of this fraud is.

As stated in the Overview on the SBS website about the program listed above,
"The frauds are elaborate and sophisticated. Scammers spend months building relationships, sending photos, calling and emailing. When family or the police intervene, **many victims refuse to believe it's all a lie**." (my emphasis).

Despite the warnings of a number of friends, I refused to believe it was a scam.

The scammer perpetrated the fraud by establishing an emotional relationship such that I agreed to marry him. He continued emphasising the we had a special partnership for life, and in such partnerships, I believed it's not my or his money, but our money, and was needed to ensure out future together.

The belief in the imagined 'relationship' that has been built is all encompassing. In this context requests for money were made to me. I paid the scammer close to $80,000 in personal funds, exhausting them. I extended a credit card and took out a new credit card, providing an additional $30,000. Then I used the SMSF funds, which I had set aside to invest in property so as to provide for my retirement. A total of $270,000 was given away in response to this fraud.

He also repeatedly said that they money would come back to me ten-fold. He even showed me bank statements (copies provided to the police) showing that the funds were there, in England, but not currently accessible, increasing my belief in this.
This promise of return of funds was made **repeatedly for all the funds given**, and was believed. It was believed for the first small payment, and for the larger payments from my personal funds, and the additional credit was also taken on this basis. By the time I accessed the SMSF funds I was unable to counter his emotional arguments of need, and unable to differentiate that these funds were different from the personal funds or credit funds that I had paid and make a different more prudent decision about these funds. I was not in effective control of my actions.

Antifraud news.com   http://www.antifraudnews.com/scam-victim-consequences/   published April 3, 2013, in an article called Scam Victim Consequences By Thomas Clark states,
"**Escalation and reinforcement:** As you make payments to the scammer, he will contact you more frequently, bombarding you with calls and emails and allowing you to think of little else. Simply the act of paying multiple times will reinforce your belief in the scam and make it easier to pay in the future, and to take ever greater risks to make payments to the scammers. You may re-mortgage your property, sell family heirlooms, borrow money, steal money from your family or embezzle money from your employers. You may steal relatives' identities in order to take out loans or credit cards. **You will do all this in the firm belief that you are about to be paid a huge amount of money, and that you will soon be able to pay it all back.**" (my emphasis – this is what happened to me)

In the last part of this fraud, I gave away money that I had just received in wages, and needed to buy food for myself and pay bills in the following fortnight. In the process there were some bills which did not get paid. I have also had to seek help from family members to get through.

Survivor

When the scam was revealed, at the individual level it was unbelievable, devastating, emotionally and financially debilitating, shaming, and crippling. I saw a counsellor several times, but was still in such a state of isolation and withdrawal that my close friends expressed concern for me. I remained isolated for the following year, with little contact outside of close family and work.

As soon as I agreed to pay the scammer **any** money, I was **not in effective control**, as he had effectively set up an emotional manipulation mechanism with me that I was unable to counter. This allowed him to put forth continued reasons for need for funds, and have me believe him and provide the money by whatever mechanism I could. If I expressed any reluctance, I was badgered until I agreed. Those reasons were increasingly of threat and violence and danger towards him, and the urgency of getting him out of Dubai.

The fraud was not only that he was in need, but that **he was going to pay the money back**. I strongly believed that he would. This 'justification' to myself became so strong, such an ingrained belief, that I even put this forward to the ATO as a reason to explain my access to money in the fund well after the activity of the scammer had ceased.

Any belief in or expectation of the return of money was **a foundation of the fraud** and was not true. In using this rationalisation to the ATO as a justification, shows that I was still caught in the thrall and justification of the fraud to some degree. In hindsight, now I understand the full extent fraud, it was never reasonable or rational to expect the money to be returned. Having the belief that it would be returned meant that I was **not in effective control of any balanced or well-judged response** to any of his demands for money, which would have been to refuse to pay any money, and to refuse to take the money from my SMSF.

Detective Superintendent Brian Hay, of the Queensland Police states in the attached Insight transcript,
"Because I've spoken to so many victims, intelligent articulate people that have led immaculate lives, made good judgments, good decisions, and all of a sudden you think well how could they make a decision? Why could they not see the obvious? But their vulnerability at that point in their life means they wanted hope. We go out and buy - how many, how many of us go and buy a Lotto ticket for a big jackpot coming up because we live in hope."
And further:

"Look, we are all vulnerable - no one is excluded from that statement. If you are approached with the right story at the right time in your life, you may very well fall victim to a scam."

If the fraud had taken place purely in Australia, there may be the opportunity to locate the perpetrator and prosecute them. In that context I would be clearly seen as the victim of the crime, and may have been able to demand recompense in some way, or even have the funds located and returned as a victim in WA has recently done with the support of her State police (Project Sunbird). The international nature of the crime, the use of Internet technology and my residency in Victoria made this path to justice virtually impossible and left me feeling helpless and unable to be helped.

I exhibited due diligence when in effective control
Once the perpetrator broke off contact, and the scam was revealed, I reported the matter to the police. Only later did I realise the deep-seated nature of the fraud.
Understanding that I had taken money from the SMSF when I shouldn't have, I reported the matter to the ATO. I have followed all direction and been compliant with undertakings required of me and have wound up the fund.

In self-reporting, I believe I have exhibited due diligence in my administration of the fund as required by law. I have not sought to cover it up, or delayed any discovery of my actions, and have been up front about what has occurred to have me act in this way. This is consistent with my normal demeanour, which is reasoned, well managed, serious and considered.

This self-reporting activity is in contrast to the inappropriate access to the funds, showing again that when I did take the funds I was a victim of this fraud and I was not in effective control.

Consideration of the financial and emotional impact on me
As a victim of a fraud, to insist that the accessed funds be included in my assessable income for that year (2013) and be taxed at the top rate is in effect a significant fine, **an emotional and financial punishment for being an unwitting victim.**

This is very unbalanced, given there is no opportunity to address and redress the fraudulent actions of the perpetrator. For this reason I ask for the Commissioner's discretion to be exercised to exclude the superannuation benefits from my assessable income.

Survivor

There is repeated comment in the Reasons for Decision about the need to maintain moneys for the purpose of being available in retirement. Does this not go both ways, and be morally if not legally a consideration for the Commissioner? Hence I ask for discretion to be applied.

I am already 60, and now have a reduced timeframe and capacity to rebuild any retirement income. Yet this decision would create further burden that would exponentially hinder any chance of this, and make certain that I would not have any personal retirement income, and be solely reliant on the Aged Pension.

Again, quoting **Detective Superintendent Brian Hay,** who has seen many instances of this fraud and its impact on victims, "If you get people that have lost their superannuation savings and they have nothing left, now they're on the public welfare system. They once had private health cover, now they're on the public health system."

The financial burden on me would include (not exclusively)
  i. Progressive payment of the tax bill of approximately $75,000, plus interest at the ATO general interest charge rate, over a future period that could not reasonably be done on my current income/expenses within my working life on top of normal living expenses, even though I have recently moved to reduce my rental payment.
  ii. Additional expenses as a result of being in a higher tax bracket, such as Medicare expenses.
  iii. Inability to pay down my current fraud instigated credit card debt due to paying the tax bill, causing additional interest expenses to be paid over an extended time (prior to being scammed I was able to pay off my card every month and have statements to prove this).
  iv. The potential that additional expenses will be put onto the credit card because I no longer have savings to buffer any additional unexpected expenses, without any expectation of ever being able to clear the card, especially once on the aged pension.
  v. Entering retirement with no financial resources and a negative financial position, ensuring a life of poverty as I age.

The current and future financial burden would be excessive and directly impact my retirement income as well as the Australian taxpayers of the future. Hence I request the Commissioner to exercise discretion.

To not have the funds included in my assessable income, in contrast, would allow me to
    i. Pay off my current personal debt, over a reasonable time
    ii. Put more money into superannuation and partially rebuild my retirement income, even though it would be significantly reduced.
    iii. Not be plunged into poverty on retirement.

In WA and QLD, the Fraud Police operate by looking at the money going out of the country, and contacting those who are sending it and warning of the fraud. In WA this stops money going out of the country 60% of the time. If I had been resident in WA or QLD, the Fraud Police in that state may have intervened early in my FRAUD, preventing funds being taken from my SMSF, and this situation arising. As such the 'punishment' of the additional tax burden appears at the whim of my state of residency, compounding my experience of inequity. Hence, I request the Commissioner to exercise discretion.

Action Requested
1. That in the light of the facts already raised, and highlighted above the objection to the private ruling be allowed, and
2. That the Commissioner, in consideration of these matters exercise discretion to exclude the superannuation benefits from my assessable income for the 2013 income year.

I submitted the objection to the ATO on May 23rd, 2014, and included for reference as well as the ATO related documents:

- Queensland Police Bulletin 347 on Internet Romance Scams
- Project Sunbird Factsheet, from WA
- Transcript of the SBS Insight program.

Done!

One of my girlfriends added some insight about shame as she read an early draft.

> "You have done so well with this! I think pars 11 and 12 are great too, because the point about shame is a strong one. ... (Brené Brown's research reveals that Shame needs 3

things; secrecy, silence and judgement, all of which were driving the isolation you felt and contributing to the difficulty that we had in reaching out to you.) And the quotes that you've now included from the Qld police are spot on"

In writing this objection, I had obtained further understanding for and of myself.

I now owned what had happened. I had been professionally defrauded and abused, not just made a mistaken response to a 'trick'. I did not any longer have to believe it had been my fault, or that I should be ashamed of my actions. I further understood why I had not been able to extract myself from the ongoing circumstances of the scam. I had been in a deliberately set up 'altered state'. I had colluded with both of these, but the scam included manipulation of me to secure my collusion. I realised that regardless of the results, and I had no idea what they would be, it had been worthwhile for me to undertake this action and write the objection myself.
I was now a **survivor**, not a victim of an internet romance scam.
I wasn't sure what response I would get. It felt like it did not matter, however there was still the tax money to deal with.
The response came through on July 17th, 2014. They did not allow the objection. The main arguments, extracted from the document so starting at Point 29, were as follows:

29. The above AAT decisions found in all cases that the superannuation benefit did not arise in circumstances beyond 'effective control of the recipient' and that the taxpayers should have been aware that the release of benefits was outside the fund rules.
30. It is also clear from these judgements that there are expected standards of a trustee when making decisions concering Fund assets. This is supported in the trustee covenants under section 52 of the SISA. Paragraphs 52(2)(b) and (c) of the SISA specifically state that the trustee of a superannuation fund is:
  a. to exercise, in relation to all matters affecting the entity, the same degree of care, skill and diligence as an ordinary prudent person would exercise in dealing with property of another for whom the person felt morally bound to provide
  b. to ensure that the trustee's duties and powers are

performed and exercised in the best interests of the beneficiaries.
31. It is considered that a prudent trustee exercising their duties and powers in the best interests of the fund would:
    - ensure they were knowledgeable of the SISA payment and investment standards
    - seek professional advice when making investments or paying benefits from the Fund
    - conduct due diligence on any proposed 'loan arrangements'
    - ensure any loans are conducted on commercial terms, including written agreements, application of interest, regular payments and sufficient security.
32. The Commissioner does not dispute that you were defrauded by the internet scammer and that you made some serious errors in judgement due to your belief in the scammer. However, in this particular circumstance it is difficult to conclude, without a certified medical opinion, that you were not in effective control of your decision making due to emotional and/or psychological disability. There is also no precedent case law to support exercising discretion for similar circumstances.
33. Based on the available information and despite your emotional attachment to the scammer, albeit through an 'emotional manipulation mechanism', a person of your standing and knowledge would have been fully aware that taking money from the Fund was not in accordance with the SISA payment or investment standards. The decision to make the payments to the scammer was not beyond your control as:
    - you had a choice to make the payment or not
    - the decision was made by you and you controlled the Fund
    - you kew the payment would breach the payment or investment standards, and
    - you failed to conduct the minimum due diligence requirements of the transactions.
34. Overall, you have not exercised your duties and powers in the best interests of the Fund. This resulted in the Fund contravening sections 31, 34 and 62 of the SISA and you as member receiving superannuation benefits outside the payment standards. Your circumstance is not sufficient for the Commissioner to exercise discretion in accordance with subsection 3-4-10(4) of the ITAA 1997.

I summarise it to notify my close friends and family, at least the ones I did not talk to regularly:

> I received notification last night that my objection to the ATO to having to pay tax on the money I took from my super fund has been disallowed. Whilst the response showed much more understanding of the circumstances, they basically said that without verifying medical evidence that I was not able to make a decision, they could not accept this as there was no precedent. And also that as the fund trustee it was ultimately my responsibility to preserve all funds for future use.
> I will now put my tax return in, and will have to negotiate with the tax office about a payment plan.
> In the meantime, I am comfortable, have a good job, and life goes on.
> Many thanks for your support over this difficult journey.

Responses come back quickly:

> Thanks for letting us know. It has been an honour to support you.
> I bless the holistic viewpoint you have been able to create around this.
> I also have a payment plan on tax, I set it low as the interest rate is much lower than credit card interest. It's between 9 and 10 per cent.
> Much love to you,

And:

> Ditto!!
> You know that you have done everything you could and this is now clean and clear. You are moving onwards and upwards!

And another:

> Thanks for letting me know.
> I am sad and disappointed for you. Just one more question: Would there be any chance to get a medical certificate now?????? How about that psychologist you went to at work? Any chance at all? You have gone that far and now they have given you some information that might be

helpful?..
I also understand if you want to put it behind and move on with your life...
We all have to deal with what life throws at us, surrender, accept and find ways to move on. Hopefully enlightened ways.....

From a family member:

So sorry this happened. You will always have my love & support, & really admire the attitude you have taken in the light of this decision.

And other friends:

I'm speechless. It is so difficult for me to accept this decision of theirs.
I feel your strength in your words. If you want to talk, I'm home this evening.
Gosh - good on you for giving it another go
I am glad you are focussing on all the wonderful things you have in your world including good health, friends that love you and a good job with heaps of opportunity
No precedent.
You were subjected to fraud. I wonder how long it will be before someone sets a precedent about this situation. You made your decision based on false information. I feel sad this has happened to you. :(
Wish I could help more, but yes you do have a good job, you are safe and comfy, a fluffy catster loves you and life goes on!

As one friend identified, there was one last possibility mooted in the ATO decision, to try and create a precedent by getting medical evidence that I was not in effective control, but I am undecided about this. I write to my lawyer and accountant:

Hi, please find attached the response to my Objection which I received on Thursday, for your files.

I am satisfied with the process to date - putting in the objection, and the response in this decision, was in a way therapeutic for me to come to terms with what happened.

I may explore the possibility of getting some medical confirmation of my situation - that seems the only opening remaining at this stage, though it seems a long shot. I will keep you in the loop if I do that, but if you hear nothing it means I have not taken the matter further and will take this decision as final.

I do some research and find that the term 'medico-legal' covers those who are writing such reports for the courts. I do put out for an expression of interest and costs from such a specialist on my circumstances and get back:

I was sorry to hear of your predicament.
Do you have a lawyer acting for you.
Our office acts on the request of the lawyer on your behalf. We could meet your timelines and cost is likely to be around $2500 +GST (which includes time for assessment of yourself in person, reading the documents and compiling a report)

Whilst I am thinking about whether to proceed with this, circumstances at work overtake me, and I do not proceed. In late August, 2014 I was retrenched from my job (more on that later).
I am left with the fact that I have to pay tax on the amount of money taken from my SMSF, at 46.5%. In effect I have been fined for my wrong-doing.
At no point in the interchanges with the ATO was there any recognition of the financial impact of this on me, even though it had been mentioned in my submissions multiple times.
So, all the burden was on me. In their mind all the fault was on me. If there was an impact of paying this tax on my future, even if it cost the government, they did not care. There was, as I expected, no compassion from them. And what I expected from the use of the term discretion, the ability to show compassion in certain circumstances, was legally proscribed from my situation.

Recovery Begins

Over the year of responding to the ATO, I continued to review the information online about romance scams. I was surprised to find, when I began to look at the medico-legal practitioners, that there was some research into the topic, done in the U.K.

This excellent report details research and I include the Executive Summary below to whet your appetite. I commend it for a full reading.

Whitty, M. T., & Buchanan, T. (2012). 'The Psychology of the Online Dating Romance Scam Report.'
University of Leicester.

Executive Summary
- This report summarises a year-long project, led by Professor Whitty, which examined the online dating romance scam. The three main aims of the project were to: identify psychological characteristics of individuals which raise their risk of becoming victims; examine the persuasive techniques employed to scam victims of the online dating romance scam; examine the psychological consequences of being a victim of the online dating romance scam.
- Drawing from the qualitative work conducted in the project a summary of the anatomy of the scam is made.
- Study 1 considered the types of people more at risk of this scam. The only finding was that those high in romantic beliefs were more likely to be victims, in particular those who have a high tendency toward idealisation of romantic partners. Contrary to statistics gained on the reporting of this crime, middle-aged women were not more likely to be victims of this crime.
- Study 2 examined the three main objectives of the project. This study examined 200 posts on a public online peer support group. Some victims wrote they had previous abusive relationships. The fake profile contained stereotypical characteristics that men and women look for in a potential mate. Through the use

of ICTs 'hyperpersonal relationships' were developed. The 'Scammers Persuasive Techniques Model' is developed here to explain the success of these scams. A range of psychological impacts is also reported.
- Study 3 examined the three main objectives of the project. In-depth interviews were conducted with 20 victims. Most of the women had experienced a highly abusive relationship earlier in their lives. Some of the men reported a history of mental health problems. Further support was found for the 'Scammers Persuasive Techniques Model'. In addition, it was found that victims were also drawn in because of the 'unconditional positive regard' displayed by the criminal. Victims experienced a double hit from the loss of monies and the loss of a relationship. Victims found it very difficult to let go of the relationship and visualise that it was not real even when they believed they had been scammed. Victims went through the stages of grieving after learning they had been scammed and those in denial were vulnerable to a second wave of the scam.
- This report concludes by providing advice to online dating companies, law enforcement, policy makers and health professionals. Online dating companies need to make information about the scam visible on their sites. Others need to be aware that victims are vulnerable and special care needs to be taken when the news is broken to victims."

This site has a good bibliography of the topic and useful resources, as well as presentations given by Monica Whitty on the topic over 2011/12:

http://www2.le.ac.uk/departments/media/people/monica-whitty/online-dating-romance-scam-project

At some stage during the next year I had a realisation. I had been dreaming, fantasising about winning the lottery, which I would then use to build a house suited to the needs of my disabled mother, to get her out of the aged care situation in which she lived, and organise carers to take care of her individually.

It came to me that this was very similar to what had happened with the scammer. I would use money to 'rescue' someone I loved, over and above my own needs. I realised that this was inherently my nature, was how I expressed my love.

I was doing what I always did with loved ones. It was nothing to be ashamed of.

Realising this allowed me to come to terms with another layer of what had happened to me.

My Emotional State

Through much of 2013 I was withdrawn and depressed. I put on weight, eventually weighing in at one hundred kilos. If I had not had my cat, as another living being to take care of, who knows what I would have done.

Family and friends were supportive of me, but it still felt like there was a cloak hanging over me. Whilst I took responsibility for what had happened, I did not like myself for doing it and did not go looking for friends because I did not think others would like me either. I was definitely not outgoing during this period.

After writing the objection, I was able to be more forgiving with myself, and during 2014 began to go out again, doing some courses with Adult Education and attending a gym for regular exercise.

Early in 2014 I also came to the emotional place where I was able to act on the realisation that, even with the good job I had and the removal of discretionary spending that I had already done, I needed to do further financial 'downsizing' and find somewhere cheaper to live. This would help me pay down my credit card debt faster.

I moved several suburbs further away from the city in Easter 2014, reducing my rent by about a quarter. It was into a new but snug apartment, with its own courtyard, one bedroom and a study. Both my brothers came to help me move and it all went smoothly.

As you know, I even went onto online dating again, and started going out with a man. However, after a few weeks of going out he declared that he was distressed about my financial situation, and could not see how we could be together in a

comfortable financial way as he would lose some of his pension if we lived together, so he called it off.
After that I did not look for anyone again.

On Sex

As part of my ongoing research, I came across a blog on recovery from being scammed. A blog discussion about cybersex hit home with me.

I was shocked to read:

"You Believe You Had Cybersex with the Scammer
...
The most important thing to remember about cybersex, or even intense flirting or playful, joking banter, flashing, or sending suggestive links, is that any type of sexual teasing, seemingly sexy flirting, or cybersex engaged in during the scam was not a form of online sex or flirting, but a form of online sexual assault or harassment. You never consented to the sexual talk or activity because you never consented to that type of talk or activity with the person you were actually talking to. Tricking someone into sexual talk or activity they would not want is a form of sexual abuse. The scammer did not seduce you, they abused you. This may be difficult to remember, but it is important to keep in mind when embarrassment, guilt, or fear creeps into your mind."

http://scamsoftheheart.blogspot.com.au/2014/02/sex-and-scams.html

I was shocked because I had not viewed it that way, but had still considered it an act of intimacy. For me, at the time, it was a form of consummation of our impending marriage.

I had been a willing participant.

When I saw it written like this I realised it was abuse. I did not consent to the intimacy with the scammer. I have not told anyone before now that I was afraid that some of that activity might have been recorded and then be published on the internet. I have not even told friends explicitly about this activity either.

I had heard of someone else whose videos were published on the web, with their name, to devastating effect.

I just hoped and prayed that it would not happen to me. It did not, at least that I know of.

Retrenchment

Initially the retrenchment from my job in late August 2014 was a shock. My skill area was one that had been growing in my company and I had not seen it coming. I had been sensing that something was wrong for a couple of weeks prior to this announcement though.

I was conscious of a sense that I was being assessed and being found wanting. This was so strong that I became very anxious about it and even went to my doctor, who prescribed some anti-depressants and referred me to a psychologist who worked in his practice.

When I was retrenched I realised that my sense was, in fact, correct, that I had been intuitively picking up on something that had been happening, though I did not know it at the time.

I had not experienced retrenchment before, and expressed to the people retrenching me that I did not have any resilience left to deal with it. It had taken so much out of me to deal with the aftereffects of the scam, that I did not believe I had any inner resources left to deal with the retrenchment. They would not have known the reason why I said this though, as it was not public at that time.

My way of dealing with the retrenchment was to contact the support agency engaged as part of the retrenchment package to help me. Initially I felt too overwhelmed to even consider it, but was able to pull myself together and think of my future. I contacted them the next day, and the counselling, training and support they provided over the next few months was critical to maintaining my balance and looking forward in my life.

Over time, I have come to see the retrenchment as a gift. Part of that gift was money, a pay-out which at least initially meant I could manage financially.

Having already planned a holiday to do a watercolour painting course in North Western Victoria as part of the Grampian

Brushes program, I decided to go ahead and do it. This allowed me to not focus on having to find work, to take a break, and to explore my creativity, for a few weeks at least.

Whilst after this I did all the right things to find more work, it did not come. Despite having many years of experience, I did not even get interviews for jobs that I should have been a prime candidate for. In truth, when I looked deeper inside myself, I did not want the work.

In the space provided and supported by my retrenchment money, I wrote Part 2 of this book, with the intent of finding a publisher for it and to begin public speaking about this topic.

As I now had less specific time commitments, apart from volunteering in order to receive unemployment support money from the Newstart Program, I also started to do some online coaching programs.

Feminine Power Mastery, a twelve-month program, encouraged taking on a project which, "speaks to your inner yearning, creates the structure of accountability that's critical to manifesting the biggest things in our lives, as it creates the conditions to show up in big ways." I took "showing up in big ways" to heart. I knew I needed to generate more than just my book, that I needed to connect with others as well.

From this space I decided to set up a support group for people who had been scammed.

I knew, from my professional study and career as a social worker earlier in my life, that I could manage a group interaction appropriately. I knew the power of sharing one's story and having it heard by others is often transforming in its own right.

So, in January 2015 I went onto Meetup and set one up. Meetup is great. It links similar types of meetings together, and publicises new meetups so anyone interested can join.

https://www.meetup.com/

I put up the notification on January 1st, and a week later I had twenty-five people joined up. That month I ran three meetings with six to eight people, men and women, young and old. The stories were many and varied. Some lost a little money, some lost a lot, but the financial impact of that loss was always comparative to the person's financial situation, and their ability to recover.

Some stories were of straight romance scams, whilst others were of legacy, or gold enticements. One woman did not know she was being scammed and was contacted by the WA police (Project Sunbird) because she was sending money to a bank known to be used by scammers. Many of these victims were professional people, or office workers, or artists. They brought evidence of their own stories and their research to the meetings to help others.

Within a week I was contacted by ABC Local Radio, and invited to do a story and an interview with them. I had thought that I would do this under an assumed name, to protect myself, but found that I was using my name.

This was the crunch point. Would I 'go public' about what had happened? Very quickly I realised that this was the easiest way to proceed. Out of this connection a story was posted online,[1] and that evening, 6th January 2015, I was part of a panel discussion on ABC Local Radio with George McEncroe, being broadcast nationally.[2] Other people on the panel included a psychologist, Sue Malta, and a specialist on scams, Nick Johnson.[3]

This was to be the start of a big year, a survivor year, that included radio, television, newspaper and magazine press, and a series of speaking engagements across my local library network. I set up a website called Romance Scam Survivor, and began blogging regularly on the topic of Romance Scams. That big year also included not finding a publisher for my book, totally running out of money and having to move again in desperation. Towards the end of the year I was offered change management work and began to work again.

But all that is rushing ahead.

---

[1] http://www.abc.net.au/news/2015-01-07/support-group-for-online-dating-fraud-survivors/6004208

[2] Show: *"Summer with George McEncroe"*(national ABC Local Radio program, analogue, digital, online and via ABC Radio app) 7 - 10 PM Australian Eastern Summer Time.

[3] Nicholas J. Johnson, The "*Honest Conman*", comedian and scam enthusiast. Has travelled the world researching different scams and swindles. http://www.abc.net.au/local/stories/2014/07/07/4040707.htm
Sue Malta, PhD, Research Fellow, Health Promotion Division, Adjunct Research Fellow, Swinburne University. http://nari.unimelb.edu.au/

My Survivor Year

From that Meetup group posted on January 1st, 2015, and the online news piece that followed within the week, many more inquiries came. On 22nd January I did a piece with television show 'A Current Affair'(ACA). They spent several hours interviewing and filming, then cut it down to about four minutes.

What was most illuminating, with the story posted on Facebook,[4] was the type and nature of comments that this generated. This was my first experience of the direct negativity towards myself, in the comments about the story. Whilst some comments were supportive, many were negative, blaming, and even personally offensive.

Someone posted "Only a mother would love this face," referring to the picture that ACA had used of me, which was unflattering, I agree. I have to say that this comment was removed by the site moderator and was not there the next time I looked.

Types of comments included:
- Reports about unsatisfactory dating websites, or even profiles known to be of scammers.
- People saying they too had been scammed because they went online to address loneliness or depression.
- Queries about why people have not taken heed of the many warnings and similar stories about this, "when are they going to learn?"
- Boredom or frustration with same or similar stories being recycled or repeated.
- Understanding of what it took for me to say what had happened, to warn others, and calls for compassion and understanding for my situation.
- People not understanding how I could part with $250,000, calling me gullible, stupid, naïve, more money than brains, sad, total desperate dipshits, silly, and many more like this.

---

[4] https://www.facebook.com/ACurrentAffair9/photos/a.133294666776919.22143.129086560531063/658065337633180/?type=1&theater

- Men saying don't trust women, they are only after your money, or others wishing the money had been given to them.
- Links to other sites such as a Blogspot on scams.[5]
- Direct blame for what happened, with comments such as, "it's your own fault, you get no sympathy for me, shame, fancy telling everyone."
- And more on similar themes to those above.

Though I can no longer locate the video, the ACA story is still there on Facebook if you wish to review for yourself. Luckily, I have a tough skin and did not take it personally. It just shows their lack of understanding, the need to push it away from themselves and to proclaim covertly that it would never happen to them.

The following month, timed to coincide with Valentine's Day, I was invited by Consumer Affairs Victoria to do a 'My Story' feature for their website, warning about scams. This was covered in the Channel 9 News. You will find links to these and all other press activity on the Media Presence[6] page of my blog 'Romance Scam Survivor'[7].

I created my blog (http://romancescamsurvivor.org) in February 2015, taking the jump to buy websites and WordPress, and teaching myself as I went, after first reading 'Blogging for Dummies'.

My first real blog was in March, starting at the beginning about how I came to get scammed. I added MailChimp, and sent out regular notifications to a growing list of those interested and to friends, and posted links on Facebook, LinkedIn and later Twitter.

This meant that another layer of friends, including colleagues from my old job in Brisbane, came to know about what had happened to me. It also drew from them a number of contacts who wanted to find out more and express horror at what had happened. All of these approaches were supportive in nature. In March I was contacted by people doing media campaigns

---

[5] http://agustinetutut.blogspot.com.au/

[6] http://romancescamsurvivor.org/media-presence/ Items listed by month, with most recent at the top.

[7] http://romancescamsurvivor.org/ See also pages on Support for victims, Research, and Victim's stories.

for the Australian Cybercrime Online Reporting Network (ACORN), asking if I would be willing to speak on behalf of victims.

In those early days it was thought that I may have to go to Canberra to be part of campaign launches with the Minister for Justice, Michael Keenan, but this did not happen. Nonetheless I was proclaimed an Ambassador for ACORN, which meant I was on their list of people who could be contacted by the press. This led to many other press approaches from this source, and these still occur to this day. I was given a logo which I use in my email signature and on my website.

The month of May included International Fraud Awareness Week, which triggered interviews for articles in newspapers The Age and the Daily Mail, the latter reprinted in Nigeria.

Other media activities this and the following year, where I was the primary person the media was about, or was mentioned, included (see my blog page Media Presence for links):

- Newspaper Articles
    - Herald Sun expose, 4th July 2015.
    - Daily Mail, response to Starts at 60 rebuttal (see below), 30th August 15.
    - Geelong Advertiser, 16th September 2015.
    - Huffington Post Australia, 12th October 2015.
    - Sydney Morning Herald, 12th February 2016.
- Television
    - Channel 9's Morning Program, with Facebook Link, 14th July 2015.
    - Channel 7 News story, 12th February 2016.
- Magazine Story.
    - Take 5 Magazine, 30th July 2015.
- Podcast
    - RMIT Journalism Student Project, 11th August 2015.
    - Scamapalooza, by Nick Johnson, who had been with me on the panel on that first ABC Local Radio forum, a fifty-four-minute interview, February 16th.
- Website Contributing Blog

> o Starts at 60 guest contributor, 20th August 15, and then rebuttal comment.

I have taken the stance of accepting most requests from the media, to spread the word about the dangers, even though at times my story was sensationalised in order to warn others.
Personally, I found that telling my story, explaining what and why it had happened, gave me back some self-respect, and allowed me to bear witness to the error in judgement I had made.
I received no recompense financially from most of these, with only the Take 5 Magazine providing a modest recompense for my story. Some of the people commenting on my various stories seem to think I would have been getting huge sums of money for my efforts.
By the time I provided my contribution to the Starts at 60 website, I had been blogging for half a year, writing on a fortnightly basis, and covering many aspects of the experience of and recovery from scams.

Guest Contributor

After an incident free move from Brisbane, and starting my new job, I settled into my new abode in Melbourne. I knew Victoria was diverse, beautiful and worth exploring, so went online to a dating site looking for a companion to do this with. I had not done any online dating before, but felt ready to give it a go. I wasn't expecting to fall in love.

Surprisingly the first person to contact me was not local, but a good looking grey-haired engineer from America, but with an English home base. I wrote back asking, "Did you know I am in Australia?" He answered that he would go anywhere for the right person.

And so it began. It was not till contact was finally broken, 72 days later, that I realised I had been scammed, and that I would not get the over $260,000 that I had sent him back. He had promised, often, that I would get it back once he had managed to get out of Dubai and back to England. He had even shown me bank statements showing he had the money, knowing I might not believe him.

He made me feel so special, that the love that we had together was destined, magical and forever. The early questioning of likes and dislikes I had thought was just getting to know each other. At least he was a man who was interested, wanting to commit, and able to communicate, I thought. When he sent me a YouTube link to 'Bless the Broken Road' by Rascal Flatts, I thought this was his experience, and it mirrored mine. We progressed from online chats, to talking on the phone, eventually to video chats. We spent hours trying to get the settings correct, but his video just didn't work. He could see me but I could not see him.

We talked late at night, we talked in the early morning. He loved me to call him as I left for work, like the kiss of your loved one as you go out the door. By the time he took a contract fixing pipelines in Dubai, from where he was going to come on to Australia to see me, I wanted this to be forever, and I suspected he did too. I was deeply and totally in love with this beautiful man, even though I had never met him. When he finally 'popped the question' my answer was immediate and without hesitation. Yes, I would marry him.

In hindsight this was to him the verification that he had me truly under his spell, and so the requests for money started. Initially it was for tax he needed to pay in Dubai. He could not access his own funds in England as his bank account was on hold. I decided I would help him, just once I thought, out of love, and sent money. I wanted to be a full partner in this relationship. The requests for help kept coming though, for materials he needed for building; and some weeks later after threats of violence and jail, more tax.

"Was he real?" I demanded of him. "How could I imagine he wasn't", he argued back, righteously. By this time I was borrowing money, on a current and a new credit card.

Then he was bashed and robbed of the tax money on his way to pay it. I wouldn't want to know him he said, but of course I did. I took money out of my SMSF and sent it to him again. He was by now not working and needed to pay back his employers or else he would not be able to leave Dubai. I took more money out of my SMSF to send him. I wondered if it was all a scam, but what we had between us seemed too personal, too intimate.

Finally he had paid enough and could leave Dubai, and soon I would get my money back. I waited through the night for his message that he was boarding his plane but there was nothing. The next day there was a call from a 'nurse' in a hospital saying he had been in a car accident, and he had asked her to call me. As next of kin, a doctor calls me, asking for his bill to be paid so he could be released. I talked to the British embassy, who said it was a scam. I could not believe it even then and sent the very last of my money. Out of hospital he now needed more money for replacement air tickets and his accommodation, so I sent my just received pay.

Truly, now, I had no more to send... and finally he got on a plane.

"Boarding the plane my love....
I love you sooo much and thanks for everything".

Over the coming days, with no more contact, I finally understood... it WAS a scam and I would never get my money back.

People ask, "How could you give money to someone you have never met..?" But in my mind he was the love of my life. I did not know that it had all the hallmarks of a romance scam.

I know NOW that I was groomed by a skilled and professional fraudster, and that it was not personal, it was not about me. Their intent is to break down their victim's defences by exhaustion, social isolation and an overwhelming amount of attention.

The love hormone oxytocin helped me to trust him. He deliberately and successfully manipulated my emotions to get my money.

When online dating or even on other group or social media sites where you may be contacted by strangers, be aware of the potential for scams. It can happen to anyone. Early attempts to build intimacy are a red flag, as are contacts through the night.

It was interesting again to see the comments that were posted to my article, many of which echoed those from the A Current Affair Facebook post about my story as described above.
I felt compelled to write a response, included as a comment, and then posted on my own blog, calling it Right of Reply as follows:

I recently wrote a blog about my scam experience which was posted on the **Starts at Sixty** website, which I have recently joined. As with previous publications by me or others, there were many comments questioning "how could she be so stupid?", "hasn't she seen the warnings?", "why doesn't she join a club?", etc. There were also positive and supportive comments, but I felt moved to provide a 'Right of Reply' comment addressing the negative ones. The following is copied from my comment (Comment No 199) on Starts at sixty. I don't know if it will be read by those who commented on the blog, but thought it was worth reposting here.

Firstly thank you to all of you who were supportive, or understanding of my situation. Sorry for those who have suffered in a similar way, or who have friends/family who have.

Secondly, I don't appreciate being called stupid. You would not call someone who was burgled stupid, and we have learnt not to call someone who was raped stupid. Please remember that I was caught by professional fraudsters who emotionally manipulated me into sending money. If you want to know more about how this works, check out my blog, especially the one on Taking the Brain. http://romancescamsurvivor.org/2015/07/taking-the-brain/
How about calling the fraudsters criminals instead.

Many comments were about being lonely, and why not get a pet. I do have a cat, thank you, and he was certainly a god-send through the difficult times after the scam. I did not do this because I was lonely, having been alone for many years. However I did want companionship, and I was certainly vulnerable to someone's loving attention. These are not the same. I had not seen previous warnings because I had never thought I would need them, never considered going onto a dating site.

All those news programs and warnings you have seen this year most
likely have had me in them. There are not many people willing to speak out about what has happened, but I am, so I have been in the press quite a bit – sorry if its getting a bit tedious for you. The latest figures show that romance scam is still the largest area of money lost to all types of scams, about $27 million across Australia last year. There is still a need to put warnings out there.

How could I give money to someone I had not met? In my mind at the time this was the person I was most intimate with, not a stranger. I was speaking to him many times a day. We had agreed to marry. Would you not help out your life partner if they were in need?

Why do I speak out? Because I will not let the shame of what happened shut me down and not be truthful about what happened. I know those calling me stupid, or sad, want me to do that, feel shame and shut up. I will not. Talking out lets me regain my self respect because I am truthful about what happened. This story is an authentic representation of what happened to me and I now know it is nothing to be ashamed of. Yes I made a mistake and did not see the red flags. I lost a lot of money as a consequence that I could not afford to lose. I still have not recovered from this loss, and maybe never will. I was caught and manipulated by expert and skilled fraudsters.

I will not be put under a rock because of this. I have learned lessons from this that in speaking out I hope to pass on. I have moved from being a victim to a survivor. I will continue to speak out, educate others and stand up for those who have unwittingly become victims of these professional fraudsters...   as I did.

Enough said!

This blog was picked up by the Daily Mail, in another article from them.
I found blogging fortnightly very therapeutic, and was able to delve into various aspects of the experience of being scammed, and of recovery from being scammed. I would combine some research into the topic with reference to my own situation and understanding. I liked finding and adding photos to break up the text as well.
In particular, I found the exploration of shame very illuminating, including research into the work of Brené Brown. I also found a great article by Nicholas de Castella on the topic. This greatly encouraged me to continue to speak out, knowing that this breaks the shame cycle. In doing this, I hoped to encourage others to do so.
A key blog I wrote is called 'Taking the Brain', referring to an article I found which had interviewed an ex-scammer who described the process from the scammer's point of view. This describes how scammers manipulate you to fall in love, knowing that when you do, they have 'taken [control of] the brain'.
I set out to do some public speaking on the topic, and in late June did my first formal speaking engagement. It was with the Watsonia Probus Group, and unpaid because it was my first. I had done many presentations in my work, and like public

speaking, so was happy to do this, with slides to guide the presentation and a give-away on types of scams.

As part of my Newstart Activity requirement in order to get unemployment money during this year, I was required to do fifteen hours a week of volunteering.

I wanted to do some work teaching seniors how to use iPads, and when I met with someone from the regional library network for my area, mentioned my speaking about being scammed. She offered me to speak across the nine libraries in the network for the upcoming Seniors month. This was duly quoted, booked and I did nine speaking engagements across October 2015.

In these speaking engagements, though not to huge audiences, I felt clear, in my element, and believe I spoke well and engagingly about the topic. This was a true expression of who I was at this time. I could truly claim to be a survivor. I gained a lot of satisfaction in doing those talks.

As a result of the Meetup group and the media coverage and my blog, I would regularly get contacts from people who had just realised they had been scammed, or from someone who had a family member or friend who they believed was being scammed. These would come through by email, and either I would respond by email or would have a phone conversation with them about their situation.

Many who had been scammed were in dire circumstances, having lost money and having to adapt to a different, and generally lesser, financial expectation for their future without this money. People had to sell houses or other goods to get by. I would make time to talk with them, knowing that there were few people they could talk to who would fully understand what they had gone through. I was able to talk the truth about the situation, help them see that they had been a victim of skilled manipulators intent on fraud, and that the love that the scammer had professed was a lie, all done in order to get their money.

For the second group, those calling on behalf of a family member or friend, I felt in a dilemma. I felt that the person contacting me may want me to fix a situation that I did not have authority or capacity to intrude upon.

I knew that people engaged in scams would push away anyone they thought was saying they were in a scam, encouraged by their scammer to do this. I felt that they would not listen to others whilst in the midst of a scam. I also felt that if I did agree to talk to the victim I would be incorrectly creating expectations for the person contacting me that I could bring about a resolution to the situation, when I could not. So I took a stance that I would not call the family member, the scam victim, but was happy to talk to them if the victim themselves made the step of contacting me.

I did give advice to the contact, trying to explain the state of mind of the victim, and what they could possibly do to get through to them. This continues to be a situation where I do not know what works, and advise the contact to not allow the victim to push them away, though this may have costs on the relationship.

It is important that the victim not be made to be wrong, as this can just get their defences up more. I suggest they try and break the contact the victim has with the scammer by taking a holiday or something similar, to get them out of the clutches of the scammer for a while, and hopefully inject some reason into the situation in this gap.

As I add a final word in Dec 2017, the blogging, interviews and contact with family and friends continues on a regular basis, from people from around the world looking for solutions to this problem. From all assessment, romance scamming continues to occur, and huge amounts of money are lost.

On the plus side, there is some evidence of extraditions of perpetrators from South Africa to America and criminals put in jail, but no-where near enough.

Research has been done, and published by Professor Mark Button, and Dr Cassandra Cross, in "**CyberFrauds, Scams and their victims**," Routledge 2017. This not only explores scams and how they work, but also analyses the policing that surrounds this. It is a seminal text on this topic and a must for anyone seriously interested in this topic, both in Australia and internationally.

Part 4: Analysis

Who is Culpable?

In the process of being caught in a scam, whether it is a romance scam or other types of relationship based or active money laundering scams such as inheritance, investment, advance fee or lottery scams, who are the culpable parties? Who bears responsibility for what happens?

This is not just a simple two-way transaction between a scammer and a victim, with no other inputs. The situation and scam process is much more complex. What follows was originally written by me as an essay, but as you will see it is too long for a blog post. It looks at the various parties, and raises questions about levels of involvement.

The Victim

Some of our own culpability, when we are the victim of a scam, lies initially in not knowing the dangers and risks inherent in being online, and so not being able to guard against them.

This is why it is often thought that older people are more vulnerable to scams, because they tend to have less experience of the online world, and therefore a skewed or naive view of its risks and dangers. Maybe it is partly the attitudes of the older generation, who have been trained to be able to pick up on social cues through face to face interactions, and are unable to do this so readily online. There are also manners and mores which have changed with the generations, which may mean that older people act 'politely' and are automatically responsive to approaches, even from strangers, who might contact victims via social media. Whatever the reason, we expose ourselves to risks in how we respond to an initial contact.

Even though looking for love is a natural activity, it involves laying ourselves open to the potential of finding love. It is a stance of vulnerability, openness and trust, though the latter may not be earned.

If we are forewarned, this does not mean we are necessarily forearmed. When submerged in the scam, we are caught in a vortex of emotion and hormones deliberately created by the scammer. We are caught in an altered state, which takes us outside of what we would normally and rationally do.

This emotional state encourages us to bypass our doubt or overlook the discrepancies that might be there, and instead to trust. We are not in control of ourselves, and respond to requests for money as if it is from our lifetime partner. We will do things such as give away our savings, sell items to raise money, take mortgages and loans that perhaps we cannot afford, even steal money from others to pass on to our scammer. We believe the scammer is our loved one, our fiancé, in distress and needing our help.

We will often defend them against friends who might warn us, and believe that someone with whom we have built a strong intimacy, even though we have not seen them in person, could not possibly be scamming us.

Once we realise we have been scammed, and we have moved beyond the initial shock and the grief, we deem ourselves as primarily to blame, and believe we are at error for not seeing through the scam. Many of us conclude that we are faulty human beings because we colluded in the scam by responding to the scammer's manipulations with love and money, even to the detriment of our own financial and physical well-being.

This attitude captures us in a cycle of shame that it is difficult to shake off. These feelings can lead to secrecy, isolation, reduction of self-esteem, lack of self-worth and potentially depression and suicidal thoughts and even actions.

Is it our fault? Maybe some others have some culpability as well.

What/Who Are Those Other Parties?

The Scammer

The next place to look is at the perpetrator, the scammer. From my understanding, they are a professional fraudster, possibly part of a gang, are often of Nigerian or South African origin and possibly, but not always, located there.
Other groups of scammers include Russians, but scammers may be located anywhere in the world and may be part of a dispersed group from these areas to other parts of the world.
From my personal experience, the Nigerian scammers in particular are highly skilled at emotional manipulation, using tried and tested scripts to great effect. A visit to one of the sites that posts scammer profiles and interactions with victims shows the commonality of the stories, and the words used.

As well as emotional manipulation, scammers:

- Steal photos of unsuspecting people.
- Steal identification.
- Set up fake profiles, including fake phone numbers.
- Fake documentation, including passports.
- Hack computers.

As levels of computer sophistication grow, so do the skills of scammers. It is nothing for them to use phone numbers that make them look like they are local to you, though in reality they could be anywhere in the world.
They will always have a logical reason why they are unable to meet with the victim in person. They are highly skilled with internet subterfuge, and have often been known to record cybersex and then use this to blackmail their victims.
Once a victim, you are on their list. Scammers will target you with follow-on or secondary scams, including offers of finding and charging the scammer, getting your money back in return for more money from you.
The primary motivation of the scammer is to get your money. They, in using the scripts, lie and act a character of an ideal lover, business partner or professional with no compunction or conscience. Some say they are possibly psychopathic,

Analysis

lacking any empathy or conscience.

Though the activities that scammers undertake are clearly fraudulent and criminal, the fact that our Australian legal system takes no action against them means that scammers have a free reign in the Australian landscape. They probably know this, and may actively target Australians to take advantage of the lawlessness and lack of consequence in this sphere of criminality.

Scammers are often described as 'dodgy', and not so often described as criminal fraudsters. The 'dodgy' label implies that it is easy to identify them, and also minimises the expectation that legal or police action will be forthcoming against them by say it is "just a little thing".

In reality, scammers are criminal fraudsters in every sense of the phrase. They are fully responsible for their actions and should be held accountable in a criminal justice system.

Unfortunately this is not so easy with the global reach of this crime.

The Websites

Internet dating sites and social media sites sit on a continuum according to how actively they take precautions against scammers.

There are Australian Best Practice Guidelines for Dating Websites available.[8]
These specify that dating websites should:

- Display warning messages about scammers.
- These messages should be prominently displayed.
- Messages should meet industry best practice.
- Sites should ensure that it is easy to report would-be scammers or suspicious activity.

These guidelines focus on education of users and active prevention, but do nothing to address scams that have taken place.

---

[8] https://www.accc.gov.au/publications/best-practice-guidelines-for-dating-websites

Some websites actively take precautions against scammers and test for fake profiles by checking for scammer red flags such as:

- Language.
- Commonly scripted phrases in profiles.
- Known scammer IP addresses.
- Reverse searching on photos to see if they are stolen.

These checking activities are done by the best sites, and not done at all by the poorer quality sites. The consequences are:
- The sites not doing this expose their members to greater risk of becoming a scam victim. Their legal levels of responsibility have not been tested.
- The fact that the better sites do undertake these activities is an acknowledgement, or at least a recognition, of the risks inherent in providing the communication link between two parties. The consequences for their paying members if things go wrong is devastating.
- Those sites at the wrong end of the continuum could be seen as culpable, living off the ill-gotten earnings of providing a platform for scammers to ply their trade with unsuspecting victims.

So where should we draw the line of negligence for companies who take little or no precautions and do not meet the "best practice guidelines"?
Should these be more than guidelines?
What come-back do victims have, and what further, more stringent regulation should be put in place?
Also, why don't more victims take legal action against dating or social media sites? Perhaps one reason is the financial cost of legal action is prohibitive, especially for someone who has been scammed of their money.
With the growing use of social media sites such as Facebook there is increasing pressure on them to moderate the posted content more actively in order to remove unacceptable content. In some countries this is defined by governments. Could and should scamming activities, fake profiles and the like, be included in the moderation of such sites?

Analysis

The Local Police (State-based in Australia)

When we think of criminal fraud, we think of the police, and expect them to be involved. In Australia, reports by victims of fraud to the Australian Cybercrime Online Reporting Network (ACORN) are passed on to state-based local police services, but items reported to ScamWatch are not.

The activities of local police services differ in approach and quality across the different states, but can include at the negative end of the spectrum:

- Refusal to take the matter seriously, including displaying victim blaming attitudes[9].
- Police may not even be willing to make a report, citing that because the victim paid the money, and because the scammer is internationally based, they can do nothing.
- They may actively discourage victims from having any expectation of action by the police or expecting to get any money back.
- If they did want to do something, they may lack the cyber investigation skills necessary to investigate further. Skilled Private Investigators, in comparison, have been able to identify scammers, gangs, and place reports through to international police.

Recently the Minister for Justice, The Hon Michael Keenan MP, announced[10] a new training for financial intelligence analysts, specifically targeting these skills. It is the first time such training has been offered in Australia and identifies the deficiency of skills in this area.

Through lack of action the policing system in Australia has contributed to a climate where scammers know they can ply their trade with impunity in Australia, and they do. In this way

---

[9] See research by Cassandra Cross et al, http://www.crg.aic.gov.au/reports/1617/29-1314-FinalReport.pdf

[10] https://www.ministerjustice.gov.au/Mediareleases/Pages/2017/FirstQuarter/World-first-training-to-create-a-new-breed-of-serious-financial-crime-fighters.aspx

257

the police acquiesce to scammer activity. Hopefully better training will help in the future.

Links to international police such as Interpol and relationships with other national police forces, such as the Nigerian Police force, would help.

After the death of Jetta Jacobs from Western Australia, the WA Police worked with the South African and Nigerian Police to arrest the culprit, which shows it is possible to generate mutually beneficial relationships across countries, even at the state level.

Why is this not done more often, and by all states?

Why does it take a death to instigate the level of contact needed?

The Banks

Any financial agency is required by law to have systems in place to identify and prevent money laundering[11].

Where they have concerns about individual transactions, they should report to AUSTRAC[12] as an incident report. In fact, all major overseas transactions are reported to AUSTRAC.

Money laundering is a common aspect of some scams, where scammers send money to the victim, which the victim is instructed to send the money on to someone else.

Why are our transactions to scammers not identified and flags raised about what we are doing by the banks themselves?

Surely the banks have the capability to identify unusual transactions, especially to suspect countries?

They do it for credit cards, don't they? Perhaps our financial loss could and should be stopped at the source.

The ACCC's 'Scam Disruption Project'[13] mostly successfully alerted potential victims that the money they are sending overseas may be to a scammer.

Financial intelligence is used to identify Australians who are sending funds to countries such as West African nations, then

---

[11] Anti-Money Laundering and Counter-Terrorism Financing Act 2006 (AML/CTF Act)

[12] Australian Transaction Reporting and Analysis Centre, http://www.austrac.gov.au/

[13] https://www.accc.gov.au/consumers/consumer-protection/protecting-yourself-from-scams/scam-disruption-project

contacting and advising them there is a good chance they have been the target of a scam.

I assume they have sourced this detail from the financial institutions directly, or from their reporting to AUSTRAC. Whichever is the case, the information is known!

Cassandra Cross, our leading researcher on this topic, makes the point that this project needs to be broadened out to cover other suspect countries[14]. This project, and the similar Project Sunbird in WA found a sixty to sixty six percent reduction in money transfers over three months, and a reduction in amounts where payments were still being made.

Why is this left up to the ACCC? Are the banks being negligent in the operation of their AML/CFT (Anti-Money Laundering and Counter-Terrorism Financing Act 2006) obligations in not identifying our transactions as being suspicious, and at least asking questions at the source?

Some would say yes! I made two very large overseas telegraphic transfer transactions that were very out of character without a single question being asked.

In hindsight, I am shocked by this. Are the banks watching what goes through credit cards but not through bank accounts?

Are banks enticed by the transfer fees that they are paid, and would thus lose if they identified and stopped potential transactions paid to scammers? In effect are they facilitating scammers through their inaction?

In not identifying and preventing our loss of money at the source, I believe banks are contributing to a culture where scammers can operate with impunity. This is especially the case where money laundering is taking place.

I hope some of these questions will be raised in a Royal Commission into the banks, when this occurs.

Money Transfer Agencies/Agency Operators

Money transfer agencies such as Western Union and MoneyGram make their money from fees for transactions.

---

[14] https://theconversation.com/how-to-tackle-cyber-crime-before-people-even-know-theyre-a-victim-38385

Perhaps they do not want to interrupt this lucrative trade of money transactions sent to scammers. As a response to recent USA investigations, both companies have admitted to facilitating scams through their lack of suitable training and compliance systems and have set up funds to pay money back to victims[15].

I assume these activities are also prevalent in Australia, where agency operators such as Australia Post must be included as a major agency providing a Western Union service.

Despite there being $10,000 limits on transactions, on numerous occasions I was able to transfer multiple times $10,000 on the same day and in the same branch. Unfortunately agencies take no responsibility for their operations, despite being required to meet the requirements of the AML/CTF Act.

Western Union and MoneyGram are already being found culpable overseas for supporting money being transferred to scammers, though not yet in Australia. They would be well aware of known scammers and suspect countries.

It is about time these agencies are assessed for culpability here too.

Regulation Agencies Who Oversee the Banks and Money Transfer Agencies

It is possible to get records from AUSTRAC about our transactions reported to them, via FOI, but this does not include if there has been a Significant Incident Report raised by the bank or reporting agency.

This means we do not know if the banks or agencies are flagging scam activities to them or not. Nonetheless, there is little or no evidence of them taking actions that would protect victims.

AUSTRAC knows about romance scams and how they operate. They even have a New Zealand case study of a romance scam on their website[16], which states that the original transaction of "multiple wire transfers over a matter of days, and wire

---

[15] See Media release from the Federal Trade Commission
MoneyGram pay 18 million to settle FTC charges
MoneyGram admits anti-money laundering and wire fraud violations
[16] http://www.austrac.gov.au/romance-scam

Analysis

transfers to high risk scam jurisdiction," should have raised concerns about a scam. It was only when money laundering became more evident that the bank raised an incident report. Banks are required to self-report their compliance with the AML/CTF Act. Recent insights from this is that many financial organisations are not meeting their requirements very well, if at all, and are 'lip-synching' the act[17].

The question arises, does the regulation agency have the required systems and processes to do the job, and the teeth required to police the legislation, or is it just a reporting entity?

Or, are they only concerned about commercial entities, and not about the impact on individuals, even though collectively the amounts of money lost are staggering.

AUSTRAC seems a toothless tiger, and in being so, and not using its systems to encourage or force the banks and money transfer agencies to prevent money being sent to scammers, allows scammers to continue unrestrained and unfettered.

Governments

Federal

In government eyes, romance and similar scams come under the heading of Cybercrime, and are just one of many types of scams currently being perpetrated in Australia. Responsibility resides in the Attorney General's Department, which includes Cybercrime and Fraud Control.

In the National Cybercrime Plan[18]:

"Governments have identified six priority areas for action shaped around the critical contributions governments can make in strengthening our national response to cybercrime-- areas where we must focus our efforts for the short to medium term in building our response to cybercrime:

---

[17] http://www.austrac.gov.au/businesses/obligations-and-compliance/insights-compliance-assessments

[18] https://www.ag.gov.au/CrimeAndCorruption/Cybercrime/Documents/national-plan-to-combat-cybercrime.pdf

- Educating the community to protect themselves.
- Partnering with industry to tackle the shared problem of cybercrime.
- Fostering an intelligence-led approach and information sharing.
- Improving the capacity and capability of government agencies, particularly law enforcement, to address cybercrime.
- Improving international engagement on cybercrime and contributing to global efforts to combat cybercrime.
- Ensuring an effective criminal justice framework."

Australian Cybercrime Online Reporting Network (ACORN) is set up as a combined effort of a number of policing agencies to facilitate cybercrime reporting agency, as a response to this plan. ACORN forwards reported incidents to the state based police forces.

Evidence so far is that the local police response to these reports lack timeliness, and victims report that state-based police are mostly not inclined to take these reports further (see previous section on Police). The reason often given is that the perpetrator is overseas, so they can do nothing.

You may think another federal agency, the Australian Federal Police, would be involved. However, "The Australian Federal Police investigates frauds committed against a Commonwealth Government department or a Commonwealth Authority," and clearly refer all other matters back to state based police.

I have heard from one victim that they were advised that individual cases could not be put to Interpol, that only a group of victims could. Yet policing response seems to be only handled at the individual victim level, with little investigation of the perpetrators as a group[19] (assumed to be overseas). As least that is what can be deduced from outside.

Another joint support agency is IDCare, which supports those who have had identities stolen. Whilst this ostensibly provides care to those who are victims of ID theft, there are no other victim support mechanisms or organisations.

---

[19] Conversations I have had with other victims reveal that Personal Investigators have been able to identify scammer gangs, and referred these to the police, but nothing seems to be done.

Analysis

The federal government has set up a new Cybercrime Unit, but we still have to see what effect this has.
Do they have the mandate and skills to do the job?
Are they focused on business crime rather than individual victims, even though there are millions of dollars lost to scams?
Federal government does take a preventative approach with education of the dangers and risks when using online dating and social media, but from the victim perspective seems to do little in the other areas to close the loop.
Educational programs are akin to telling the rape victim to not wear a short skirt, to stay inside at night, and place the responsibility on the victim, not the perpetrator.

State

State based police take referrals of reports from ACORN (see the previous section on local police) as well as from individuals directly. If investigations are to happen at the state level, the state based police need to be trained and equipped to operate in this area, and undertake the cross jurisdictional activities required.
Currently there are questions as to what extent that is so, given the common complaint that is given by victims that local police will do nothing.
State based services should be supporting victims, assisting them to deal with the consequences, as these are impacting at the most personal level.

Consumer Affairs

State based departments of Consumer Affairs, such as Consumer Affairs Victoria, do have some concern about victims of scams operating in their jurisdiction. However, in this instance there is little that they can do.

On the CAV website they state:

"Although we cannot actively respond to or investigate every report we receive, all intelligence is helpful to us.
We frequently use the information we receive about scams to

warn other Victorians, and rely on the public to tell us about any issues within our jurisdiction that may cause widespread harm to consumers.
We often share information we receive about scams with state and federal regulators, so that we can better protect Australians from scams.[20]"

Again, they take an educative approach, not a criminal investigation approach, but refer these on to relevant police.

Society at Large

A commonly voiced attitude is "It's your fault for sending money. How could you be so stupid!"
Thus it is not surprising that only an estimated ten to twenty percent of those scammed actually report it. The applied shame is too great with this attitude so prevalent in society.
"Shame needs three things to grow exponentially in our lives: secrecy, silence and judgement," says Dr Brené Brown, in an interview with Oprah.[21]
The victim blaming that occurs ensures that shame is present, and keeps many people from speaking out about what has happened. When they do, the press often sensationalise the outcome, reinforcing the responsibility of the victim and their stupidity in sending money, whilst neglecting the responsibility of the criminal fraudster.
There is little understanding in the general community of the process of being caught in a scam, the nature of the scam hook, or how being caught in a scam affects the individual victim after it is revealed.
The most visible approach of government is to provide education and warning to be wary of "dodgy scammers". If this warning is missed and the individual is still caught in a scam, it's the victims fault and their problem. The lack of acknowledgement that there is a criminal fraudster, even if overseas, as well as the lack of evident government or police action against criminal fraudsters, reinforces the overall

---

[20] https://www.consumer.vic.gov.au/contact-us/report-an-issue/report-a-scam
[21] http://www.huffingtonpost.com/2013/08/26/brene-brown-shame_n_3807115.html

attitude. We did something stupid, but we are not stupid people.

Scammers are let off the hook.

The victim blaming approach, rather than placing responsibility on criminal fraudsters, maintains the status quo, disempowers victims and lets the scammer get away with it.

The latest work of Dr Cassandra Cross highlights the need for more simple messages to reinforce the education provided by victim's stories, as scammers will adapt their scams even with one victim. These messages could focus on not revealing personal or bank details, and on not sending money, especially overseas.

What Needs to Change?

From the previous chapter, many different organisations can be seen as culpable, as well as victims for their own even if manipulated behaviour. All have a role in a 'successful' scam event. As well as the questions already raised, and the implied changes that might be required, here are some further specifics as take-aways of this book.

1. **Language makes a difference.**
   Calling it a scam enables it to be trivialised, and it is not trivial. It should always be made clear when people are talking about romance scams and scamming behaviour that it is a deliberate and professional fraud. It is not just a trick, the scammer is a criminal fraudster and is responsible. The word fraud has much more gravity and is the more correct one to use.

2. **The professional nature of scamming activity needs to be made clearer.**
   Calling it a scam makes it seem like a one-off event. It is a business, with professionally skilled teams of people (actors) and scripted scenarios being followed. These have been fine tuned to deal with every likelihood to ensure they get the best outcome - the most money they can. It is a deliberate and professional fraud.

3. **Scammers have a world-wide reach, the location of the person is irrelevant.**
   Romance frauds have been linked frequently to Nigeria, Ghana and Russia. This may be where the money ends up, but has nothing to do with where the victim thinks that person is located, according to their profile. Scammers increasingly utilise technology to hide their real identities and locations. Cross-jurisdictional approaches to the problem need to be developed and implemented by our law enforcement agencies with more rigour and vigour. This has led to convictions in America and elsewhere.

4. **More education is needed.**
   Whereas some dating agencies are putting warnings on their websites, and may even be doing some ID security checks, there needs to be more education about this matter. One example might be a compulsory online tutorial for all new members of dating and social media sites. Another option could be inclusion of classes on cyber security, in all its forms, in schools. This would need to include the basics of how to check photos, emails and IP addresses. However this does not necessarily reach older potential victims. Clear and succinct educational and warning messages need to be developed.

5. **Faster police responses, nationally and internationally, to deal with this matter.**
   It should not be left to television programs to do 'stings' on the perpetrators. We have built up the expectation from television police dramas that they can find culprits quickly, given the right clues. Many victims have these clues and expect police to act upon them, and achieve an outcome. The inability of our police to do this is baffling and demeaning to many victims. From better police work, better and faster ways to get money returned would be appreciated. This includes the ability to respond to concerns of family and friends when they see someone activity caught in a scam, and intervene on their behalf.

6. **Greater legislated compliance.**
   There is increasing compliance required for prevention of money laundering activities. The transfer of large sums of money needs to be given much higher levels of surveillance, wherever and whenever it occurs. One suggestion I have heard is for organisations such as Western Union transfers to have a twenty-four hour delay.

7. **Role of agencies.**
   All agencies with a role in scams need to be aware of their contribution towards colluding with the success of scams and doing what they can to minimise this, even when scams target individuals. The whole concept of money laundering needs to be broadened out to include any

international transfer of potentially criminally sourced money, including scams. Mechanisms put in place need to include the potential that they will find ways around this to send money locally.

8. **More research needs to be done into the psychological effects within a scam.**
   We need to better understand the individual triggers and depth of a romance 'thrall' and how it is developed. This would help further identify 'at risk' people, and provide more targeted education, key messaging and support for victims. It would also help when family or friends notice someone they believe is being scammed, and enable prompt and effective intervention.

9. **More research needs to be done into the psychological effects after a scam revelation.**
   We need to better understand the victim role, and how to get out of this after a scam. Understanding of the issues of shame, guilt, and silence on our behaviour is important. As well, the understanding of the process of recovery from being scammed, what steps do people usually go through, how can the process be facilitated and where and when can support most usefully be provided.

10. **Better support for those scammed.**
    More support groups, more ways to bring light into our lives about this, and how to go through the process of recovery from romance scams. How can people help themselves? Victim blaming needs to be discouraged, and blame placed on the criminals where it belongs.

11. **Finally, breaking the silence of this issue.**
    More people talking openly about their experience and how it has affected them. So that everyone learns about the risks, and how to support someone who has been affected. In the end it is a mistake, and nothing to be ashamed of.

Analysis

Finally, in the words of Dr Cassandra Cross:

> "People cope differently from this experience: some are angry, some are depressed, some talk of suicide, while others spend every waking hour trying to figure out how they were scammed and try to prevent it happening to others." [22]

I trust that you see that in writing this book I have found myself in the last of these groups.

---

[22] Cassandra Cross Love Hurts: the costly reality of online romance fraud, The Conversation 11 December 2014

Romance Scam Survivor

Appendix

Additional documentation:

Item 1

My Complaint Posted on the Website of the Dubai Financial Service Authority (www.dfsa.ae).

As reported to the DSFA.AE on 23/11/12:

> The subject of the complaint as detailed above has engaged me in an internet romance scam, inducing me to pay money to him in Dubai. Whilst I understand that this is most likely unable to be retrieved, I do wish to notify you of the entities and persons being used to gather these monies in Dubai, in the hope that you can investigate, perhaps identify and arrest people engaged in these activities, or at the very least, put a stop to the identities being used. The story is a long one, so please forgive me if I just give you the most important details as I know them, though I know they may be falsified. All of the money detailed as paid below is a result of the scam, i.e. false reasons given to extract money from me.
>
> Mr Dubhlainn arrived in Dubai, from Birmingham England (7 Carrwood Rd, Wilmslow, Cheshire East, Manchester, SK95DJ, UK) so he told me, on Sat 8/9/2012 with his 15 yo daughter Blessing Patience Dubhlainn, to stay at 318 Discovery Gardens Dubai whilst he undertook a contract replacing pipes in an oil refinery. His first request for money was to pay part taxes which he said was required to be paid up front for his work. this was paid by me via telegraphic transfer to
>
> Account name : Gbolahan David A
> Bank name   : Dubai Islamic Bank
> Acc number   : 067520030888801
> Iban   : ae070240067520030888801
> Bank address   : Sahara center dubai
> Swift code   : Duibead
>
> See receipt attached.
> Over the following month from a number of different inducements including additional taxes, supplies for his work, theft, medical expenses after an accident, I paid additional moneys via Western Union (this is being reported

to them via the Victorian Police who I have reported this to)to the following names:
Eamon Donegal Dubhlainn - 9 transaction from 17 Sept 2012 to 4 October 2012, sometimes 2 x $10000 in a day. total AUS$63,000
Hassan Waheed Adissa (supposedly his driver)4 transactions via Western union on 4 and 5 October, totalling $40,000, and a further 2 x $9750 via MoneyGram. A further $800 was paid to this name via Western Union on 10 October 2012.
An amount of $77,00 was paid via telegraphic transfer to
Bank Name : Emirate NBD
Account Name : Peace Nyerovwo Abolo
Account number: 1014442343801
Address :   Union Square Branch
Swift :   EBILAEAB

This was supposedly Mr Waheed's fiancée. I was recently contacted by my bank with a query saying that the Dubai bank was wanting further information on the purpose of this transaction. I advised it was the result of a scam and if the money was not already paid out, I did not want it paid, and if possible to get it returned. (Ref:AUEXM: 688365 with International Operations
St George Bank
Payment Services and Operations
Level 4, 68-80 George Street,
Parramatta, NSW 2150
Ph 1300 726 228
Fax 1300 726 282
internationaloperations@stgeorge.com.au)
Further money was paid out via Western union to Blessing Patience Dubhlainn (actually that was a MoneyGram)$10,000
Carla Moss 3 x transactions totalling $5300 on 18th and 19th October,
I have since found the name Carla Moss mentioned on another scam query, by Googling her name.   In total I paid out over AUD$260,000 as a result of this scam.
I am aware since this happened to me, as a result of research done on other scams via the website www.romancescam.com that there are numerous other stories of similar scams taking place in Dubai. I refer this to you for any assistance you can give to stopping this sort

of thing happening. My research shows it is consistent with Nigerian scammers doing this, but I cannot confirm this.

If there is anything you can do to stop other people being scammed, that would be useful. Any assistance you can give to refunding the bank transactions would also be gratefully appreciated.

Please request any other information that would be of use.

Appendix

Item 2

Response to me from Dubai Financial Service Authority.

27 November 2012
BY E-Mail: ▓▓▓▓▓▓▓▓▓▓▓▓▓▓▓▓
Dear Ms Marshall,
COMPLAINT REGARDING EAMON DUBHLAINN
I refer to your complaint to the DFSA on 23 November 2012.
The Dubai Financial Services Authority (DFSA) is the independent regulator of financial services for the Dubai International Financial Centre (DIFC). The DIFC is a 110 acre free zone located within the City of Dubai. The DFSA regulates firms and individuals providing financial services in the DIFC.
The DFSA has assessed your complaint and following its assessment it has determined to:
Take no further action.
A search of the both the DFSA and DIFC public registers indicate that Mr Eamon Dubhlainn is not authorised by the DFSA, nor is he listed in the DIFC Register of Companies as being involved in any of the companies which operate in the DIFC. For your information the DFSA's and the DIFC's public registers can be accessed respectively at:
http://www.dfsa.ae/PublicReqister/Default.aspx
http://www.difc.ae/browse-directory
The regulation of financial services outside the DIFC (including in the city of Dubai) falls within the jurisdiction of the Central Bank of the UAE, if banking services are provided, and the Emirates Securities and Commodities Authority (ESCA) if securities are offered. Also the DFSA in the DIFC has civil and commercial jurisdiction only, and therefore any criminal conduct is more appropriately dealt with by the Dubai Police.
Accordingly the DFSA does not have jurisdiction. As such the DFSA is unable to take any further action in relation to your complaint.
You may wish to forward your concerns to the Central Bank and/or the ESCA for consideration. Level 13, The Gate, PO Box 75850, Dubai, UAE Telephone: +971 (0)4 362 1500 Fax: +971 (0)4 362 0801 Email: info@dfsa.ae
The contact details for the Central Bank are as follows: telephone: +971-2-665 2220; facsimile: +971-2-665 2504; URL www.centralbank.ae .

ESCA's contact details are: telephone: +971-2-627-7888; facsimile: +971-2-627 4600; URL: www.sca.ae .
You may also contact Dubai Police through their electronic portal at the following URL: www.alameen.ae/en/onlineform/default.aspx , or the Economic Crimes Combating Department of the Dubai Police by telephone: +971-4-203 6341.

Should you have any queries in relation to the contents of this letter please feel free to contact me.

Yours sincerely,

Appendix

Item 3: ATO/SMSF Documentation

1. *Wording from ATO's first response to my self reporting.*

Your self managed superannuation fund obligations
For your information

Dear Trustee

We refer to your letter dated 5 January 2013, and our subsequent telephone call on 10 January 2013, in relation to the ▮▮▮▮ Super Fund (the fund).

You made the following voluntary disclosures to the fund:
- you set up the fund in March 2012 with the intention of investing in residential property
- in October 2012, without knowing it at the time, you became engaged in an internet relationship scam
- during October 2012 you removed $165,000 in smaller amounts from your SMSF account and paid them to the scammer; you knew that it was inappropriate but you felt compelled to do so
- you intended the withdrawal of the money to be a loan to your sole member and you believed that the funds would be returned within a short time with interest
- you have lost the $165,000 as well as $100,000 of your personal savings/borrowings
- you have reported the scam activity to the Victoria Police
- you are unable to repay the money to the fund
- in hindsight, you realise that it was a mistake, irrational and inappropriate and it has left you financially and emotionally compromised
- you intend to wind up the fund as there are now only minimal funds in the fund's account.

We advise that this matter has been escalated for review.

Please note that no action is required of you at this stage.

You should keep any relevant documentation relating to this matter as we will request it at a later date.

More information
If you have any questions, please phone **13 28 69** between 8.00am and 5.pm, Monday to Friday, and ask for ▮▮▮ on extension ▮▮

For general superannuation information, visit our website at www.ato.gov.au/super or phone **13 10 20** between 8.00am and 6.00pm, Monday to Friday.

Yours faithfully,

Deputy Commissioner of Taxation

Appendix

2. ATO Request for fund review documentation.

12 February 2013
Your Superannuation Fund is being reviewed
Dear Trustee
We're following up on our recent conversation and advise that the Trustee for JAN M Super Fund has been selected for review in respect of its compliance with superannuation law in relation to your voluntary disclosure date 5 January 2013.
We intend to complete this review by 7 June 2013. However this will depend on the specific details of your case.
What you need to do
To help us complete the review you need to provide the following information and documentation:

- Copy of the police report referred to in your letter dated 5 January 2013
- a clear explanation of when, how and why the fund member felt compelled to remove all of the fund monies and direct the funds to an internet source
- copy of the trust deed
- copy of the instruments varying the trust deed
- copies of meeting minutes
- copies of the fund's signed financial statements for the 2011-12 year of income
- copy of the independent auditor's report for the 2011-12 year of income
- copies of the fund's bank and other financial institution statements for the 2011-12 and 2012-13 years of income inclusive of the latest statement available
- copy of member accounts showing when the payments were made
- copies of any letters from members regarding the payment of benefits, proof of age and/or their employment status, or the type of payment being requested
- details of the investment strategy
- details in relation to any payment of superannuation benefits to members, including: amount paid, benefit type, date of the payment, the condition of release that

279

was met, evidence supporting the payment (such as deposit slips, cheque butts or withdrawal forms), and the name of the ABN/TFN of the member to whom the payment was made
- copies of any payment summaries for members
- copies of any rollover benefit statement and other transfer forms for members
- details of any commissions, fees or other payments made in relation to the setting up of the fund and/or rollover or payment of superannuation benefits to members, including: amount paid, date of payment, reasons for the payments, evidence supporting the payment (such as invoices) and name, ABN/TFN and phone number of the individual or entity to whom the payment was made
- evidence of how the fund's assets are invested (eg: term deposit statements, share or unit holding certificates, property titles, etc)
- copies of loan agreements for each loan made by the fund (if prepared)
- details in relation to the loans, including: amount loaned, how loan was provided to third party (eg. Cash, cheque, electronic transfer, etc), date of loan, rate of interest charged, period of the loan, dates specified for payment of the principal, dates specified for payment of interest, security provided for the loan, reason for he loan, the names and ABN/TFN of the persons or entities to whom the loans were made and any relationship of such person or entities to the fund, the principal outstanding on the loan, and the interest outstanding on the loan
- details of any default in payment of the principal and/or interest or other breach of any loan agreement
- details of any action taken in relation to breach of any loan agreement (eg: write-off, forgiveness, debt recovery action, legal proceedings, etc)
- any loan schedules
- copies of any letters of approval from APRA or Medicare to make payment of superannuation benefits to members of the basis of compassionate grounds
- copy of any superannuation contribution splitting applications for members

Appendix

- copies of any applications and/or letters from members regarding the rollover or payment of superannuation benefits
- details of remuneration provided to any individual for services rendered.

If you identified contraventions and rectified them or have taken steps to rectify them, you will need to provide us with:

:. a statement in writing detailing what you have done so far, and

:. supporting evidence.

Send your response by **5 March 2013** to:

Australian Taxation Office
PO Box 3578
ALBURY NSW 2640
Quoting reference ▮▮▮▮▮▮▮▮
Or fax to 1300 139 024 quoting reference ▮▮▮▮▮▮▮▮

3. My 'Statement in Writing' in response to the ATO.

Sunday, 17 February 2013
Australian Tax Office
PO Box 3578
ALBURY NSW 2640
Re: SMSF " ███ Super Fund," ABN: ███████████ ;
REF: ███████ Request for information to undertake Audit

To whom it May Concern,

Please see below my response to request points, 1, 2 and 12

Point 1: Request for Police Report.

Victoria Police (Preston Police Station Ph: 03 9479 6111) advise that they do not provide a Report, but do provide incident numbers, and the ATO can then directly request the report through FOI provisions.

Relevant numbers they have provided are:

Incident Number: 120328842
Sub-Incident Number: 120437875

Point 2: When, how and why the member felt compelled to remove funds.

When and How funds were removed?:

Funds were removed by online bank transfer to the personal account Jan Marshall (St George Bank Account) and forwarded on to Dubai as follows:

Why I felt compelled to remove funds and direct the funds to an internet source?

Appendix

At the point where I commenced withdrawing funds from the Jan M Super Fund:

Date of transfer	Amount	Amount and Method of onwards transfer			
3rd October 2012	$35,000	3-Oct	10000	435.92	Western Union
4th October 2012	$8,000	3-Oct	10000	440.42	Western Union
5th October 2012	$45,000	4-Oct	10000	435.92	Western Union
		4-Oct	10000	435.92	Western Union
		5-Oct	10000	435.9	Western Union
		5-Oct	10000	435.92	Western Union
		5-Oct	9761.8	380	MoneyGram
		5-Oct	9711.8	380	MoneyGram
			$79473.6	$3380	Total: $82853.60
8th October 2012	$77,000	Full amount payed by Overseas telegraphic transfer to a bank account in Dubai.			
18th October 2012	$1,000	Paid via Western Union			
19th October 2012	$150	Part of a $500 payment via Western Union			
TOTAL	$166,150.00				

- I was deeply involved in what I regarded as a serious romantic relationship, and believed I was engaged to be married to a man located in Dubai who had significant funds, to which access was temporarily delayed until he returned to England.
- There was a promise to repay, with interest, any funds provided within a short period.
- I expected the payment of funds to promptly facilitate the ability of the person to return to England, where his funds would become available, for repayment. He had as significant payment for his work by cheque which he was unable to cash whilst in Dubai.
- I had already provided $81,000 comprising personal cash funds and additionally approved credit card funds. I had no remaining access to other personal funds.
- During this period, reasons given for need for funds included:
1. He needed to pay $40,000 in taxes before the end of the week, or he would be arrested. They had already violently threatened arrest, which had been narrowly averted.
2. He is attacked and robbed of the $40,000 whilst on his way to pay with the money I had sent him, and

needs more to pay taxes.
3. He needed to repay part of the cheque he had received in payment for his contract, as he had not completed the work contracted for. This was with threat of violence if he did not pay before leaving Dubai
4. He was involved in a car accident whilst on the way to the airport where his driver was killed, and he and his daughter were in hospital, and needed to pay fees before being able to leave the hospital. This had been negotiated down from an initial fee to pharmaceuticals only.
5. Assistance with accommodation and purchase of additional airfares as original tickets were forfeited when he did not arrive due to the car crash.
   - During this period I became increasingly anxious to do what was necessary to get him out of Dubai, and back to England, to remove him from a dangerous situation, as well as to be able to refund to me loans I had made to him of all my available personal funds, credit, and then super fund money. It was only after he had advised that he was on a plane to England and I was unable to subsequently make contact with him that I realised it had all been a scam.
   - These people are professionals at personal manipulation. Unfortunately I was a gullible victim, having no had a personal relationship for 20 years, and desperately wanting one.
   - For information on romance scams see.. http://www.scamwatch.gov.au/content/index.phtml/itemId/694213
   - For specifics with the same photos used with me see http://www.romancescam.com/forum/viewtopic.php?f=3&p=270179
   - For more detail of the story used with me.... http://www.romancescam.com/forum/viewtopic.php?f=3&t=55151&p=289015

Point 12: Detail of benefit to Member.
All funds as listed above were paid to fund member Jan

Marshall. Funds were paid by online bank transfer, with no additional documentation. Copy of the bank statement is attached, showing bank transfer.

Transfers were paid to Jan Marshall, BSB: ▓ Account No: ▓

TFN is ▓.

DOB: ▓ ie 59 years old, and post preservation age.

Jan Marshall did, as of 30 June 2012, leave gainful employment as a contractor paid through her own company Sangam Enterprises Pty Ltd, working for the Queensland Government in Brisbane.

She has since returned to work as an employee working on a fixed term employment contract in Melbourne, and through this, continue to contribute superannuation payments to the fund.

Yours sincerely, Jan Marshall, TRUSTEE, ▓ Super Fund, with my signature

4. Scammer bank statements (x 2).

Please find attached two bank statements which show the movement from monies from my Superfund bank account, to my personal account, then the payments out of my personal bank account. I am also attaching a spread sheet of all payments made. Most were paid by Western Union, however two were made by bank transfer as follows
1. GBOLAHAN David A
Dubai Islamic Bank
Sahara centre Dubai
Acct 067520030888801

2. Peace Nyerovwo Abola
Union Square Branch
UAE
Acct AE500260001014442343801
The details given to me by the person who scammed me are (I believe **all** of this detail to be fabricated, or using untraceable pre-paid phones):
Name: Eamon Donegal Dubhlainn
Address in UK: 7 Carrwood Road, Wilmslow, Cheshire East SK95DJ, Manchester UK
UK Mobile: +44 7700 028168
Email: dubhlainneamon@yahoo.com (Email Header details comment by www.Romancescam.com "96.44.140.242 - that's OC3 Networks, bad IP, proxy, used in scams a LOT." For more details, and how often the photos supplied to me have been used in different scams see http://www.romancescam.com/forum/viewtopic.php?f=3&t=50379 . When I later did a Google search on the photos, I found them being used on 10 different sites around the world, all with different names, even different languages.)
DOB: 7 April 1963
Dubai Address: 318 Discovery Gardens Dubai
Dubai mobile: +971 55 3796376
I am also attaching a copy of emails with bank statements sent to me showing that this 'man' had substantial funds in UK but hey were on hold, upon which I assumed my funds would be returned once he was able to return to the UK. I now believe

Appendix

this to be fully fabricated. These were with Nat West bank, though the logo is no longer loading.

As provided to the ATO as part of the request for details.

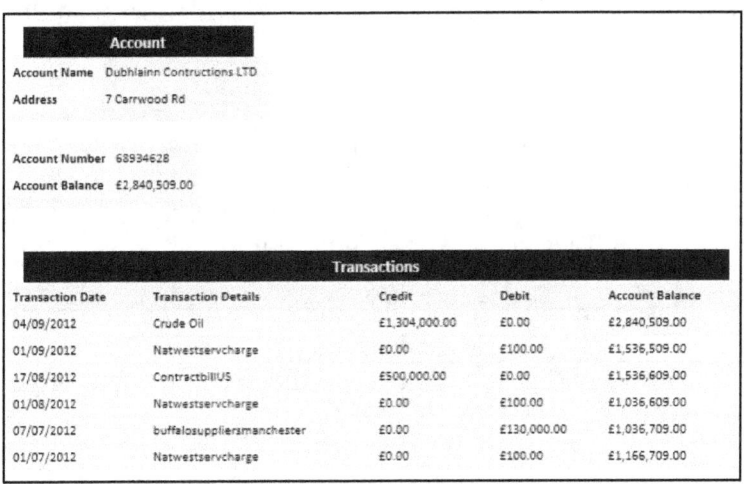

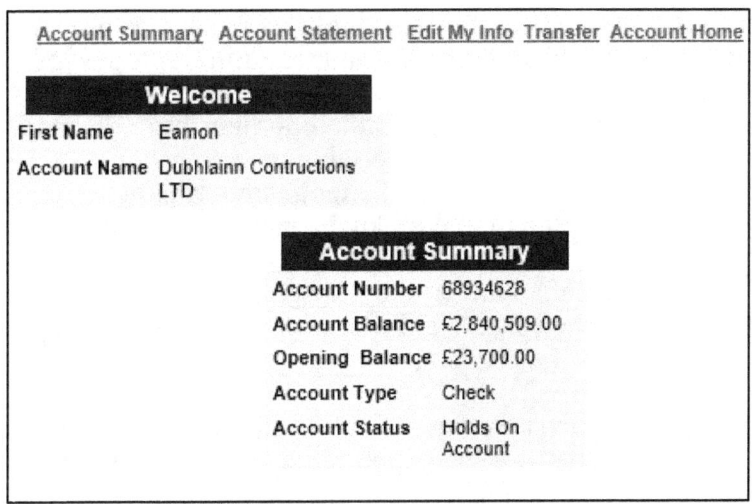

287

5. ATO Notification of Escalation to Audit

23 May 2013
Contravention of superannuation law – escalation to audit

Dear Trustee

1. After consideration of the review evidence we have decided to escalate this review to audit as we have found that you have contravened superannuation law in your role as Trustee for ▉▉▉ Super Fund.

2. Based on times for similar audits we intend to complete the audit by 16 November 2013.
   However this will depend on the specific detail of your case.

3. The following contraventions were verified to have occurred after consideration of the evidence:
   - Early Access of Benefits
   - Sole Purpose Test

We have decided to allow you an opportunity to provide a written undertaking setting out your commitments to wind up the fund.
Attached is a Position Paper which outlines our reasons for requesting you to offer an undertaking.
You are under no obligation to offer an undertaking.
If you wish to offer an undertaking you need to:
1. Consider your circumstances
2. Determine if an undertaking is appropriate for you, and
3. Ensure that you are able to meet the terms before you make your undertaking.

If the undertaking is accepted by us it will become enforceable. This means that we can apply to a court to enforce the undertaking if you do not comply with it.

Your undertaking must contain, as a minimum, the following essential items.:
- What actions will be taken to rectify the

contraventions
- The time in which the contraventions are to be rectified
- How and when you will report to the commissioner on the progress made towards completion of the undertaking
- A commitment to cease the behaviour which resulted in the contraventions
- If appropriate, the strategies require to be implemented by you to prevent the contraventions from occurring again.

A template is attached for your use if required. For further information regarding enforceable undertakings please see ATO Law Administration Practice Statement PS LA 2006/18.

If you do not accept our findings or don't believe a written undertaking is appropriate, you need to respond in writing, clearly stating your reasons. Your response should address the issues raised in our position paper.

6. Lawyer's letter asking for discretion.

It was in typical legalese. Names have been redacted rather than altered.

All legislative references are references to the *Income Tax Assessment Act 1997* (Cth) unless stated otherwise.

Background

1. Ms Marshall was the sole director of ▮▮▮▮ Super Fund Pty Ltd, the trustee of the Fund. Ms Marshall was the only member of the Fund.
2. During the 2013 income year Ms Marshall accessed $166,150 in superannuation benefits from the Fund.
3. Ms Marshall has summarised the circumstances of the early access of benefits in her statement enclosed in Annexure B.
4. The purpose of this letter is to request that the Commissioner indicate whether the amount of $166,150 (the amount of superannuation benefits accessed form the Fund) will be excluded from Ms Marshall's assessable income in the 2013 income year, prior to lodging her tax return for that year.

The Commissioner's discretion – section 304-10(4)

5. A taxpayer's assessable income includes the amount of a superannuation benefit received otherwise than in accordance with the payments standards prescribed in the superannuation laws (section 304-10(1)(b)(ii)).

   Section 304-10 was introduced in 2007 in the 'simplified superannuation' measures.
6. Parliament provided the Commissioner with discretion to exclude an amount of a superannuation benefit from a taxpayer's assessable income where the Commissioner is satisfied that it would be unreasonable not to do so (Explanatory Memorandum, Tax Laws Amendment (Simplified Superannuation) Bill 2006 at 2.84).
7. In determining whether to exclude an amount of a superannuation benefit from a taxpayer's assessable income, the legislation says that the Commissioner must consider:
    - the nature of the superannuation fund in

Appendix

question; and
- any other matters the Commissioner considers to be relevant.

These considerations are addressed below.

8. The Commissioner has not published any statement or guide on when it is appropriate to apply section 304-10(4).
9. The nature of the fund
10. The Fund was a regulated superannuation fund.
11. The Fund was established 'solely for the purpose of providing old age pensions for Members in the event of their retirement or in other circumstances approved under the Relevant Law' (clause (3) of the recitals in the Fund's deed).
12. The Fund has never had any other members, therefore no other parties were affected by Ms Marshall's actions.
13. If Ms Marshall had satisfied a condition of release (Schedule 1 of the Superannuation Industry (Supervision) Regulations 1994), all the money in the Fund would have been hers to do with as she pleased.
14. Therefore, the nature of the Fund means that no other parties have been affected by Ms Marshall's conduct.
15. Other matters for consideration
16. Ms Marshall has summarised her reasons for withdrawing the money form the Fund in her statement.
17. The legislative history of the discretion was set out by Senior Member Walsh in Mason v Commissioner of Taxation [2012] AATA 133. Senior Member Walsh stated:

24. Section 304-10 of the ITAA 1997 has evolved from the enactment of a number of similar preceding provisions of the Income tax Assessment Act 1936 (ITAA 1936), namely: (i) section 26AF of the ITAA 1936, which was enacted in 1980; (ii) section 26AFA of the ITAA 1936, which was enacted in 1984, and (iii) section 26AFB of the ITAA 1936, which was enacted in 1987. Former sections 26AFA(2) and 26AFB(4) of the ITAA 1936 each contained a discretion similar to that which is provided in subsection 304-10(4) of the ITAA 1997.

25. Former section 26AFB of the ITAA 1936 was inserted into the ITAA 1936 by Taxation Laws Amendment Act (No.4) 1987 (1987 Amendment Act).

The Explanatory Memorandum to the Taxation Laws Amendment Bill (No. 4) 1987 (1987 EM), which introduced the 1987 Amendment Act, states:
"Clause 11 will insert new section 26AFB in Division 2 of Part III of the Principal Act in order to continue the policy embodied in existing sections 26AF and 26AFA designed to prevent abuse of concessions available to approved funds by payment of excessive or unauthorised benefits, following establishment of the new supervisory arrangements. The new section will ensure that where a taxpayer receives any such benefits from a fund approved by the Insurance and Superannuation Commissioner (or a fund which was formerly approved by the Insurance and Superannuation Commissioner) then the benefits will be subject to tax unless the Commissioner of Taxation is satisfied that this would be unreasonable. As noted above, this section will apply to benefits received from those funds which have at any time obtained tax exemption under section 23FC after Regulations have been made under the Standards Act embodying requirements relating to the level and nature of benefits paid.

New section 26AFB will assume the discretion currently available under section 26AFA in order to ensure that taxpayers are treated appropriately such as where loss of tax exemption by a fund may be regarded as a sufficient penalty for a breach of the relevant standards."
[Emphasis in original]

26. The 1987 EM referred to the discretion in former section 26AFA(2) of the ITAA 1936, as follows:
"The Commissioner has indicated that this discretion would be exercised where there are no tax avoidance implications and where the excessive benefit arose fortuitously or in other circumstances beyond the effective control of the recipient or the employer."
(our emphasis)

18. We draw the following facts to the Commissioner's attention:

Appendix

   a) The policy intent of parliament by establishing the self-managed superannuation scheme will not be undermined by excluding the amounts from Ms Marshall's assessable income.

There is no suggestion that Ms Marshall deliberately abused the self-managed superannuation regime as by her own admission, she was under the genuine belief that:
- the Fund would be repaid with interest; and
- she had no choice to save the scammer's life except to loan the amounts.

   b) There was no 'fraudulent enterprise' or any suggestions of impropriety by Ms Marshall.

In the case of Brazil v Federal Commissioner of Taxation [2012] AATA 192, the Senior Member affirmed the Commissioner's decision to include the amounts taken from the AON Master Trust (an APRA regulated fund) because of the overwhelming evidence of a 'fraudulent enterprise' (at paragraph [25]).

There are no such suggestions in this instance.

   c) Ms Marshall did not receive the benefit of the money taken from the Fund, nor does she have any likely prospects of the money being returned to her. There is clearly no tax avoidance purpose in this case.

   d) While Ms Marshall always had sole effective control of the Fund (see Mason v Federal Commissioner of Taxation [2012] AATA 133), this case can be distinguished from the facts in the Mason case because Ms Marshall never received the use of, or benefit from, the money withdrawn from the Fund (unlike Mr Mason) as the money was all sent to the scam artist.

   e) On this basis, it is unreasonable to include the amounts in Ms Marshall's assessable income because she did not receive the benefit of those funds.

   f) The non-complying status of the superannuation fund is more than a sufficient fiscal penalty for Ms Marshall, together with the fact that she has been forced to return to work to start saving again. She has not obtained any 'excessive benefit', or any benefit at all, from the withdrawal of the funds. In addition, she has suffered emotional distress and embarrassment.

She has also incurred professional fees to rectify these

matters.

Based on the above facts, we request that the Commissioner exercise discretion to exclude the superannuation amounts from Ms Marshall's assessable income under section 304-10(4).

Requested action

We ask that the Commissioner exercise discretion to exclude the amount of $166,150 (the amount of superannuation benefits accessed form the Fund) from Ms Marshall's assessable income under section 304-10(4) after she lodges her 2013 income tax return.

Appendix

7. My letter to ATO

The lawyer's letter to ATO was accompanied by my statement, a summary of the facts in a personal tense, explaining what happened, remedial action taken and the long term financial consequences on me.

I was the sole member of the ▮▮▮▮ Super Fund (Fund). I was also the sole director of ▮▮▮▮ Super Fund Pty Ltd, the trustee of the Fund.
The Fund was established on 9 March 2012 and became a regulated fund on 23 April 2012.
I have worked in the computer industry for 25 years in various sales and support positions and since 2000 work in the specialised field of Change Management. For 20 years I have operated as a consultant or contractor, and invoiced for my services through my company ▮▮▮▮▮▮▮▮▮▮▮▮▮▮▮▮▮▮▮▮▮▮▮▮▮▮. For the 6 years up until June 2012, I worked for the Queensland Government, my last position there being as a ▮▮▮▮▮▮▮▮▮▮▮▮▮▮▮▮▮▮▮▮▮▮▮▮▮▮.
At this time I retired and moved to Melbourne.
My intentions when establishing the Fund
I began the Fund by rolling over amounts from my BT Super Wrap fund ▮▮▮▮▮▮▮▮▮▮▮▮▮▮▮▮▮▮, totalling $154,196.00.
The initial rollover was my life superannuation savings at the time, minus a minimum amount of $5000 to maintain my insurance with BT Super Wrap. I was 59 years old at the time.
I intended to establish the Fund because I wanted to have the capacity to maximise my potential retirement income through selected investment activities.
At the time when I established the Fund, I had not met the person who would later turn out to be a scam artist.

Why I chose to withdraw my superannuation
In August 2012, I joined the dating website Plenty of Fish, as having moved to Melbourne I was keen to meet someone with whom I could explore the environs of Melbourne and Victoria. I had never used internet dating prior to this time so I had

295

little experience of its dangers.

Within several days I was approached by a man purporting to be an engineer working in America, who indicated he was willing to move anywhere to be with the right woman.

He finished his job in America, and moved back to Manchester, where his home base was. We were now talking on the phone, and he had suggested that we communicate on Yahoo messenger.

We were soon talking several times a day, for long periods, via message, phone and internet video, and were becoming more deeply involved.

After being emotionally involved over a period of 2 months, we became extremely close. I was deeply involved in what I regarded as a serious romantic relationship. He asked me to marry him, and I agreed. I had not been in a serious relationship for over 20 years and was extremely excited about this new relationship.

At the time of entering into the relationships I was feeling extremely lonely, and wanted more intimacy and companionship as I entered into retirement.

Eventually, I was convinced that I was engaged to be married. He talked about buying a house for us together in Melbourne, and asked me to start looking. He indicated that he could fund a purchase up to $2 million from his savings, and still retain his properties in Manchester.

This man had me believe that he was undertaking a new engineering contract in Dubai where he was replacing/maintaining an oil pipeline, a contract that would take about 8 weeks, after which time he would come to Melbourne. That is where the trouble began.

It was only after a few weeks that he made his first request for money due to "miscalculations" about the Dubai work environment; he told me that he was requested to pay tax on his project earnings up front.

He told me that he owed $40,000 in taxes in Dubai. He also told me, and I believed, that he had been threatened with violence by the police and was soon to be arrested if he did not repay the money he owed in taxes.

I agreed to loan him $43,000 to assist with his taxes and some living and business expenses.

The agreement was that he would repay me with interest when

Appendix

he returned home to England. He told me that he had significant wealth in England but for one reason or another was unable to access his money in Dubai. In particular, he told me that he had access to a large cheque from business in Dubai that was only able to be cashed in England.

On this basis, I felt I was sufficiently protected and decided to lend the money.

I paid $35,000 on 1 day and $8,000 the next day. I used my personal savings to do this, not money from my superannuation fund. He assured me that the money would be a loan and he could repay me as soon as he returned to England.

He proceeded to use a series of ploys asking for more money. He told me that that he had been robbed and all the money I had given him to pay the tax was gone. I was immediately convinced about fears of his personal safety and wellbeing. I felt there was no other option but for me to continue assisting him.

After exhausting my savings, I drew on my credit card, extended the available balance in it, and took out an additional card. This allowed me to source an additional $40,000 in funds.

Once again, he assured me that the money was a loan and he could repay me as soon as he returned to England

Around 8 October 2012, he told me that he was forced to repay part of a cheque received from his employer in Dubai. His employer (I don't know details) would not allow him to leave Dubai until he paid back the money. He provided me a copy of a bank statement indicating that he had sufficient money available in England. After I saw the bank statement I felt confident that he would repay all my money as he appeared to have significant cash resources.

Repaying his work cheque appeared to me to be the last hurdle for him to return home to England where he could cash his other cheque and repay my money.

The next day, I received a phone call supposedly from a hospital saying that he was involved in a car crash and was hospitalised. He had hospital and medical expenses that he could not afford to pay and I felt that his chances of a full recovery would be compromised if he did not have money to pay for the hospital bills. This reinforced my concerns about his personal safety and seemed to back up his story about the threats of violence.

I decided to loan him a total of $78,150 to cover his work cheque, hospital expenses and medical bills.

While my judgement was severely diminished, I definitely would not have made any of these payments if the man had not told me they were loans (not gifts) that he would repay with interest. I viewed the withdrawals as short-term loans from the Fund. My judgement was so impaired, and I felt there was some urgency to get him out of a violent environment so I did not obtain professional advice before making the loans.

I would have never compromised my financial security and my retirement if I did not genuinely believe the Fund would receive the money back.

I was in shock when I realised the funds would not be returned. I had to get personal loans from friends to get through the first month after this as I had compromised my personal financial situation so severely.

I did not keep any of the money from the Fund for myself. My actions were borne out of, what I felt, was a moral obligation to assist this man who I believed to be my fiancé, and I did not act out of self-interest.

I am currently receiving free counselling services and I am suffering ongoing depression.

I have forced myself to continue working throughout my depression in order to ensure I have funds to pay back the credit cards and loans I had incurred

Remedial action

I have taken all steps to notify the Victoria Police. I also made several enquiries with agencies and banks in Dubai in an effort to contact or at least identify the man, including Emirates NBD (a bank) as well as the Dubai Financial Services Authority. Despite many attempts, the authorities have told me there is little they can do for my situation.

I have contacted my own bank (St George) and they have told me that they are unable to help.

I voluntarily wrote to the ATO to admit to the amounts withdrawn from the Fund once I realised the 'loans' were never going to be seen again. I have cooperated fully with the ATO.

I have complied with all the ATO's requests of me, including

Appendix

providing undertakings to wind up the Fund and to close the bank account for the Fund.

My personal finances

I only started to withdraw money from the Fund after I had completely exhausted all other avenues.

After depleting all of my savings, I turned to credit cards and I now owe around $10,000 on a Mastercard and another $12,000 on a Visa card.

I own a property at ▮▮▮▮▮▮▮▮▮▮▮▮▮▮▮ but this property is mortgaged. Due to the property market and current valuations, I expect I have very little equity if I were to sell now (which I have considered on numerous occasions). I currently rent the property to tenants so I can pay for the mortgage, but it does not provide enough income to also support me.

I am now forced to return to work at age 60. I realise I will have to continue working well into my sixties to rebuild my life.

As a result of these actions I now have no superannuation and I predict I will need to rely on a government pension as a form of supplemental income for living expenses.

An amended assessment by the ATO would leave me in severely crippling financial circumstances. I have already lost $260,000 that I sought to rely on in retirement due to this scam and I cannot fathom how I will survive for the rest of my life if I have a further tax debt in the vicinity of $80,000.

I am severely embarrassed about being defrauded and I now have grave concerns as to how I will survive for the rest of my life without the financial security I had built up in the Fund.

I have read everything in this statement. I have had the opportunity to correct the statement and have done so where necessary, initialling any corrections.

Everything contained in this statement is true and correct to the best of my knowledge.

Romance Scam Survivor

Appendix

Useful Information

Websites

Romance Scam Survivor
This is my blog. I post frequently on topics relating to romance scams. I have done a lot of research, so there are separate pages on support and research information, latest media and victim's stories.
http://romancescamsurvivor.org/

Scamwatch
ACCC Govt site for reporting all scams.
www.scamwatch.gov.au (also on Facebook)

Australian Cybercrime Online Reporting Network (ACORN)
Combined Police site for reporting all scams where money was lost.
http://www.acorn.gov.au/

Stay Smart Online
ACCC Govt site. Have a scam alert email service.
https://www.communications.gov.au/what-we-do/internet/stay-smart-online (also on Facebook)

Seniors Online Security
Community Safety and Crime Prevention Branch and the Fraud and Corporate Crime Group, conducting research with seniors with Dr Cassandra Cross. The Seniors Online Security package, was done under the auspices of the Police Citizens Youth Clubs, Queensland.
http://www.pcyc.org.au/Clubs/Carindale/SeniorsOnlineSecurity.aspx

Project Sunbird, WA

Government of Western Australia, Project Sunbird is a joint Project between WA Police Major Fraud Squad and Department of Commerce, to identify and prevent consumer fraud in Western Australia. Unfortunately this project has now closed.
http://www.scamnet.wa.gov.au/scamnet/Fight_Back-Project_Sunbird.htm

Consumer Affairs Victoria

General information and real-life stories.
http://www.consumer.vic.gov.au/resources-and-education/scams   (also on Facebook)

Scam Disruption Project

Has great information on how to identify a scam in email content or online profile behaviour. Unfortunately this project has now closed.
http://www.accc.gov.au/consumers/consumer-protection/protecting-yourself-from-scams/scam-disruption-project

Other Websites

Various sites collecting information about scams and scammers. I recommend a Google search, which will show you many more, including Facebook pages.
www.romancescam.com
www.romancescams.org
www.scamdigger.com
www.scamwarners.com
https://romancescams.wordpress.com/

Books

Dr Cassandra Cross and Professor Mark Button, *"CyberFrauds, Scams and their victims",* Routledge 2017.

Jon van Helsing and Anna Aldern-Tirrill, *"Cyber Love's Illusions: Romance Scams... a Virtual Pandemic",* White Cottage Publishing Co., 2010.

Jon van Helsing, Tom Mack and Anna Aldern-Tirrill, *"Cyber Love's Illusions: The Healing Journey",* White Cottage Publishing Co., 2010.

Elina Juusola, *"Love on the Line",* Xlibris 2016.

Sofija Stefanovic, *"You're Just Too Good to be True",* Penguin Specials 2015.

Acknowledgements

I wish to acknowledge Anne Robotham and Celia Taylor for feedback and editing on my first draft, and Karen Collyer for editing my final manuscript, Bryan McNally for proofing, and Tashia Hales for my book cover. I have learned that it takes much more that the initial writing to create a book.

For my friends Sue, Rosie, Lael and Doris, for proving ongoing support, including financially, prior to, through and after the scam. To Darryl Hoare and Kay Clark for feeding me and supporting me emotionally and financially especially though the tough times.

To Carolyn Jury of YPRL for providing a venue for me to speak my truth, and all those who interviewed me for press engagements who listened openly, and allowed me to regain my self respect.

To Dr. Cassandra Cross for her much needed ongoing research of this topic, contributing to my Romance Scam Survivor blog, and helping me to understand.

To Whittlesea U3A members for encouragement to 'get it done'.

Lastly my mum, Amitabha Phillips, who never understood how and why it happened, but loved me anyway.

Author Information

Having spent 30 years in the IT industry Jan Marshall had reached a senior level in her professional field, earning a six figure income.
After an interstate move in 2012, Jan looked to online dating to find a companion with whom to explore her new location. Unfortunately, this developed into an online romance scam where Jan lost more than $260,000 over several months. This lead to grief, shame, financial devastation, and a shattered self image. Jan credits having her Ragdoll cat called Cookie with helping her get through the tough recovery process, lasting over two years. Much of this book was written as part of her recovery.

Early in 2015 she set up a support group for other victims, created a blog, and became an Ambassador for the Australian Cybercrime Online Reporting Network (ACORN). She regularly speaks to the press, TV, and community groups. he has become the face of an internet scam victim in Australia, and is an active advocate for other victims. She also provides peer counselling to other victims and their families.

Jan comments that going public "allowed me to regain my self respect", because she was no longer hiding in shame about her experience. Through these activities she discovered her writing ability, and after this book, wishes to keep on writing about other topics of interest.

In her spare time Jan paints and draws, and enjoys time walking and swimming. She remains single, having not ventured back to online dating.

For more information, check her
Blog site: www.romancescamsurvivor.org.
Twitter: @JanCarMar   Web: www.janmarshall.com.au
LinkedIn: https://www.linkedin.com/in/janmarshall53/

www.ingramcontent.com/pod-product-compliance
Lightning Source LLC
Chambersburg PA
CBHW051935290426
44110CB00015B/1986